THE
FIRST
SAMURAI

THE
FIRST
SAMURAI

THE LIFE AND LEGEND OF THE WARRIOR REBEL
TAIRA MASAKADO

KARL F. FRIDAY

John Wiley & Sons, Inc.

Library of Congress Cataloging-in-Publication Data:

Friday, Karl F.
   The first samurai : the life and legend of the warrior rebel Taira Masakado
/ Karl F. Friday.
      p. cm.
   Includes bibliographical references and index.
   ISBN 978-0-471-76082-5 (cloth: alk. paper)
   ISBN 978-1-68442-589-1 (paperback)
   1. Taira, Masakado, 903 or 4-940.   2. Generals—Japan—Biography.   3. Japan—History—Tengyo Revolt, 938–940. I. Title.
   DS852.T3F75 2007
   952'.01092—dc22

                                                            2007035510

Printed in the United States of America

For Chie, who makes it all worthwhile

Ambition is an idol, on whose wings great minds are carried only to extreme; to be sublimely great or to be nothing.

—Robert Southey

CONTENTS

Illustrations follow page 85.

ACKNOWLEDGMENTS

No book writes itself, and no author works entirely on his or her own. This project could not have been undertaken without help and support from dozens of friends and colleagues on both sides of the Pacific, to all of whom I express my profound appreciation and gratitude.

A special round of thanks goes to my editor, Stephen Power, and my production editor, Rachel Meyers, at John Wiley & Sons for shepherding the book from conception to publication; to Peter Hoffer for his advice and counsel throughout; and to Tanaka Atsuko, Nick Adams, Wendy Giminski, and Money Hickman for their work on the maps and illustrations that adorn this volume.

Some of the research for this study was funded by grants from the Japan Foundation, whose support I gratefully acknowledge. I am also deeply indebted to professors Kondō Shigekazu, and Ishigami Eiichi and the rest of the faculty and staff of the University of Tokyo Shiryōhensanjō who gave me a place to work and took time away from their own labors to assist me with mine.

This book is part of a larger project reexamining warrior "rebellions" in Heian Japan that began with a paper delivered at a conference held at Harvard University in June 2002. My thanks, therefore, to Mikael Adolphson and Edward Kamens, whose invitation to participate in this event got me started. And an extra thank-you goes to Mickey, for his invaluable bibliographic and editorial help.

Once again, however, my greatest debt is to Chie, my wife and the wind behind my sails. She listened patiently to my ideas, graciously ignored my frustrations, and kept me going with enthusiastic responses and cogent suggestions. Most important, she gives me a reason to go home at the end of each day.

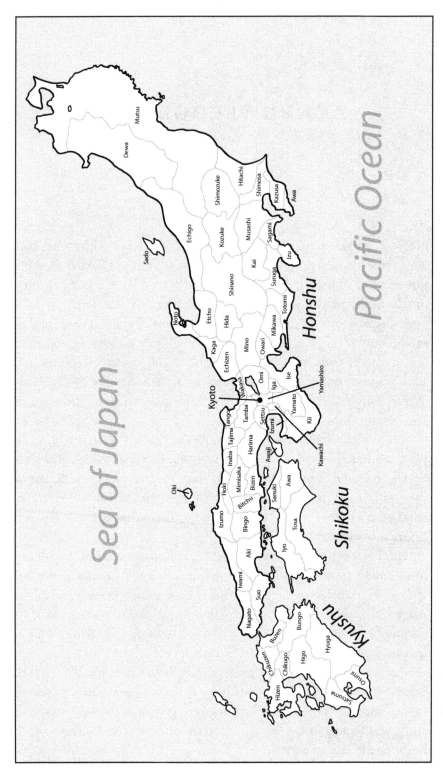

Japan in the tenth century

Chapter 1

Masakado and His Legacy

The history we read, though based on facts, is,
strictly speaking, not factual at all, but a series
of accepted judgments.

—Geoffrey Baraclough, *History in a Changing World*

Ignorance is the first requisite of the historian, ignorance
which simplifies and clarifies, which selects and omits.

—Lytton Strachey, *Eminent Victorians*

On the twenty-fifth day of the second month of 940, according to the old lunar calendar,* the capital was all atwitter with the news that Taira Masakado, the warrior rebel who had held the city and the imperial court in terror for the past two months, was dead—slain twelve days earlier in battle with imperial forces led by Fujiwara Hidesato and Masakado's kinsman Taira Sadamori. Ten days later, official dispatches from Hidesato and from the provinces of Kai and Shinano confirmed the news.[1]

Excitement, anticipation, and anxiety intensified over the next few weeks as further messengers reported that Hidesato and Sadamori were on their way to Kyoto, and rumors that Masakado's warriors were

---

*Until the late nineteenth century, the Japanese used a lunar calendar that featured twelve unnamed months of twenty-nine or thirty days each. The year began later than it does in the modern Gregorian calendar, with New Year's Day falling between January 21 and February 19. The twenty-fifth day of the second month of 940 would thus correspond to April 5 in the Gregorian calendar. I have followed the convention of converting years to the Gregorian equivalents but have left months and days in the lunar calendar format.

marching on the city to avenge their master swirled through the streets. In the end, however, the rumors proved baseless. Nearly two hundred of Masakado's core followers had died with him, and the rest of his men and allies scattered or were tracked down and killed in a matter of weeks. The court breathed a collective sigh of relief and sat back to discuss appropriate rewards for the victors, while Kyoto waited eagerly for the arrival of Masakado's head.[2]

The gruesome custom of gathering enemy heads after a battle (*buntori*, literally "taking one's share") became common practice in Japan at least as early as the seventh century, when the imperial state (*ritsuryō*) legal codes laid out a flexible point system for assessing battlefield merit and awarding promotions in rank. "Points," explained the Statute on Military Defense (*Gunbōryō*), "have no fixed meaning. In one year's battles one point may require the taking of ten heads, while in another year's fighting five heads can make a point."[3]

By the tenth century, warfare and law enforcement had become the preserve of professional warriors who fought for rewards for their services paid by the government or private employers. Recompense, however, required proof of success, making careful accounting and confirmation of one's kills a matter of considerable importance. Warriors concocted numerous devices toward this end, ranging from marking arrows with their names to commissioning illustrated accounts of their exploits, but the cardinal warrior trophies throughout Japan's premodern epoch were the heads of those they were contracted to run down. Heads were severed in the heat of battle, usually by means of a warrior's short sword (*katana*), or in the aftermath, as a substitute for live prisoners when capture or transport of the latter was impractical. Heads collected in accord with government warrants were assembled, identified, marked with the names of their former owners, and brought to the capital for inspection. Those belonging to important criminals were paraded through the streets and placed on public display.[4]

Hidesato and Sadamori reached the capital on the tenth day of the fifth month of 940 and entered the city through the Rashōmon gate to the south, where they were met by envoys from the Office of Imperial Police (*Kebiishi-chō*). The heads of Masakado and his men had previously been marked with red tags attached to the topknots and packed in salt to preserve them for transport to Kyoto. Now they were removed from the packing material, impaled on the tips of spears, and paraded north-ward up Suzaku Grand Avenue, while on both sides of the route "the carts and horses of high and low gathered like clouds" to watch the spec-tacle. An Imperial Police officer in full armor and on horseback led the procession, bearing a brightly colored banner announcing Masakado and his crimes. Behind him followed five armored foot soldiers carrying Masakado's head and guarding it with bared spears. Next rode Hidesato and Sadamori, also in full armor, but without their helmets so that they might be more easily recognized. And behind them came three or four dozen mounted warriors and foot soldiers who served Hidesato and Sadamori, followed by other Imperial Police officers, bearing the heads of the rest of Masakado's lieutenants. The parade ended outside the gate to the East Market, where Masakado's head was ceremoniously hung from a tree for display.[5] (See the illustrations on pages 86–87.)

Reliable historical records have little further to say about Masakado's remains. But popular rumors and legends, which had found their way into print by the early medieval period, relate that his was no ordinary head. For three months, they say, it hung outside the East Market, its eyes never closing and its color remaining unchanged, while in the evenings "it gnashed its teeth and wailed, 'Where is my mortal form, that which was cut away? Come to me, that this head might do battle once again.' And all who heard it trembled in fear." This howling continued night after night until one passerby at last had the presence of mind to answer it, reminding Masakado where he was and how he got there. At that, the now-chastened head grinned wistfully, sighed, closed its eyes, and fell silent.[6]

Shortly thereafter, however, Masakado's head was once again in search of its missing body, this time breaking free of the tree from which it had been hung and flying off toward Masakado's home in the East. One account relates that along the way an attendant of the Nangū shrine, in what is now Gifu prefecture, shot it with an arrow. Today the spot at which the head fell is marked by a small shrine called the Okashira Jinja ("Shrine of the Honorable Head") in a village called Yadōri ("Arrow Path"). Prayers offered there are said to be especially efficacious for cur-ing ailments of the head and neck.[7]

But the most famous accounts of Masakado's head indicate that it did not stop its journey after being shot in Gifu. Instead it continued on until it exhausted its remaining strength and came to rest near a small temple in a village called Shibazaki, in what would eventually become the Ōtemachi district of Tokyo. As it landed, the ground rumbled and the sky darkened, terrifying the local villagers, who washed the head and buried it on the grounds of the Kanda Myōjin shrine. Ten years later, in the ninth month of 950, an eerie cry issued from this grave site, the darkness was rendered by a flash of light, and a strange warrior appeared— and then vanished. The locals thereafter attended to Masakado as a potentially dangerous spirit and conducted rites to keep him pacified. By the late thirteenth century, this tomb had apparently fallen into disrepair, and Masakado's spirit was said to have been voicing its displeasure by causing one natural disaster after another. In 1305 a visiting priest had the grave site restored and bestowed the Buddhist name Hasuamida-butsu on Masakado, engraving this sobriquet on a stone stele that he erected next to the tomb. After that, the calamities ceased—at least for a while.[8]

When Ieyasu, the first Tokugawa Shogun, established his headquarters in Edo (now called Tokyo), Kanda Myōjin was moved to its present location in nearby Chiyoda ward, but Masakado's ancient grave, which had come to be known as the Kubizuka ("tomb of the head"), was left in its original spot, on what then became the estate of the Sakai, a prominent *daimyo* house. In 1868 the last Tokugawa shogun resigned, ostensibly returning power to the emperor. This event, known as the Meiji Restoration, marked the beginning of Japan's modern era. It also marked the beginning of new tales of troubles spawned by Masakado's restless spirit.

The new regime tore down the Sakai mansion in 1871 and erected offices for the Ministry of Finance on the site, but the Masakado Kubizuka was left in place on the grounds. Oda Kan'e's 1908 account describes Kubizuka as having, at that time, consisted of an earthen mound just under 7 meters high and about 30 meters in circumference, standing just to the southwest of a lily pond in front of the main entrance to the ministry offices. About 2 meters east of the mound stood a 2-meter by 3-meter foundation stone adorned with a garden lantern, on which, Oda contended, "there can be no doubting once stood" the stele (which had apparently disappeared sometime during the Tokugawa period) bearing Masakado's Buddhist name, Hasuamida-butsu.[9]

In 1874, just prior to the Meiji emperor's visit to Kanda Myōjin, the government issued a formal declaration condemning Masakado as having been "an enemy of the emperor" and ending Masakado's status as a principal divinity at the shrine.[10] Oddly enough, Masakado appears to have taken this insult in stride, for no significant troubles were reported to have followed immediately. But during the Great Kantō Earthquake of 1923, the Ministry of Finance offices burned to the ground and the Kubizuka site was seriously damaged. Ministry officials took advantage of this opportunity to excavate the site but found only an empty stone chamber. Determining that Masakado's head had probably never been there at all, the ministry filled the pond, razed the site, and put up a temporary office building over it. That, however, soon proved to have been a poor decision.

Construction workers and ministry officials began dropping like proverbial flies. Within two years, fourteen had died—including the minister of finance, Sasoku Seiji, himself—and large numbers of others suffered falls and other accidents in the new building. As rumors spread that Masakado's vengeful spirit was behind the troubles (the majority of the maladies involved the feet, lending credibility to gossip that blamed the victims for treading on Masakado's grave!), the ministry at length decided, in 1928, to tear down the buildings and restore the Kubizuka. Morita Shigetani, the chief attendant to Kanda Myōjin, was engaged to hold a pacification rite (ireisai), attended by the new minister, Mitsuji Chūzō, and large numbers of other ministry officials.[11]

On June 20, 1940, very nearly a thousand years to the day following Masakado's death, the Communications Ministry offices were struck by lightning. The resulting fire spread rapidly through Ōtemachi, burning down nine government offices, including the Ministry of Finance. Jumping once again to the obvious conclusion, Kawada Retsu, the minister of finance, swiftly summoned attendants from Kanda Myōjin to perform another pacification rite and had the foundation stone that had been removed after the 1923 earthquake rebuilt. For good measure, he also restored the stone stele bearing the name Hasuamida-butsu. A few months later, the Ministry of Finance moved its offices to Kasumigaseki, a few kilometers to the southwest, and the land surrounding Kubizuka became the property of the Tokyo municipal government.[12]

Allied air raids on Tokyo during the war virtually leveled Ōtemachi, but the Kubizuka site somehow survived amid the wreckage. In 1945, however, the Occupation forces decided to build a large motor pool garage on the site. But as construction began, one of the bulldozers struck the Kubizuka foundation stone and overturned suddenly, killing its operator. Ōtemachi ward chief Endō Seizō hastened to SCAP (Supreme Commander for the Allied Powers) headquarters with a delegation of neighborhood residents to explain the importance of Masakado's tomb and succeeded in persuading Occupation authorities to cancel their building plans and to cooperate in the restoration of the site. In 1970 a person or persons unknown made off with Masakado's

The Kubizuka today

stele, later returning it broken into three pieces. To avoid further wrath from Masakado, the monument was hurriedly recarved. The following year, the Tokyo government declared the site a municipal cultural treasure. And in 1984, in response to public pressure arising from a Japan Broadcasting Corporation (NHK) television series on Masakado, he was restored to his position as a principal divinity enshrined at Kanda Myōjin.[13]

While Ōtemachi has once again grown up around the Kubizuka site, stories abound of the lengths to which surrounding companies will go to appease Masakado's spirit—and the penalties some have suffered for failing to do so. Mitsui Finance Corporation's sudden bankruptcy in 2002, for example, is commonly attributed to plans to sell mineral rights to the land under the site. Most of the companies in the neighborhood contribute to the upkeep of the monument, some require employees to make regular pilgrimages to Kubizuka and/or to Kanda Myōjin, and many take pains to arrange office desks so that no one sits with his or her back facing Masakado's grave.[14]

Masakado in History

Taira Masakado is perhaps the most famous samurai you've never heard of. Celebrated as a populist hero, denounced as a rebel and a state criminal, or feared as an avenging spirit, he is the subject of national history, folklore, literary imagination, and local legends passed down in more than three hundred fifty places across Japan. Stories about him appear in some forty-five medieval or early modern literary works, as well as hundreds of modern books, articles, and novels. A score or more of Shintō shrines claim to be burial sites for parts of his body—his head, torso, hands, or the like—or to house bits of the armor he wore or the weapons he carried when he died.[15]

Such enduring fascination with a tenth-century warrior chieftain is less strange than it may seem at first consideration, for Masakado's story is operatic in its themes of fate and destiny: The scion of a prominent noble lineage and "a descendent, in the fifth generation, of Emperor Kashiwabara," Masakado served the imperial court in the capital as a youth, then settled down to the life of a country gentleman in the provinces of eastern Japan, to the northeast of modern-day Tokyo. His troubles began in 935, when he was suddenly attacked—ambushed—by another prominent local warrior, Minamoto Tasuku, at a place called Nomoto, near the convergence of Hitachi, Shimozuke, Musashi, and Shimōsa provinces. The nature of Tasuku's grudge against Masakado is hazy, but his decision to pursue it in the field set in motion a complex and momentous chain of events. Within months, Masakado found himself embroiled in conflicts with several of his kinsmen, led by his paternal uncle and father-in-law, Taira Yoshikane. Yoshikane, who was Tasuku's brother-in-law, had (so goes the tale) been at odds with Masakado since 931, "owing to a trifling quarrel over a woman."[16]

For the next four years, Masakado managed to keep his squabbles within the boundaries of imperial law, but in the eleventh month of that year, his fortunes took a radical turn when he entered Hitachi province at the head of a thousand troops, ostensibly to plead with the provincial government on behalf of one of his followers. Whatever his intentions might have been in leading armed men into Hitachi, he ended by attacking and occupying the provincial government headquarters. With this action, he crossed the proverbial line: no longer just a (for-the-most-part) law-abiding provincial warrior drawn into a feud with local rivals, he was now in rebellion against the state.

Seeing no avenue of retreat, Masakado chose instead to surge forward, seizing, in rapid succession, the provincial government headquarters of Shimozuke, Kōzuke, Musashi, Kazusa, Awa, Sagami, Izu, and Shimōsa. Then, according to most versions of the story, he threw down the most direct challenge to the authority of the imperial throne in three centuries—and the most direct that would be offered for four centuries hence—declaring himself the New Emperor, and setting about building a new capital near his home and appointing officials to staff his new court.

But his reign as New Emperor was to be short-lived. Within a month of his assumption of the title, the court had issued edicts calling for his destruction and commissioned several warrior notables—including Sadamori and Hidesato—for this task. Thus, on the fourteenth day of the second month of 940, "the punishment of Heaven descended upon Masakado." As he squared off against government forces in northwestern Shimōsa, "his horse forgot how to gallop as the wind in flight; the man lost his skills. Struck by an arrow from the gods, in the end the New Emperor perished alone, like Ch'ih Yu battling on the plain of Cho-lu."★

Masakado's insurrection ranks among the most dramatic episodes in the early history of the samurai. Coinciding with earthquakes, rainbows, and lunar eclipses in the capital, uprisings in the north, and pirate disturbances in the west, it threw the court and the capital into a panic and earned Masakado the worst sort of moralizing opprobrium. An edict issued by the Council of State, for example, intoned:

> Since creation this court has seen many rebellions, but none that compare to this. Now and again there have been those who yearn with treasonous spirit, but such meet always with the calamity of obliteration. The Heavenly Sovereign shall visit upon this Masakado the punishment of Heaven![17]

In this same vein, the most important source for information on the events of 935–940, a chronicle titled *Shōmonki* ("The Masakado Records"), ends melodramatically with a report from Masakado suffering in hell:

> Masakado now dwells in the village of the Eight Difficulties, in the town of the Five Modes of Existence, in the district of the Six Ways of Rebirth, in the province of the Three Realms. Nevertheless, an envoy from the Transitional Realm reported these words:†
>
> "While I dwelt on the earthly plane I did not one good deed, and for this wicked karma I spin through evil incarnations. At this very moment 15,000 souls indict me—how painful that is! When I did evil deeds, I gathered followers and through them committed my crimes. But on the day of judgment, I took on all my sins, and suffer alone. My body has been cast into the Forest of

---

★Ch'ih Yu was a rebel from Chinese mythology who met his end in a battle with the illustrious Yellow Emperor near Cho-lu, a plain in Hopei province. Quotations from *Konjaku monogatari shū* 25.1; *Shōmonki*, p. 129.

†Masakado's address in the next world follows the format of more mundane Japanese addresses, with place names drawn from important Buddhist concepts and principles.

Sword-leaf Trees and made to suffer, while my liver roasts over coals in an iron box. . . . My courage in life brought me no honor after death. In reward for my arrogance I have gained only bountiful suffering."[18]

All the same, Masakado's reputation was rehabilitated quickly. *Shōmonki*, our most expansive record of Masakado's adventures, is thought to have been completed sometime shortly after Masakado's insurrection ended—perhaps as early as a few months later—and is certain to have been finished sometime prior to 1099, the date recorded on the oldest surviving copy.[19] Intended for a court audience, the chronicle harshly condemns Masakado's actions after 939, but it also treats him sympathetically throughout, portraying him as a victim of circumstances and poor choices rather than as an evil man per se.

By medieval times, Masakado had become literally larger than life. He was now thought to have been, as one text put it, a man "the likes of which the world has seldom known. He stood over seven feet tall, his corporeal form was all of iron, and he had two pupils in his left eye."[20]

The idea that Masakado's body was made of iron—that he was indestructible—rapidly evolved into a belief that, like Achilles some two millennia earlier, he had but a single weak spot and that Hidesato's discovery of this secret (betrayed to him by one of Masakado's consorts) was the real cause of his doom. The location of Masakado's vulnerable point varies from tale to tale. Some legends give it as being his temple, while others identify it as his forehead, between his eyes, or his right eye. One particularly colorful version of the story relates that his mother had been a giant serpent, who made him invulnerable by licking him all over his body shortly after birth. Unfortunately for Masakado, however, she somehow neglected to lick the very top of his head, leaving that as his one point of weakness.[21]

The First Samurai

Masakado has long captured the imaginations of historians, as well as those of the general public in Japan. His life and his insurrection mark the advent of an era: the coming of age of the order of professional fighting men in the capital and countryside that we know as the *bushi* or *samurai*. The records concerning Masakado's misadventures are among the first in which this warrior order can be clearly seen—the first that confirm if not its maturity, certainly its adolescence. Many of the weapons and tools that became characteristic of samurai for the remainder of the classical and early medieval epochs—the curved sword (*tachi*), the open platform stirrups, the saddles, the bridles, the *ōyoroi* and *haramaki* styles of armor, the antlered, sweeping-brimmed helmets—were developed around Masakado's time.

The warbands led by Masakado and his adversaries were raised, organized, and bound together in a manner that would characterize samurai military forces for the next thee hundred years. The strategies and tactics they employed reflected the political, economic, and social structure of Masakado's world, as well as the priorities, ethics, and values that shaped Japanese warfare until modern times. And the court's methods of dealing with Masakado, his enemies, and his crimes illustrate the key principles and practices of the state's military and police system, along with the methods and the dynamics through which the civil nobility managed and dominated warriors for more than three centuries.

Masakado was not, of course, literally the first samurai. That warrior order emerged gradually over the course of the ninth and early tenth centuries in response to changing military needs and accompanying reforms to the state's military and police system.[22] The *ritsuryō* military system, the system of the imperial state, had been designed in the late seventh century, in the face of internal challenges to the sovereignty of the court and the regime, and the growing might of Tang China, which had been engaged since the early 600s in one of the greatest military expansions in Chinese history.

Most of Japan at that time was controlled by a confederation of great houses, among which one—the royal, or Yamato, house—stood as a kind of first among equals. Some of the other houses were entirely dependent on the Yamato for their positions, but the majority had their own geographic bases of power, which they ruled with considerable autonomy. In theory, these regional chieftains drew their titles from the court, but in practice, their positions were permanent, hereditary, and only nominally related to the king's authority. In fact, the principal role of the royal court—and of the countrywide polity—was little more than to serve as a vehicle for cooperation among the great houses in matters of "national" concern. All of that changed—rapidly, fundamentally, and sometimes dramatically—during the seventh century, as this polity gave way to a centralized imperial regime.[23]

The changeover accelerated after the sixth month of 645, when a radical clique led by the future Emperor Tenji seized power by hacking their political opponents to pieces with swords and spears in the midst of a court ceremony. In the wake of this spectacular coup d'état, Tenji and his supporters introduced a series of centralizing measures collectively known as the Taika Reforms, after the calendar era in which the first were launched. Over the next few decades, the great regional powers were stripped of their independent bases and converted to true officials of the state, while the Yamato sovereigns were restyled in the image of Chinese emperors: transcendent repositories of all political authority.

The reformers succeeded through an esoteric combination of cajolery, cooptation, and coercion, aided in no small measure by widespread apprehension over the very real—or so it seemed at the time—threat of a Chinese attack on the homeland. Specters of Tang invasion fleets looming over the horizon served to mute opposition to losses of local or hereditary privilege and to promote support for state-strengthening reforms, as central and provincial noble houses set aside their differences in the face of a perceived common enemy. For it was obvious to all concerned that the Yamato military organization was far from equal to the task of fending off the Tang.[24]

"National armies" of the confederation era were knit together from forces raised independently by the various noble houses, who then led them into battle under the banner of the Yamato sovereign. Recruitment, training, and mobilization varied from province to province—and sometimes from conflict to conflict. So did organization and control. Overall command of the army was also eclectic and sometimes divided between multiple "Supreme Commanders."[25]

The post-Taika military structure placed the whole of the state's military resources—weapons, auxiliary equipment, horses, troops, and officers—under the direct control of the emperor and his court. Henceforth, centrally appointed officers and officials oversaw all military units and activities, and direct conscription—supervised by the imperial court—replaced enlistment of troops through provincial chieftains.

Under the new system, all free male subjects between the ages of twenty and fifty-nine, other than rank-holding nobles and individuals who "suffered from long-term illness or were otherwise unfit for military duty," were liable for induction as soldiers, or *heishi*.[26] Conscripts were enrolled in provincial regiments (*gundan*), which were militia units, akin to modern national guards. Once assigned and registered as soldiers, most men returned to their homes and fields. Provincial governors maintained copies of regimental rosters, which they used as master lists from which to select troops for training; for peacetime police, guard, and frontier garrison duties; and for service in wartime armies.

The model for the *ritsuryō* military system was Tang China, which is hardly surprising in light of the concerns that inspired it. Contrary to the images that still dominate many popular histories, however, the new institutions—like the rest of the imperial state structure—were not simply adopted wholesale. The architects of the imperial state carefully adapted Chinese practices to meet Japanese needs and circumstances. At the same time, the planners all too often contended with conflicting priorities and accordingly incorporated some rather unhappy compromises into the final product. The original foibles of the system were, moreover, exacerbated by changing conditions: by the mid-eighth century the needs and priorities of the Japanese state differed considerably from those of the late seventh.

One of the difficulties the government faced was enforcing its conscription laws. Under the imperial state polity, military conscription was simply one of many kinds of labor tax, and induction rosters were compiled from the same population registers that were used to levy all other forms of tax. For this reason, peasant efforts to evade any of these taxes also placed them beyond the reach of the conscription authorities.

Far more important than the reluctance of peasants to serve in the military, however, were the fundamental tactical limitations of the *ritsuryō* armies. Like their Tang archetypes, the regiments that formed the backbone of Japanese imperial armies were mixed weapons-system forces: predominantly infantry but augmented by heavily armored archers on horseback. This infantry-heavy balance was the product of both design and necessity.

The architects of the *ritsuryō* polity seized on large-scale direct mobilization of the peasantry as a key part of the answer to both of the perceived threats that concerned them (a Chinese invasion and regional insurrections led by the old provincial chieftains). The system they created enabled the court to corner the market on military manpower—incorporating all or most of the bodies that could be drawn off to serve as soldiers into the state's armed forces—and to create loyalist armies of daunting volume, thereby effectively closing the door on military challenges to imperial power or authority. An army of imposing numbers was also, of course, precisely what would have been needed to fend off a foreign invasion, while a militia structure made it possible for a tiny country like Japan to muster large-scale fighting forces when necessary, without bankrupting its economic and agricultural base as a large standing army would have.

But the court had opted for size at the expense of the elite technology of the age, choosing, as a matter of logistical necessity, a military force composed primarily of infantry. The problem, however, was that the premier military technology of the day was mounted archery, not foot soldiers.

The state did try to maintain as large a cavalry force as it could, but efforts to that end ran afoul of major logistical difficulties. Foremost among these was the simple truth that fighting from horseback, particularly with bows and arrows, demanded complex skills that required years of training and practice to master. It was just not practical to attempt to develop first-rate cavalrymen from short-term peasant conscripts. The court addressed this problem through the straightforward expedient of staffing its cavalry units only with men who had acquired basic competence at mounted archery on their own, prior to induction.

This policy had far-reaching consequences for the shape of military things to come in Japan. It meant, first, that only a small portion of the imperial armies could be cavalry. It also meant that the cavalry would be composed solely of the scions of elite elements of Japanese society. For if the prerequisite to becoming a cavalryman was skill with bow and horse, cavalrymen could come only from families that kept horses, a practice that did not spread beyond the nobility and the very top tiers of the peasantry until the tenth century or later.

None of this mattered a great deal initially: the *ritsuryō* military structure was more than adequate to the tasks for which it was designed. But by the middle decades of the eighth century, the political climate—domestic and foreign—had changed enough to render the provincial regiments anachronistic and superfluous in most of the country.

The Chinese invasion that the Japanese had so feared simply never materialized. Whatever real peril there might have been ended by the late 670s, when the kingdom of Silla forced the Tang out of the Korean peninsula and checked its eastward expansion. Later, a rebellion (lasting from 756 to 763) by a Turkish general named An Lu-shan shook the Tang dynasty to its foundations, making it abundantly clear to the Japanese that the danger of Chinese warships approaching their shores was past. The likelihood of violent challenges to the central polity from the regional nobility had also dwindled rapidly, as former provincial chieftains came to accept the imperial state structure as the arena in which they would compete for power and influence. The passing of these crises all but ended the need to field large armies and prompted the court to begin restructuring its armed forces.

In the frontiers—particularly in the north, where the state was pursuing an aggressive war of occupation—large infantry units still served a useful function. But the martial needs of the interior provinces, the vast majority of the country, quickly pared down to the capture of criminals and similar policing functions. Unwieldy infantry units based on the provincial regiments were just not well suited to this type of work. The sort of military forces most called for now were small, highly mobile squads that could be assembled and sent out to pursue raiding bandits with a minimum of delay. In the meantime, diminishing military need for the regiments encouraged officers and provincial officials to misuse the conscripts who manned them—borrowing them, for example, for free labor on their personal homes and properties.

The court responded to these challenges with a series of adjustments, amendments, and general reforms. The pattern of edicts issued from the 730s onward indicates that the government had reached the conclusion that it was more efficient—and cheaper as well—to rely on privately trained and equipped elites than to continue to attempt to draft and train the general population. Accordingly, troops mustered from the peasantry played smaller and smaller roles in state military planning, while the role of elites expanded steadily throughout the eighth century. The provincial regiments were first supplemented by new types of forces and then, in 792, eliminated entirely in all but a handful of provinces. In their place the court created a series of new military posts and titles that legitimized the use of personal martial resources on behalf of the state. In essence, the court moved from a conscripted, publicly trained military force to one composed of professional mercenaries.

These measures served to make the acquisition of martial skills an attractive path to personal advancement for provincial elites and low-ranking central aristocrats. In the meantime, expansive social and political changes taking shape in Japan during the ninth and tenth centuries spawned intensifying competition for wealth and influence among the premier noble houses of the court, which in turn led to a private market for military resources, arising in parallel to the one generated by government policies. State and personal needs thus intersected to create broadening avenues to personal success for those with military talents.

From the late eighth century, skill at arms increasingly offered ambitious young men a means to get their feet in the door for careers in government service or in the service of some powerful aristocrat in the capital. The greater such opportunities became, the more enthusiastically and the more seriously such young men committed themselves to the profession of arms. The samurai thus came into being as an order of mercenaries in the capital and the provinces, for whom military service represented a means to broader—"civilian"—career ends.

By the middle of the ninth century, perhaps as early as the late eighth, fighting men in the provinces had also begun to form themselves into privately organized martial bands. By the third decade of the tenth century, private military networks of substantial scale had begun to appear, centered on major provincial warriors like Masakado, who, we are told, could charge into battle "leading many thousands of warriors," each himself leading "followers as numerous as the clouds."[27]

Although the government initially opposed such networks, it soon came to realize that they could be useful in filling a gap created in the state military system by the dismantling of the *ritsuryō* regiments in 792. For without the regiments, the court had no formal mechanism by which to call up troops when it needed them. During the early tenth century, however, it began to co-opt private military organizations to provide just such a mechanism, now transferring much of the responsibility for mustering and organizing the forces necessary for carrying out military assignments to warrior leaders, who could in turn delegate much of that responsibility to their own subordinates.

Thus by Masakado's day, Japan was ruled by a government that, outwardly at least, lacked both an army and a police force. Without troops of its own, the court turned instead to private forces directed by private warriors for its martial dirty work. And, as most readers are no doubt aware, the descendants—both genealogical and institutional—of these warriors became the political masters of Japan's medieval and early modern epochs. Juxtaposed in this fashion, these two developments suggest an appalling shortsightedness or naïveté on the part of the court nobility, which would seem to have adopted military policies tantamount, in the words of one popular author, to "sowing dragon's teeth." This led, inexorably, to the court falling under the domination of its own military servants.[28]

In this light, Masakado's insurrection—which, in the conventional reckoning, culminated in his proclaiming himself emperor over an independent new state in the east—seems eerily like a harbinger of things to come, a presage of the Gempei War of the 1180s, the Jōkyū War of 1221, and the Nambokuchō wars of the late fourteenth century, which, step by step, ushered in the medieval era of warrior rule. And, indeed, that is precisely the way historians have traditionally cast the events of the 930s.

But there are numerous problems with this scenario, not the least of which are the rather inconvenient facts that Masakado was not able to break free of court control and that he was brought down by other samurai. Even more important—and more telling—the first successful steps toward warrior autonomy and political power came nearly two and a half centuries after Masakado's death, and real samurai rule was yet another two centuries in the making after that.

These gaps are awkward and difficult to explain in the context of traditional assumptions about Masakado's insurrection: If provincial warriors, who by the mid-900s already constituted the government's only significant military forces, began a struggle to break free from court political control in the tenth century, why did it take them so long—nearly four hundred years!—to achieve this goal?

The short answer is that the rise of the warrior class as a political and economic power is a tale of the thirteenth through the sixteenth centuries, not the tenth, eleventh, and twelfth. Masakado's career and circumstances were typical of his class; he was an exemplar of his age, not a pale foreshadowing of the medieval future.

As the following chapters will reveal, a careful look at Masakado's insurrection illuminates both the structure and the inherent stability of his social and political world. Court supervision of the provinces became less direct than it had once aspired to be, and local freedom of action expanded. But the core premises of the imperial state persisted, and the bonds between capital and countryside endured.

Chapter 2

Masakado's World

All government—indeed, every human benefit and
enjoyment, every virtue and every prudent act—
is founded on compromise and barter.
—Edmund Burke, Speech on the Conciliation of America

Alliance, n. In . . . politics, the union of two thieves who
have their hands so deeply inserted in each other's
pockets that they cannot separately plunder a third.
—Ambrose Bierce, *The Devil's Dictionary*

For Masakado and his contemporaries, the center of the known world
was the capital city of Kyoto, known in their day as Heian-kyō, "the
Capital of Peace and Tranquility." Nestled in a bowl of low-rising
mountains near the southwestern tip of Lake Biwa, the city spanned a
little under 24 square kilometers between the Katsura and Kamo Rivers,
just north of where they joined the Yodo River, which in turn connected
the city to the Inland Sea, 30-some kilometers to the southwest.

Like the Tang Chinese capital at Chang'an (present-day Xi'an) on
which it was modeled, Kyoto was laid out in a rectangular grid of streets
that defined twelve hundred blocks of almost uniform size. The imperial palace enclosure (Daidairi)—about twice the size of the modern-day
imperial palace compound in Tokyo—stood at the northern end of the
city. From there, Suzaku Grand Avenue, nearly 85 meters wide, ran
southward to the Rashōmon gate made famous by Kurosawa Akira's
1950 film, dividing the city into Right (*Ukyō*) and Left (*Sakyō*) Capital

districts, each with its own state-sponsored temple (the Tōji in the east and the Saiji in the west) and state-administered market.[1]

Kyoto was Japan's fourth Chinese-patterned capital city, but it was the first enduring home to the government and the noble houses the government comprised. During the seventh century, the court's location had shifted with each new sovereign, in response to changing political alignments and fears of ritual pollution brought about by the death of the preceding monarch. In 694 Emperor Mommu established a more ambitious seat of power at Fujiwara, in west-central Yamato province, but this was abandoned in 710 for the much grander city of Nara (then called Heijō), about 15 kilometers to the north. Emperor Shōmu moved the capital three times between 741 and 744, and then back to Nara in 745.[2]

In 784, Masakado's forebear, Emperor Kammu, ordered the construction of a new capital city at Nagaoka, about 30 kilometers northwest of Nara. This area had been a political and economic stronghold for both sides of Kammu's family for generations, but it proved an ill-fated choice for the new capital. In 785 the official in charge of construction there was murdered, and the crown prince, Kammu's younger brother Sawara, was implicated in the crime. Sawara was deposed and ordered into exile, but he committed suicide before the sentence could be carried out. There followed a series of famines, floods, and epidemics that the court's diviners attributed to Sawara's vengeful spirit. By the spring of 793, Kammu had had enough and ordered work on Nagaoka halted. Construction on Kyoto, a few kilometers to the northeast, began the following year and continued until 805.[3]

The new capital was an awe-inspiring place. It was—and still is—a city of remarkable beauty. Encircled by thickly forested hills and mountains with slopes and valleys decorated by abundant rivers, lakes, springs, and waterfalls, its urban landscape was defined by broad tree-lined avenues, the splendor of the imperial palace enclosure, and the mansions of the powerful. The high and mighty lived gracefully in Kyoto in airy, spacious wooden homes that featured elegant stone walls, ornate gates, and stylish gardens complete with artificial lakes and islands.

More than just the political capital, Kyoto was also the center of culture, a hub for the leading religious establishments, and the axis of the country's manufacturing and market networks. In Masakado's time, its surrounding earthworks and moats enclosed a population of ten thousand or so nobles, lesser officials, police and military officers, and clerics, together with ninety thousand or more servants, craftsmen, merchants, entertainers, bandits, and beggars.

But Kyoto represented only one pole of Masakado's world. The other lay some 450 kilometers to the east, in the region then known as the Bandō ("East of the Slopes") or Tōgoku ("the Eastern Country"). The richest and most populous portion of this vast semifrontier region was the great Kantō plain, Japan's largest expanse of open farmland—more than 32,000 square kilometers—stretching along the southeastern sea coast, across the provinces of Sagami, Musashi, Kazusa, Shimōsa, Hitachi, Kōzuke, and Shimozuke (see map on page 22).

The term *Kantō* (literally "east of the barriers") refers to the lands east of three barriers described in the *ritsuryō* codes: *Suzuka no seki* in Isei province, *Fuwa no seki* in Mino, and *Arachi no seki* in Echizen. These were military checkpoints stocked with troops and weapons, under the authority of the provincial governors. Their principal function seems to have been to prevent rebels and criminals in or near the capital from escaping to the east.

Kantō fell out of fashion as a general label for the eastern provinces by the middle of the eighth century. Thereafter the region was most often referred to as the *Bandō*, which specifically pointed to the lands east of the Ashigara hills in Sagami province and east of the Usui hills in Kōzuke. *Tōgoku* also came into common usage about this same time.[4]

Masakado's homeland lay at the northern end of this plain, in what is now Ibaraki prefecture and was then the Toyoda and Sashima districts of northern Shimōsa province. Travelers today can get there from Kyoto in just four or five hours by train, but in the tenth century, the east was a distant realm. Even rapid messengers (*chieki* or *hieki*), changing horses every 20 kilometers at each postal station along the way, took eleven days or more to race from Shimōsa to the capital. For more ordinary travelers, the journey required fifteen to thirty days by horse or on foot along the sea coast or across the mountains of central Japan.[5]

Sashima and Toyoda were set between the Kogai and Watarase Rivers, which closely followed the borders with Hitachi to the east and Musashi to the west. Across the Kogai from Shimōsa lay the Niihari, Makabe, Tsukuba, and Ibaraki districts of Hitachi, a landscape dominated by Japan's second-largest lake, Kasumigaura, and by the twin peaks of

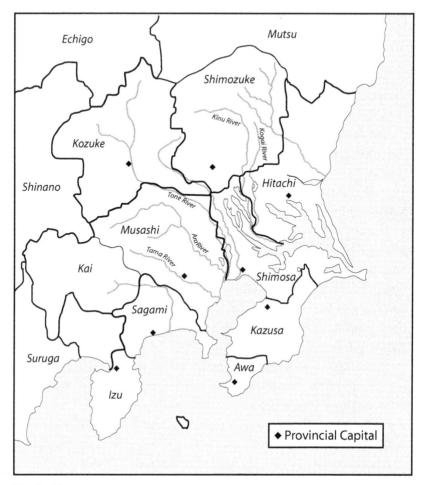

The Bandō

Mt. Tsukuba, rising some 870 meters above sea level and guarding the entrance to the Japan Alps (see the map on page 46).

In marked contrast to the urban splendor of the capital or the dramatic mountains and valleys that surrounded it, northeastern Shimōsa and southwestern Hitachi was a sparsely populated realm of low-lying forests and alluvial plains. A few kilometers south, west, or east of Mt. Tsukuba, the land flattened, sloping slightly to the south but nowhere rising more than 30 meters above sea level. To the west, the Kinu River system fed numerous small north-to-south-running streams, splattering the landscape with marshes. The largest of these, the Iinuma, about 20 kilometers in length and 2 kilometers across, formed the border between Sashima and Toyoda.

Prior to extensive drainage projects during the early modern period, there were relatively few rice paddies in this region, and those that were actively farmed were mostly small scale. Residents of the area drew their livelihood from fishing, hunting pheasants and migratory birds, lumbering, and dry field agriculture that produced millet, melons, and mulberry. They lived in diffuse hamlets consisting of a dozen or so houses scattered in small clumps across areas the size of two or three football fields.[6]

The authority of the central court in this region—as in the rest of the countryside—was most clearly symbolized by the provincial government office compounds, or *kokuga*. These were square complexes, about 100 meters on each side, built as scaled-down models of the office compound of the imperial palace enclosure in the capital (see the illustration on page 88). Each featured a main hall, identical in shape and construction to the Great Audience Hall (Daigokuden) in the palace, standing at the north end and facing onto an open courtyard flanked on the east and west by long secondary halls. Surrounding walls, and massive gates at the south end, allowed the compounds to double as military fortresses.

Provincial governors held audience with lesser functionaries, military commanders, and other provincial notables in the main hall, in close imitation of the emperor's audiences in Kyoto. Such ceremonies emphasized and symbolized their role as the emperor's representative in the province and the subordination of the provinces to the court.[7]

Eastern Japan was a world in flux long before Masakado and his enemies turned it into a world at war. Masakado's life and career highlight an era of change, in which old paradigms of power and wealth were giving way to new ones; innovative technologies of agriculture, governance, and warfare were reshaping life in the provinces. Masakado epitomized a new kind of provincial aristocrat ascendant in the tenth century. Son and grandson of nobility and great-grandson of royalty, he obtained no posts or court rank of his own; yet he became, for a time, one of the most powerful men in Japan. To appreciate how this could be and why Masakado failed so utterly in the end, we must first pause to ponder the political and social realm that both made and ruined him.

The Court and the Countryside

The imperial state's provisions for ruling and taxing the countryside were calculated, above all, to establish centralized control and to produce revenue for the court. They cast the whole country as a giant manor on which the farming population served as peasant tenants and over which the court—the imperial house, the major religious institutions, and the great noble houses—functioned collectively as lord.[8]

This basic conception of the proper order of things changed little between the creation of the *ritsuryō* state in the seventh century and Masakado's era. But the court's priorities did shift, evolving from a strident assertion of direct central oversight at the dawn of the new polity to an emphasis on maintaining centralized authority while delegating responsibility for many of the workaday functions of government. As a result, the mechanisms of control and exploitation—resource collection—did change dramatically, particularly from the late eighth century onward.

The *ritsuryō* codes defined a four-layered system of administration and supervision, establishing fifty-eight (later increased to sixty-six) provinces (*kuni*) gathered into seven circuits (*dō*) and a capital region (*kinai*), and subdivided into districts (*gun*), which were further divided into townships (*sato* or *gō*). Of these, the provinces and districts proved the most important.

Officers of the provincial governments were envisioned as a network of loyal mandarins stationed across the country to supervise, and supersede, the local elites who had ruled as largely autonomous chieftains under the earlier confederation. The principal officials—the governor (*kami*), assistant governor (*suke*), secretaries (*jō*), and inspectors (*sakan*)—were all central nobles dispatched from the capital. They served four-year terms, after which they moved on to new positions in other provinces or in the central government. (See the illustration on page 89.)

As representatives of the emperor, governors and assistant governors had jurisdiction over—and were held responsible for—almost everything that went on in their provinces, including the maintenance of census registers, promotion of agriculture, maintenance of law and order, oversight of military affairs and training, oversight of religious ceremonies, and collection of taxes. Their authority was restricted only from above, by the court, ensuring that the power of the central government, justified by the authority of the emperor, checked and overrode the role of provincial elites in local and regional governance.

While the nobility in Kyoto tended to view postings to provincial offices as a hardship, and sometimes used them as a form of exile, an appointment as provincial governor could be extremely lucrative. Under the *ritsuryō* system, the state—the emperor—claimed ownership of all rice-producing lands. The largest portion of these were allotted to peasant cultivators, apportioned according to household size. Such fields became essentially the private property of the family that held them, although they could not be sold or used as collateral for loans, and they were subject to rearrangement and redistribution every six years.

All other rice fields under cultivation at the time the first allotment took place in the 690s were placed under the supervision of the provincial governor and his staff. A good bit of this land was assigned to the support of the powerful, under a system in which aristocrats and religious institutions were awarded the tax receipts from designated "office lands," "rank lands," and "temple lands." The remainder was leased to local peasants, who paid a fifth of the annual yield as rent collected by the governor and sent to the capital, along with other tax receipts.[9]

As a compensation for having to work in the boondocks, governors were assigned office lands, and laborers to work them, in their provinces of appointment. Because they could directly supervise cultivation and could exploit their powers of office to appropriate free labor from the pool of military conscripts and corvée workers under their jurisdiction, provincial officials usually found their office lands to be significantly more profitable than those held by aristocrats who remained in the capital.

Governors were also in charge of a system of government-operated loan sharking, called *suiko*, under which peasants were compelled to borrow seed rice in the spring and repay it, with interest as high as 50 percent, after the fall harvest. This practice, which predates the imperial state, seems to have served three useful purposes: (1) it helped promote the expansion of paddy rice agriculture (which made cultivators less mobile and therefore more easily governed than dry field farmers); (2) it provided the government with revenue; and (3) it functioned as a kind of welfare system, because borrowers could be forgiven the interest payments in times of crop failure or famine. In order to encourage continual expansion of the system, officials were directed to add a portion of the interest collected to the principal lent out the following year and were allowed to keep the interest on this portion of the loans for themselves.[10]

Provincial officials also enjoyed another perquisite that stemmed from provisions for expanding the state's taxable land base to keep up with a growing population and rising government expenditures. Because of the heavy costs involved in the construction of new rice paddies—which needed to be perfectly level, set off by dykes, and connected to irrigation systems for flooding and draining them at the appropriate points in the growing cycle—the law encouraged provincial governors, temples, and high-ranked aristocrats to open new fields using their own resources and operate them as private lands for specified periods, after which they would revert to the public treasury. Under the original terms of the *ritsuryō* codes, new fields were to be held by the developer for the duration of his lifetime, or of his term in office, in the case of provincial governors. But this proved insufficient incentive to inspire enough land reclamation to keep up with the court's need for revenue, and in 723 the law was amended to allow possession of reclaimed fields for three generations. In 743 it was amended again to allow possession in perpetuity.

In addition to being allowed to open new lands for themselves, and to having at their disposal ready sources of legal and illegal labor to develop and work them, provincial governors were charged with overseeing all paddy construction, a function that included the power to confiscate illicitly opened fields for the public treasury. In practice this assured governors a powerful—and profitable—role in any efforts by aristocrats and local elites to acquire lands in the provinces.[11]

Premise, Reality, and Adjustment

The institutions and procedures of the early imperial state were born from an intriguing blend of idealism, wishful thinking, pragmatism, and compromise. Few survived wholly intact for more than a few decades, although the spirit of the system—particularly the principle of centralized authority culminating in the emperor—remained strong into the fourteenth century and beyond.

By Masakado's time, landholding, tax collection, and social structure in the provinces bore scant resemblance to the letter of the *ritsuryō* law. A new gentry was emerging in the countryside and absorbing a burgeoning share of both the revenues produced and the responsibilities of government there.

Nevertheless, the medieval world of "feudalism"—nearly autonomous baronies contesting among themselves with minimal regard for the wishes or prerogatives of the court—was still very far off. The prospect of such an unraveling of central authority would likely have seemed every bit as improbable to Masakado and his contemporaries as it would to twenty-first-century Americans. Indeed, the ties binding capital to countryside were growing stronger, not weaker, in Masakado's day.[12]

This odd mixture of centrifugal and centripetal development transpired because the provincial gentry and the court nobility embraced fundamentally different notions of what constituted wealth and power. The Kyoto aristocracy viewed wealth in terms of rice and other products and viewed power as a function of administrative oversight. The provincials, in contrast, saw both in terms of hands-on control over productive resources—land and people. So long as they were allowed a share of the profits from the land, they were content to acquiesce to central authority and to focus not on ultimate ownership but on actual control—management of the agricultural process, collection of taxes and rents, and other domanial sorts of authority. The result was an evolving series of accommodations among the court, provincial governors, and rural elites. Provincial governors arriving from Kyoto quickly discovered that they simply could not govern without coming to terms with their subordinates.[13]

Tax Farmers, Princes, and Bandits

One shortcoming of the landholding and tax structure established in the late seventh century was that it presumed a countryside populated by a largely undifferentiated mass of peasant households. The peasants were to be assigned—or leased—fields to cultivate, from which they would draw their livelihood and in exchange for which they would pay taxes and rents to sustain the emperor, the court, and local officials. But the theory behind this system failed to account for differences in individual ability: Some peasants proved to be better—or simply luckier—farmers than others. Some were able to make a profit year after year; others found themselves incapable of making ends meet, let alone meeting their tax obligations.

Allotment fields could not legally be sold or pawned outright, but families in rough financial straits learned to skirt the law, mortgaging future crops to more successful neighbors, who would then assume responsibility for the taxes, while the nominal owners became essentially tenants on their own fields. Another way out was to moonlight, raising extra income by hiring out family members to work lands belonging to others. Still another solution was simply to run away, abandoning assigned fields and resettling elsewhere, where absconders could easily find work on lands belonging to government officials or local elites.

Thus some peasants grew wealthy, while others were forced to become dependents of their neighbors, who increasingly organized the populations around their homes under their own control. A gap was developing between the structure of provincial society as envisioned by the architects of the imperial state and reality in the countryside. And, as the gap widened, tax collection through the procedures set down in the *ritsuryō* codes became increasingly difficult.[14]

In a remarkably pragmatic effort to reconcile old premises to new realities, the court responded with an updated paradigm: henceforth, tax collection was to be a problem between the central and provincial governments, rather than one between the court and individual subjects. Revenue quotas were set province by province, and governors were made accountable for seeing that they were met—making up shortfalls out of their own pockets, if necessary. The means by which the taxes were actually collected were left largely to the discretion of the governors, who in turn delegated most of the burden to local elites charged with assembling whatever revenues were deemed appropriate from the specific locales in which they had influence.

Governors and local managers alike welcomed such policy measures as opportunities for increasing their personal wealth and power. In a matter of decades, the new tax structure turned everyone involved—except peasant cultivators—into tax farmers collecting revenues beyond their assigned quotas and pocketing the surplus.[15]

Governors, for their part, demonstrated a less-than-noble inclination to regard their provinces chiefly as revenue-producing resources and became increasingly indifferent to the needs and welfare of residents. Gubernatorial posts became more lucrative than ever: a reasonable estimate suggests that a typical governor could skim off as much as 10 percent of the total production of his province, an enormous sum for an individual.[16]

By the end of Masakado's century, the court was receiving a steady stream of petitions demanding the impeachment of rapacious governors. The most famous of these, filed in 988 by the "district officials and taxpayers" of Owari province, accuses the governor of tax fraud, extortion, nepotism, murder, and a host of other greater and lesser crimes. He was said to have collected nearly three times the prescribed amount of taxes, often beginning his collection efforts as much as four months ahead of the traditional schedule and using agents who stole even the furnishings from the lodgings provided for them as they made their rounds. His relatives and followers, it was charged, were allowed to seize lands throughout the province and operate them as private, tax-exempt holdings. They also "commandeered" horses and cattle from provincial residents, and then sold them back several days later for three to five times their fair price.[17]

The extent of gubernatorial abuses of power can be imagined when one considers that during the whole of the ninth century, only forty-four provincial governors were officially designated "Good Officials" (ryōshi). This was less than 3 percent of the approximately fifteen hundred appointees who served over this time span, and even those who earned the appellation were most often cited not for positive contributions but simply for having managed to avoid doing anything unusually wicked.[18]

The aristocracy and religious institutions in the capital were also working to create and expand private sources of revenue and influence outside the official government structure. Such efforts became a persistent source of trouble for provincial residents and officials from the middle decades of the ninth century onward.

Council of State edicts from this period railed against "temples, shrines, princes and officials behaving like peasants, contesting over peasant paddy fields, stealing moveable property, ignoring governors and district magistrates, and using their prestige and influence" to intimidate provincial residents. "Agents of temples, shrines, government officials, and great houses," we are told, were "confiscating boats, carts, horses and men by force," "robbing tax shipments," and "causing much suffering for the people."[19]

In the meantime, provincial elites were learning new and better ways to flex their political and economic muscles. One of the defining characteristics of the imperial state was the monopolization of power by the nobility of the capital region in west-central Honshu. Regional nobles elsewhere, who had once been the peers of this group, were—in principle, at least—relegated to the political and social back benches. But the old regional chieftains never fully surrendered their wealth or their familial authority in the agricultural villages, and by the early Heian period (794–1185), their descendants and other rural elites were challenging gubernatorial power in myriad subtle—and many not-so-subtle—ways.★

Most of these challenges took place within the bounds of the law. More overt resistance, when it did occur, was small scale and certainly did not rise to the level of rebellion, but it did sometimes involve violence. From the turn of the ninth century onward, the court issued a steady stream of complaints about armed marauders "burning people's homes and using weapons to rob," "striding about the villages opposing government officials and intimidating the poor," "harming public morals," and interfering with tax shipments—stealing not only the tax goods themselves but the horses and boats used to transport them.[20]

Alliances and Immigrants

Masakado's eastern provincial world roiled under a competition for wealth and influence between three groups: (1) governors, (2) provincial resident elites, and (3) "temples, shrines, princes, and officials" of the court. At the axis of this competition was the class from which both Masakado and his chief opponents derived: the middle-ranked court nobles whose careers centered on appointments to provincial government offices.

★The Heian period, most commonly dated from 794 to 1180 or 1185, is the era in which the apex of political control rested incontestably in Kyoto (Heian-kyō)—that is, the period between the relocation of the capital from Nara to the establishment of the Kamakura shogunate.

Compelled by a need to defend themselves and their prerogatives against outlawry and armed resistance, as well as by the desire to maximize the profits that could be squeezed from taxpayers, many governors included "warriors of ability" among the personal entourages that accompanied them to their provinces of appointment. A substantial number also took up arms for themselves and established reputations as military troubleshooters. Fighting ability was, in fact, useful not only in intimidating armed residents of their provinces but also as a means to speed the advance of their careers by opening doors to posts in court military units or to the private service of important court figures.[21]

Tenth-century Japan was a rigidly stratified society in which functionally unbridgeable gulfs of station separated the top tier of court aristocrats, the lower- and middle-level nobles who served as provincial governors, and the residents of the countryside. A complex system of court ranks, created by the *ritsuryō* codes and similar in purpose to modern civil service rank systems, was used to classify both the central and the provincial nobility. A man's rank determined his status, his eligibility for government posts, and his place in the complex protocols for official and social events. There were nine main ranks, beginning with the initial rank and continuing upward from the eighth to the first. The first, second, and third ranks were subdivided into senior and junior grades; the senior fourth through junior eighth ranks were further divided into upper and lower categories. There were also four initial ranks: greater initial rank, upper grade; greater initial rank, lower grade; lesser initial rank, upper grade; and lesser initial rank, lower grade.

As one might expect, each stratum in this hierarchy had access to specific types of government posts, rights over land, and forms of income. What made things particularly interesting, however, was that the rights and privileges of each stratum were sealed from below as well as from above, so that high-ranked courtiers were as effectively barred from provincial or local posts as provincial elites were from becoming top court officials.

This arrangement generated intense competition and rivalry among peers—including siblings—who contested in circumscribed and ever more crowded arenas for the same baskets of fruit. But it also formed a basis for cooperation between members of different strata, because neither party could challenge the prerogatives of the other, and each member of the alliance could aid the others in obtaining rewards for which he was himself ineligible.[22]

Over time, connections between hereditary status and office-holding became progressively deeper and more firmly entrenched, and eligibility for posts became limited to smaller and smaller numbers of houses. As the prospect turned more and more predictable that descendants of particular families would hold the same posts generation after generation, many offices—and the tasks assigned to them—became closely associated with certain houses, and key government functions came to be performed through personal rather than formal public channels, rendering "public" and "private" rights and responsibilities harder and harder to distinguish.[23]

By Masakado's time, court society and the operations of government were dominated by a handful of high-ranked courtiers and their families, the most powerful of which was the Fujiwara *Sekkanke* or Regents' House, whose heads served as hereditary regents or chancellors to emperors. Men of the provincial governor class and other low- and middle-ranked nobles would attach themselves to Fujiwara regents or other senior courtiers, who would become their patrons and sponsor their advancement at court. In exchange, the clients served on the patron's household staff and vouchsafed his interests in the course of their official duties in the posts he obtained for them.

This patron-client relationship was rooted in mutual need and worked to the advantage of both parties: it permitted top courtiers to exploit the administrative talent and the private wealth of provincial governors in the administration of their private affairs, and it assured lower-ranking nobles of continued appointment to lucrative posts.[24]

Alliances were also developing between senior court figures and provincial elites, as the latter learned to use their connections—real or pretended—with the former to gain greater autonomy from the provincial government. By the late 800s, court edicts complained that the great houses and religious institutions of the capital were "by-passing the governor and issuing private house edicts directly to district magistrates and functionaries within the provincial government," as well as "sending agents, who led followers through the provinces," disrupting peasant households and government business; and that "natives and drifters claiming to be housemen of princes and government officials did not fear the authority of the governor and did not obey the injunctions of district magistrates."[25]

The "natives and drifters" cited in these documents included a new group of provincial residents. For members of the career provincial governor class (*zuryō*), the heightened competition, factionalism, and atmosphere of hereditary prerogative that characterized court politics during the ninth and tenth centuries meant diminishing prospects in the capital for themselves and their children. At the same time, many were finding that they could use the power and perquisites of their offices and the strength of their court connections to establish landed bases in their provinces of appointment and to continue to exploit the resources of these provinces even after their terms of office expired.

As former officials settled in the countryside, they quickly became powers to contend with, competing with subsequent governors, district magistrates, and older gentry houses for resources and influence. The newcomers seem to have been, among other things, continuing to collect taxes—especially back taxes—just as if they were still officials. Ironically, then, the settlers, driven out of the capital by waning opportunities there, were forming similar personal networks in the provinces and through them establishing themselves at the top of provincial society— creating a new, provincial-level system of hierarchical alliances.[26]

The central government initially saw the emigration of ranked nobles to the countryside as a threat to provincial order and attempted to prohibit it. Court documents from the late eighth to the late ninth century railed against "officials who have finished their terms of office, and sons and younger brothers of princes and court officials" who were "settling down in their [former] areas of jurisdiction, where they hindered agriculture, gathered up the peasantry like fishermen gathering fish, and constructed plans for their own evil gains."[27]

By Masakado's time, however, the court had given up this effort and was instead coming to terms with the emigrants. Former provincial officials and their children began to gain appointments to assistant governorships and other provincial offices.[28]

Nevertheless, few of the nobles who "settled down" in the countryside actually abandoned life in the capital for a provincial existence. Some individuals and branches of families became more thoroughly committed to rural life than others, but most were still careful to maintain their ties to the capital. They had to, for cutting themselves off completely from the court would have meant severing themselves from the source of official appointments and from critical personal connections, and would thereby have ended all hope of maintaining the family's social and political position—even in provincial society.

Typical exurban provincial officials built homes and held packages of lands scattered about the countryside, providing them with income. At the same time, they continued extensive contact with political affairs in the capital and often maintained homes there, to which they shipped most of the profits from their rural enterprises. To provincial governors and their families, Kyoto was the source of the human and physical resources that made their provincial business activities possible, as well as the marketplace for the goods they obtained in the country. By the same token, they used their provincial activities to reinforce their footholds within the political and official world of the capital.[29]

The carpetbaggers competed with longer-established provincial elites, but they also formed alliances with them. Most importantly, they intermarried with provincial families. Edicts forbidding this practice make it clear that provincial officials were taking wives and sons-in-law from provincial elite houses with considerable frequency.[30]

Curiously, marital ties of this sort were often stronger than direct blood ties among the elite warrior houses of the East. This may have been because marriage-based alliances were newer—and thus more individual—than direct blood ties.[31]

Marriages in Masakado's world were polygamous or serially monogamous and usually involved not just separate bedrooms but separate residences. Women most commonly continued to live in their birth homes or in other residences provided by their fathers, while husbands lived in houses of their own, visiting as frequently as circumstances and inclinations allowed. Children reckoned descent primarily from their father and took his surname. But they were usually raised in their mother's home and inherited much of their material property from her. Often when the bride's family was of significantly higher station than the groom's, the children—and sometimes the new husband—adopted the surname of the bride's father. As a result, court-derived surnames like Taira, Minamoto, and Fujiwara gradually supplanted those of the older provincial noble families.[32]

The Taira in the East

The two most illustrious warrior names of the Heian age, Taira and Minamoto, both had their beginnings in efforts to prune the imperial family tree and dispose of extraneous princes and princesses. The *ritsuryō* codes provided special stipends, rank lands, and other advantages to imperial offspring down to the fourth generation. But in a society in which emperors and ranking courtiers routinely carried on romantic liaisons with dozens of consorts, concubines, ladies-in-waiting, and other court women—and in which all or most of the children born from such encounters were recognized as legitimate heirs—the numbers of privileged imperial progeny could easily swell to levels that threatened the solvency of the public treasury. This problem was made even worse by profligate royals who got themselves into debt and then paid off the loans by adopting the creditors as heirs, thereby entitling them to the rewards of princely status.[33]

Fortunately, however, the court and the imperial house rescued themselves from floundering in a sea of dissolute princes and princesses through the simple expedient of granting surnames to unwanted heirs and demoting them from royal to commoner status. Taira and Minamoto were the most common family names awarded in this fashion. There were seventeen major lines of Minamoto and four of Taira, all descended from different emperors.[34] Branches of two of these—the Seiwa Genji deriving from Emperor Seiwa (r. 858–876) and the Kammu Heishi from Emperor Kammu (r. 781–806)—became famous as warrior houses.★

Seiwa had nineteen sons, the descendants of nine of whom bore the Minamoto surname. The lines that produced samurai claim descent from Seiwa's sixth son, Prince Sadazumi, through his son Tsunemoto, who received the Minamoto name just a few months before his death, in 961, and played a small but important role in Masakado's story.

The Kammu Heishi actually comprised four main lineages, each descended from a different prince. The line that produced warriors began with Kammu's eldest son, Katsurahara, through his son Takami and

---

★The term *Genji* derives from the Sino-Japanese reading of the surname Minamoto. Similarly, *Heishi* comes from the Sino-Japanese reading of the surname Taira.

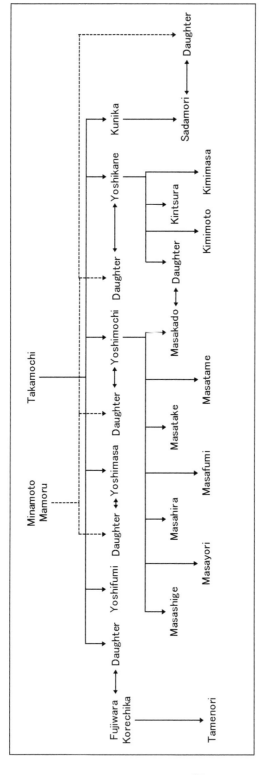

The eastern Taira

grandson Takamochi. According to tradition, Takamochi, who was presented with the Taira surname and appointed assistant governor of Kazusa in 889, acquired both the appointment and the name as rewards for his military heroism in suppressing an attempted coup d'état at court. This story is probably not true; nevertheless the fact that Takamochi's descendants believed in—or created—such a venerable military tradition for their house is worth noting.[35]

All of Takamochi's wives appear to have come from provincial families, and the majority of his children were probably born and at least partially bred in the east. He fathered eight sons, all of whom served as officials and established bases for themselves in various eastern provinces. The descendants of four continued to obtain posts in provincial and central government offices and developed formidable reputations as military servants in the capital. The others appear to have committed themselves to a more thoroughly provincial existence within a generation or two. Takamochi also had several daughters who married into prominent local houses, further extending his circle of allies in the countryside.[36]

Three of Takamochi's progeny played key roles in Masakado's story. The eldest of these was Kunika, who carved out a landed base and a personal following for himself in and around the provincial capital of Hitachi, where he became a senior secretary (*daijō*). Sometime near the middle of his career, he also served as commander of the Pacification Headquarters in Mutsu, a post that proved most valuable to him as a symbol and a tool toward forging his military reputation and standing, strengthening his position in Hitachi upon his return. He seems, in fact, to have brought some of the men he commanded in the northeast back to Hitachi with him and to have passed their services on to his son Sadamori.[37]

Takamochi's second son, Yoshikane, fared even better for himself professionally, rising to junior fifth rank, upper grade, and serving as assistant governor of Shimōsa. Curiously, however, there is no evidence of his having held lands in Shimōsa. His main base, which he probably inherited from his father, appears instead to have been on the northern tip of Kazusa, in the Musata district. He also maintained a home called Hatori-no-shuku in the western part of Hitachi.[38]

Takamochi's third son, Masakado's father, Yoshimochi, also enjoyed a fruitful career that included a stint as commander of the Pacification

Headquarters and ended in his rise to the junior fourth rank, lower grade.[39] He may also have served for a time in the Shimōsa provincial government. In any event, he married a daughter of Inukai Harue, the head of a prominent district magisterial house in Shimōsa's Sōma district, and established a home in the Toyoda district, to the north of Sōma.[40]

As already noted, this was a marshy area not well suited to paddy rice agriculture. In consequence, few public paddies had been established there in the early years of the imperial state system, and many that were started quickly went out of cultivation. This situation offered Yoshimochi and his family plentiful opportunities to reclaim fields and build a large portfolio of lands. His most important source of income came, however, not from farming but from livestock. Yoshimochi was a cowboy, or rather, a horse and cattle baron.[41]

Among the least successful provisions of the early imperial state system were those concerned with ensuring an adequate supply of warhorses for the state's armies. The *ritsuryō* codes originally established royal pastures in every province, under the authority of the Ministry of Military Affairs and administered by the provincial governor and a Pasture Master (*makichō*) appointed from the provincial gentry. This plan was, however, rapidly done in by the advance of agriculture. By the mid-eighth century, most of the pastures in the home provinces around Kyoto—and in other areas amenable to cultivation—were being turned into rice fields or simply taken out of use because they now bordered too closely on paddy lands.

A second generation of court-owned pasture lands came into being, mostly in the frontier regions—the east and the extreme southwest—and often bordering on private pasture lands owned by court families or local elites. By Yoshimochi's day, the pasture system had much in common with the new tax system emerging at about this same time. Prominent locals holding usually inheritable appointments as Royal Wranglers (*bokushi*) bred horses and cattle on a bewildering mixture of public, private, and semiprivate pasture lands. The court requisitioned an agreed-upon annual quota of animals from each pasture, and the wranglers were allowed to do as they pleased with the rest.[42]

This proved an extraordinarily lucrative arrangement for men like Yoshimochi, for horses were a valuable commodity in Heian Japan. To begin with, they were the favored gift offered to powerful court nobles in exchange for favors and influence-peddling on one's behalf—the stable currency of political commerce.[43] They were also an essential item of military accoutrement for the emerging warrior class, which, as we have seen, was defined by its mastery of mounted archery. Thus Yoshimochi's, and later Masakado's, access to a supply of quality warhorses bought them access to aristocratic patronage in the capital and enabled them to recruit and equip followers, greatly enhancing both their political and military strength.

As inhospitable as the Sashima-Toyoda-Sōma region may have been for rice growing, it was unusually good terrain for pasture lands. Relatively level and conveniently chopped into small islands and peninsulas by the various rivers and wetlands, it was easily turned into pastures using ditches and fences to augment these natural features, in order to keep horses and cattle from wandering off or straying into agricultural fields or residential compounds. An early tenth-century compendium lists thirty-nine horse and cattle pastures under the nominal control of the Ministry of Military Affairs. Twenty-four of these were devoted to horse breeding, and, of these, five were located in Shimōsa.[44]

Both of Masakado's principal homes—which he inherited from Yoshimochi—fronted on royal pastures. A reasonable estimate suggests that the two pastures together supported some six hundred horses and a similar number of cattle. This would have represented a substantial herd and enormous wealth for Yoshimochi and Masakado, who used the income obtained from ranching as investment capital to purchase agricultural tools and to open new farm and pasture lands.[45]

Masakado was Yoshimochi's third son. No records of his birth or early life survive, but we can surmise at least a few basic bits of information from circumstantial evidence. We know, for example, that his childhood sobriquet was Kojirō ("Little Second Son") and that when he emerged into the historical limelight in 935, he was his father's principal heir.[46] Together these facts suggest that at least one of his elder brothers must have died before Masakado was born and the other before Yoshimochi passed on, sometime in the 920s or early 930s. Similarly we can place Masakado's birth year somewhere around 900, because accounts of his adventures in the mid-930s speak of his having children young enough to be still in the care of their mother but make no mention of adult children.[47] He was most likely born and raised in Sōma, near his mother's childhood home. In all likelihood, he also accompanied his father to Mutsu for at least part of the time when Yoshimochi served as commander of the Pacification Headquarters.[48]

At some point during his late teens, Masakado was sent to the capital, where his father had arranged—presumably with bribes of gold and horses from Mutsu, which were very much in demand in Kyoto—for him to enter the service of the future regent (*sesshō*) and chancellor (*daijōdaijin*) Fujiwara Tadahira. In spite of this powerful patron, Masakado failed to obtain court rank or significant office, although he may have served for a time in the Takiguchi, a special guard unit attached to the Chamberlain's Office (*Kurōdo-dokoro*).[49]

Masakado's failure in the capital seems odd, inasmuch as he should have been well prepared and positioned for success. He had an illustrious pedigree, an influential patron, and ample resources for providing the right sorts of gifts to the right people. His later history also demonstrates that he was intelligent, courageous, politically astute, and persuasive in debate. By all reckoning, then, his time in Kyoto should have launched a prosperous career in government.

Instead, Masakado returned to Shimōsa empty-handed, perhaps overwhelmed by the competition in the capital or perhaps simply feeling the need to personally secure his inheritance following the death of his father. Shortly after his return, he married a cousin, a daughter of his uncle Yoshikane, and settled into what might have been a comfortable life as a country warrior-gentleman.

Fate, however, had other plans for him.

Chapter 3

Masakado and His Uncles

One knows what a war is about only when it is over.
—H. N. Brailsford

Being mad, I take to arms, even though
there is little reason in arms.
—Virgil, *Aeneid*

Early in the second month of 935, just five or six years following his return from the capital, Masakado stumbled into the conflict that would eventually cost him his life—but earn him his immortality. On that fateful day he was riding north from his home in Shimōsa province at the head of a small band of warriors toward lands controlled by Minamoto Mamoru in northwestern Hitachi province. He never got there. A few kilometers north of the Kinu River, which marks the border between Shimōsa and Hitachi, Mamoru's sons, Tasuku, Takashi, and Shigeru, lay in wait for him near Nomoto village (see the map on page 46). As Masakado and his men rode into sight, Tasuku's troops raised banners, struck battle drums, and galloped out from hiding places, shooting and screaming as they came.[1]

The brothers seem to have planned their ambush rather poorly, however, and found themselves attacking into the wind—a decided disadvantage in a battle contested mainly with bows and arrows. Although outnumbered and taken by surprise, Masakado and his men carried the day, prevailing on a combination of luck and determination. Tasuku, Takashi, Shigeru, and most of their men were shot down; the rest fled.

Minamoto Mamoru was at the time perhaps the most powerful warrior chieftain in western Hitachi. His genealogy is uncertain, but his single-character surname marks him as a scion of the Saga or the Nimmyō Genji, the lines descended from Emperor Saga (r. 809–823) or Emperor Nimmyō (r. 833–850), not the Seiwa Genji line most famous for producing warriors. He had settled in Hitachi even before Masakado's line of Kammu Heishi, having originally been dispatched from the capital to take up the post of senior secretary (*daijō*) in the provincial government.[2] Hitachi was one of three provinces (along with Kazusa and Kōzuke) designated as *shinnō ninkoku*, provinces whose gubernatorial posts were reserved as sinecures for imperial princes, which effectively rendered Mamoru the second-ranking official in the province.*

In the decades following his arrival, he exploited the power and perquisites of that office to establish lands and residences for himself in the three districts (Niihari, Tsukuba, and Makabe) surrounding Mt. Tsukuba and the Hitachi provincial capital. Initially it appears there was some friction between his family and the later-coming Taira—Mamoru's younger brother Mitsuru fought a much-celebrated duel with Masakado's uncle Yoshifumi—but that was quickly resolved.[3] Indeed, Mamoru married three of his daughters to Masakado's uncles Yoshikane and Yoshimasa and his cousin Sadamori (see the genealogical chart on page 36), making him both literally and figuratively a patriarch and elder statesman of eastern society.[4]

Why he sent his sons against Masakado and why Masakado was leading warriors into Mamoru's bailiwick that fateful day are matters for speculation and guesses—our sources are all but silent on these questions. One account, however, suggests that Masakado may have been traveling—with

---

*The *shinnō ninkoku* system was the brainchild of Fujiwara Natsuno, who proposed it in 826. Under it, Princes of the Blood received the title of grand governor (*taishū*) and collected all the perquisites and fiscal rewards of the gubernatorial offices of Hitachi, Kōzuke, and Kazusa, while leaving all actual administrative responsibilities to the assistant governor. The first *taishū* of Hitachi was Katsurahara Shinnō, who received the title in 830. The practice ended in Hitachi sometime between 931, when Sadazane Shinnō became *taishū*, and 961, when Fujiwara Tametada became governor.

an escort for protection against bandits and the like—to visit Mamoru at the behest of another Hitachi warrior, Taira Maki, who had for some time been caught up in a dispute over the boundaries between his lands and Mamoru's. If this is correct, Masakado's purpose would seem to have been benign: to offer his services as an intermediary in order to resolve the dispute. Mamoru may simply have misread Masakado's intentions and overreacted. Whatever the motivation underlying the attack, however, Tasuku's tactic—ambush—was typical of the warfare of his age.[5]

Popular images and a good bit of the scholarly received wisdom concerning combat during the Heian period suggest a picturesque and quaintly ritualized order to battles: Challenges were issued, followed by agreements on the time and place for fighting. At the appointed hour, the two sides would draw up their lines, and messengers would exchange formal, often written, declarations of hostilities. Special whistling or humming arrows were then used to signal the opening of combat, which would commence with a general—and mostly ineffectual—exchange of volleys of arrows at a distance. After that, individual warriors would gallop forward; recite their names, pedigrees, and battle résumés; and pair up with suitable opponents for one-on-one combats that would constitute the brunt of the day's fighting. Enemy troops who surrendered or were captured were treated with respect and honor, and care was taken to ensure the safety of noncombatants on or near the field.[6]

But early samurai warfare thus envisioned bears little relationship to the battlefield exploits of real tenth-, eleventh-, or twelfth-century warriors. It arose, rather, in the imaginations of later medieval poets and jongleurs who re-created those exploits. Creative nostalgia of this sort found its most eloquent expression on the pages of the *Heike monogatari*, the classic saga of the Gempei War (1180–1185), which was until fairly recently the principal source for studies of early samurai culture.[7]

Contemporary accounts, even literary ones like *Shōmonki*, offer a very different picture of Heian warfare. They make clear that warriors, whether fighting on behalf of the state or for personal reasons, made little time for ceremony in their battles. Their concerns lay overwhelmingly with accomplishing their objectives in the most efficient way possible, with scant regard for the lives and property of women, children, and other noncombatants or for any notions of fair play.

The overwhelmingly preferred stratagem was to catch opponents off guard, using ambushes or surprise attacks. Indeed, audiences of the period considered surprise attacks so normal that an early eleventh-century text began its description of an archetypical samurai, "the greatest warrior in the land," by informing us that "he was highly skilled in the conduct of skirmishes, archery duels on horseback, and *ambushes*" (emphasis added).[8] (See the illustration on page 90.)

Indeed, one might well argue that a fondness for surprise attacks and ambushes represents one of the dominant themes of Japan's military history, visible from ancient mythology to the Pacific War. It reflects a cultural assumption that proper military readiness means always being on guard, always prepared for and expecting an attack. Considered in this perspective, taking an enemy by surprise, catching him unprepared, amounts to much the same thing in terms of fairness or sportsmanship as slipping past his defenses after the battle is under way. More importantly, surprise attacks offered a ready solution to an otherwise thorny tactical dilemma.

When both sides in a conflict are similarly armed and equipped—as samurai warbands were—it is difficult for either side to force combat on the other, for the simple reason that a retreating force can almost always outrun a pursuing one. Armies in pursuit need to remain in ranks and ready to fight, should they overtake their quarry; but armies on the run can devote their full attention and resources to escape and evasion. All things being equal, then, battle can only take place when both sides determine it to be to their advantage to stand and fight.[9]

This situation posed a serious problem for the early samurai, whose military campaigns—public or private—focused on the opposing warrior leaders. Heian samurai took the saddle either to chastise lawbreakers (as deputized agents of the state) or to pursue personal grudges. In both cases the natural objective—the definition of victory—involved apprehending or killing the enemy, not occupying his lands or driving him off them. In contrast to the later medieval period, when military might became the ultimate arbiter of political and economic right, outright seizure of land was impossible within the political framework of Masakado's day, when warrior titles over lands they claimed to own or administer were still subject to the confirmation and approval of the court. When samurai fought on behalf of the government, lands belonging to law breakers were sometimes confiscated and distributed to the victor as a reward. But warrior recourse to "self-help"—the right to pursue private ends through violence—was closely circumscribed by law and precedent. Private conflicts, particularly attempts to seize lands by force, invited government censure and punishment, most often visited at the hands of a rival commissioned to chastise whoever started the trouble.[10]

In corollary, victory for the defensive side of Heian warrior conflicts was fundamentally just a matter of survival: evasion was as good as actually winning on the battlefield. The challenge of running a slippery foe to ground could therefore be a source of considerable frustration. The simplest solution to this challenge—and the one favored by tenth- and eleventh-century warriors in particular—was to catch the opponent unawares.

Masakado's response after fending off Tasuku's ambush and scattering the attackers displayed a second archetypal early samurai tactic: he gathered additional troops and set off across southwestern Hitachi, razing and plundering the homes and property of Minamoto partisans, in the process slaughtering "thousands of the residents" and cutting a path of destruction some 15 kilometers wide.[11] *Shōmonki* paints a dramatic picture of this counterstrike:

> Masakado went about burning the homes of Nomoto, Shida, Ōgushi and Motoki, from the great compounds of the wealthy to the tiny houses of those who abetted them. Any who ran out to escape the flames were surprised with arrows and forced back into the fires. . . . Then he burned more than 500 homes in the three districts of Tsukuba, Makabe and Niihari belonging to allies [of Minamoto Mamoru and his sons], obliterating each and every one of them.
>
> How sad it was! Men and women became fuel for the fires, and rare treasures were divided among strangers. . . . That day, the voice of the flames contended with the thunder as it echoed; that hour, the color of the smoke battled with the clouds as it covered the sky. . . . People's homes became ashes scattered before the winds. Provincial officials and common folk witnessed this in anguish; relatives from near and far heard of this and grieved.[12]

Raids of this sort on an enemy's homes or fields were popular tactical expedients in Masakado's day. Their underlying strategic objective was not the real estate itself but the humans whose livelihoods depended on it. Their purpose was destruction, not seizure—raiders burned fields, plundered houses, killed inhabitants, and then moved on. Attacks on an opponent's home or economic base threatened his ability to continue to fight, depriving him of troops, allies, and supplies. Raids also offered yet another means of forcing an elusive foe to stand and accept battle (or risk the destruction of his property and the lives of his family).[13]

The scale of the destruction wrought by Masakado in 935—the razing of not just the homes of Tasuku and his fellow warrior leaders but the villages in the general area as well—reflected military organization during the period. The core of the forces deployed by Masakado and his

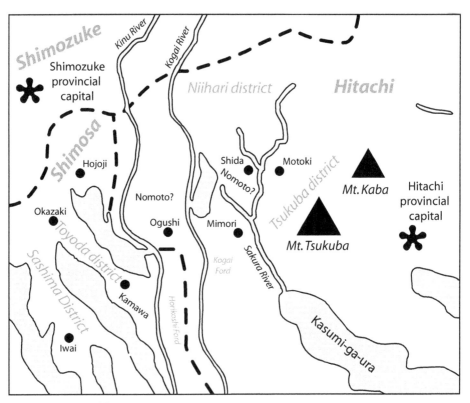

Masakado's world

enemies consisted of men who were direct economic dependents of the warriors and lived in homes in or very nearby the warriors' compounds. But in numbers such troops amounted to a few dozen at most.

For large campaigns, warriors also mobilized the cultivators, woodsmen, fishermen, and other residents of the lands in and around the estates and districts they administered. Such men were, strictly speaking, not under the warrior's control, but they often leased land from him, borrowed tools and seed from him, and conducted trade at his residence, making his home an important economic center for them. By exploiting whatever political and economic leverage they could bring to bear on these semidependents, warriors like Masakado could assemble armies numbering in the hundreds—thousands, if accounts like *Shōmonki* are to be believed.[14] This explains the breadth of Masakado's rampage: he was out to destroy his enemies' capacity to raise additional troops and strike again. It also explains why the forces brought to the field in Masakado's major battles tended, as we shall see, to break and scatter in the face of fierce opposition, even from numerically inferior forces: large hosts were composed, in the main, of semidependents whose affinity for the warrior leader's cause was often tenuous at best.[15]

The difficulty of binding followers to their banners would plague samurai leaders throughout the medieval era. Masakado's story stands as a particularly poignant reminder that this problem, which turned on the relative economic autonomy of allies and subordinates, applied even to members of the warriors' own families.

Under the laws and customs governing property and inheritance during the Heian period, estates were divided to provide independent means to all children (including daughters); wills were probated by the provincial governors and other authorities who held jurisdiction over the lands and titles bequeathed, not by clan patriarchs or matriarchs; and bequests were nearly always lineal (parent to child), not lateral (sibling to sibling). In legal and economic terms, cousins, uncles (or aunts), and nephews (or nieces) had little or no meaningful relationship to one another. The result, as can easily be imagined, was often a geometrically progressing diffusion of family property and familial identity from generation to generation.

In practical terms, meaningful bonds existed only within the smallest kinship units—that is, within nuclear families. Although the ties between parent and child were usually strong, those between siblings were relatively weak, and those between cousins, uncles and nephews, and in-laws were weaker still. While siblings might maintain a fair degree of family unity during the lifetime of their father, the various cadet houses tended to split off following his death and become independent of one another. Each new household head inherited properties and titles of his own, which he would subsequently pass on to his heirs. Each followed his own career path and maintained his own retinue or private warband. Even in cases in which fathers designated a primary heir (and they did not always do so), the primary heir's residual rights over the affairs of his brothers and sisters were minimal at best; ties between collateral lines usually did not extend beyond an innocuous consciousness of a shared heritage. The Minamoto and Taira "clans" that receive so much attention in popular literature never existed outside the imaginations of medieval and modern storytellers.[16]

Accordingly, while samurai sometimes attempted to exploit the emotional and ideological power of kindred relationships to build and strengthen their warbands—employing terminology suggestive of familial connections to designate vassals, or arranging marriages between their children and those of allies, followers, or lords—such practices usually proved to be little more than exercises in wishful thinking. For the most part, warriors joined, or refused to join, the military networks of more prestigious kinsmen out of the same considerations that might have led them to follow completely unrelated warrior leaders: based, that is, on a communality of interests, not bloodline. Conflict—even out-and-out warfare—between in-laws, cousins, uncles and nephews, and even brothers became a near-constant theme of Heian military history, visible in dozens of famous and not-so-famous skirmishes throughout the period—as Masakado was about to discover.[17]

The Alliance

Among the most important victims of the Nomoto battle and its brutal sequel were Mamoru's sons, Tasuku, Takashi, and Shigeru, and Taira Kunika (who was Masakado's uncle). Their deaths brought Masakado into conflict with two of Mamoru's other sons-in-law, Taira Yoshimasa and Taira Yoshikane.

Yoshimasa, who was either Masakado's paternal uncle or his cousin, had not been involved in the fighting until then.[18] Nevertheless, he was sufficiently upset by the deaths of his brother (or uncle) and brothers-in-law to raise troops and rush to Hitachi in pursuit of Masakado:

> Yoshimasa rolled about Hitachi like a wheel. So caught up was he in his grief for his in-laws, that he completely forgot the way his blood flowed. Thus he set about making battle plans, that he might destroy Masakado. His father-in-law [Mamoru] watched this raging fervor and smiled with delight—although one could not yet know who might win.[19]

Masakado, however, played Yoshimasa brilliantly. On the one hand, had he simply returned to Shimōsa, he would have ceded the initiative to Yoshimasa. Worse, Masakado would have left himself vulnerable to raids on his own lands, since he would not have been able to keep troops who were eager to get back as soon as possible to their lands and affairs mobilized for any length of time. A preemptive offensive against Yoshimasa, on the other hand, would, in the eyes of the law, have turned Masakado from a victim acting in self-defense to an aggressor. But Masakado managed to avoid both traps and instead was able to put Yoshimasa on what amounted to a defensive offense.

For eight months Masakado darted about Hitachi, feinting but never actually striking. This kept Yoshimasa chasing him and too preoccupied to stage an attack on Masakado's base. At length, on the twenty-first day of the tenth month of 935, Masakado led troops toward a village called Kawawa in the easternmost part of Hitachi, what is now the Yūki district of Ibaraki prefecture. Yoshimasa took the bait and rushed there to meet him. But, once again, fortune and talent lay with Masakado's side. His troops killed more than sixty of Yoshimasa's men and scattered the rest. The following day, Masakado at last rode home to Shimōsa to relax.[20]

In the wake of this humiliating defeat, Yoshimasa focused his efforts on securing allies to do his fighting for him. He began by courting his brother Yoshikane with a letter, pleading that:

It is through the aid of the wind and rain that the thunder and lightning echo; it is through the aid of their wings that swans surpass the clouds. I beseech you, then, to join forces with me, in quelling Masakado's unruly evil. Thus will the disturbances in the province spontaneously end; thus will the unrest of the high and low subside without fail.[21]

At the time, Yoshikane was the assistant governor (*suke*) of Kazusa province. He was also Masakado's uncle and father-in-law, but the two had been on uncomfortable terms for some time. One text informs us that he and Masakado had a "dispute over a woman" in 931, while another says the two came to blows shortly after this in a quarrel over lands that had belonged to Masakado's father. The initial disagreement may have centered on Yoshikane's distaste for his daughter's marriage to Masakado, whose prospects for worldly success were less than bright after his failure in the capital. In any case, Yoshikane was living in Kazusa on the far side of Shimōsa province from Hitachi at the time of the Nomoto incident and was not involved in it.[22]

Yoshimasa's entreaty presented Yoshikane with a difficult choice: should he honor his blood ties to his brother and his marriage ties to Mamoru, his blood and marriage ties to Masakado, or simply remain neutral? After mulling things over for more than half a year, Yoshikane at length elected to throw his lot in with Yoshimasa. His decision may have been prompted by his earlier quarrel(s) with Masakado, but it more likely stemmed from practical calculations. Masakado was a nobody, lacking rank, office, and even familial protection—his father being dead and his father-in-law being Yoshikane himself. Yoshimasa and Mamoru, by contrast, were major powers in the southwestern Bandō and influential officers of the Hitachi and Kazusa provincial governments. Siding with them against Masakado therefore carried much greater prospects for success, vindication in the eyes of the government, and reward—perhaps even including the lands and titles Yoshikane had disputed with his nephew. But while this was the rational, conventional choice, it was a decision that Yoshikane would live to regret—for it would prove his undoing.

On the twenty-sixth day of the sixth month of 936, Yoshikane gathered his troops and "roiled forth like a cloud" toward Hitachi. Authorities from the provincial governments of Kazusa and Shimōsa attempted to stop him, but Yoshikane brushed them off, claiming he was merely on his way to "visit his in-laws" (presumably Mamoru). Avoiding the main roads and checkpoints the rest of the way, "like an escapee in flight," he arrived the following morning at Mimori, to the west of the Sakura River (a dozen or so kilometers northwest of present-day Tsuchiura city), where he met with Yoshimasa and their nephew Sadamori. After this meeting, Yoshimasa took no further part in the conspiracy he had engineered. Instead, he ceded the initiative to Yoshikane.[23]

Sadamori, the eldest son of Kunika and a son-in-law to Mamoru, had been serving in the capital as secretary of the Left Bureau of Stables (*samaryō no jō*) when the news of the Nomoto incident and his father's death reached the capital. Obtaining a leave of absence from his post in the Bureau of Stables and an appointment to replace his father as senior secretary of Hitachi, he returned to his provincial home to attend to his mother and what were now his lands. Intriguingly, his initial impulse toward his cousin Masakado was to seek reconciliation, not revenge.

Masakado, he reasoned, was not really his enemy, his complicity in his father's death notwithstanding. Kunika's demise and whatever obligations Sadamori might have to take the field against Masakado were the result of their entangling marriage alliances with Mamoru. Against this Sadamori weighed his desire to return to the capital to continue his official career, which would be impossible until he could be sure that his lands and family in Hitachi were being safely managed and cared for. And he realized the quickest and most efficient way to accomplish this would be to make up with Masakado. Accordingly he wrote to his cousin, expressing his hope "that amity might course from capital to countryside, and spread harmony throughout the state."[24]

Or at least that is what *Shōmonki* tells us that he had in mind. An alternative account claims that Sadamori had initially "abandoned his duties at court and rushed down" to Hitachi to avenge his father. Upon his arrival, however, he quickly recognized that "he could not equal Masakado's dash and spirit, thus he remained hidden in the province, unable to carry out his plans."[25]

In the end, Sadamori's ulterior motives mattered little, for his uncles were not about to let him off the proverbial hook. During their meeting at Mimori, Yoshikane confronted Sadamori, chiding him that such an unfilial course of action was "unwarrior-like." A samurai, he argued, "must put his name before all else. Our possessions have been looted, our relatives murdered. Ought you to accept flattery from this enemy?"[26]

Sadamori may have been persuaded by Yoshikane's scolding. Or he may simply have realized that he would be unable to leave his lands and his duties in Hitachi to return to the capital and resume his career there so long as fighting between his cousin and his uncles continued to tear the province apart; that Yoshikane and Yoshimasa were not about to let go of their grudge against Masakado; and that throwing in with his uncles probably represented his quickest option for wrapping things up and getting on with his life. Whatever his reasoning, Sadamori now reluctantly agreed to join Yoshimasa and Yoshikane in their quest for revenge.

The Battle at Shimozuke Capital

A few days after his meeting with Yoshimasa and Sadamori, Yoshikane crossed into Shimozuke province at the head of a column so large that "the ground shook and the grass was swept aside" as it marched. He swung wide, heading northwest into Shimozuke, then southward into Musashi, before cutting east toward Masakado's homes in northwestern Shimōsa. His intention may have been to spare himself the trouble of crossing the numerous north-to-south–flowing streams that formed the Kinu River system, or he may have been attempting to avoid the area in which he expected Masakado to have scouts and spies operating. If stealth was his plan, however, he might just as well have saved himself the trouble of the long march. Masakado heard reports of Yoshikane's departure and, late in the seventh month of 936, set off to intercept him.[27]

His scouts caught up with Yoshikane near the Shimozuke provincial capital and reported a force numbering "several thousand troops," all healthy, fresh, and well equipped. This figure, given in *Shōmonki*, is almost certainly an exaggeration. Literary accounts of early samurai battles commonly inflate armies by factors of ten or more. Such descriptions should therefore be regarded as metaphorical, rather than as reliable estimates of troop strengths.[28] An assemblage of a few hundred men would already have represented an enormous army for the day, and is, therefore, a more probable number.

Masakado's warband was, of course, considerably more war-weary. It was also much smaller: around a hundred mounted warriors and one or two hundred foot soldiers.[29] Masakado, however, was able to turn these circumstances and Yoshikane's military prejudices to his advantage.

In urban street fights and other situations that circumscribed the arena of combat, Heian samurai often fought on foot. They also conscripted or hired foot soldiers, armed them with bows and polearms, and deployed them in most sorts of battles.[30] Such troops were active combatants, not just grooms and attendants to the mounted warriors (as they are often portrayed). At the same time, they were considerably less than an infantry.

On open ground, infantrymen can stand against charging horsemen only when they can form up with sufficient density and depth that horses refuse to collide with them, and only when they also have sufficient morale and courage to stand and face the terrifying charge. This requires that infantry units have ample numbers, as well as enough practice and experience fighting together to be able to trust their fellows to stand with them rather than break and run. Effective infantry can therefore be deployed only by a command authority strong enough to gather sufficient troops and wealthy enough to maintain them while they train or fight together long enough to develop the needed unit cohesion.[31] Samurai commanders lacked the resources to accomplish this until well into the sixteenth century.

Besides, infantry units, which could neither run away from pursuing horsemen nor run down cavalry in flight, would have been of limited worth in early samurai warfare, even if warrior leaders had possessed the wherewithal to organize them. On open ground, where mounted warriors had adequate room to maneuver, horsemen could usually stay out of range and pelt foot soldiers bearing swords or polearms with arrows. Even bowmen on foot posed no decisive threat to mounted samurai, who, unlike the French knights at Agincourt, could shoot back. While archers on foot enjoy a higher rate of shooting and greater accuracy than mounted bowmen, in Japan these advantages were largely offset by the short effective killing range of the bows—around 10 to 20 meters—and the protection afforded by the horsemen's heavy armor, which was specifically designed to shield them from arrows (see chapter 4).

Foot soldiers in samurai armies normally fought side by side with mounted warriors in mixed units rather than as discrete infantry companies. Their principal contribution was harassing and distracting warriors on horseback, whose attention could otherwise be fully directed at allied horsemen. Nevertheless, while foot soldiers were clearly an auxiliary presence on early samurai battlefields, they should not be dismissed too lightly, as Yoshikane was about to learn.

As soon as he became aware of Masakado's approach, Yoshikane drew his troops into battle formation, lining them up behind temporary walls of shields. Japanese shields resembled the mantlets sometimes used by medieval European archers and crossbowmen: self-standing wooden barriers approximately eye level in height and about the width of a man's shoulders, with poles, or feet, attached to the back by hinges that

Japanese shields (*Taiheiki emaki*)

allowed them to be folded against the shield for transport or storage (as shown in the illustration on the previous page). Typically, shields of this sort were lined up, sometimes overlapping like roof tiles, to form a portable wall that protected archers on foot. They were also placed atop the walls of fortifications and hung from the sides of boats. On occasion, they served as substitutes for other tools such as benches or ladders.[32]

Masakado halted and formed his own lines within ready sight of Yoshikane's men, but still well out of arrow range, and kept Yoshikane's attention focused on his horsemen alone—perhaps even concealing his foot soldiers in nearby paddy fields or woods. When they perceived their enormous advantage in numbers, Yoshikane's troops abandoned their positions and rushed forward "like a knife slash" toward Masakado's warriors. But before Yoshikane's men could get close enough to engage his mounted samurai, Masakado's foot archers opened volley on them, killing more than eighty horsemen and sending the rest into panicked flight.[33]

Yoshikane and some of his men were, however, able to retreat behind the walls of the nearby provincial headquarters, where Masakado could not reach them without exposing himself to criminal charges for attacking a government office and officials. Stymied, Masakado chose to remain within the law and withdrew, allowing Yoshikane and his men to escape "like pheasants spared from a hawk, joyous as birds fleeing their cages." That same day, however, Masakado filed formal grievances with the provincial authorities in Musashi, Awa, Kazusa, Shimōsa, Hitachi, and Shimozuke.[34]

In the meantime, Masakado's enemies had been doing some legal maneuvering of their own. In the ninth month of 936, he received a summons to appear at court to answer charges filed by Minamoto Mamoru the previous year. Setting off for the capital on the seventeenth day of the tenth month, he arrived ahead of Mamoru and was able to persuade the Office of Imperial Police (*Kebiishi-chō*) and the Council of State that the circumstances surrounding his actions in Hitachi mitigated against severe punishment. Two months later the court declared a general amnesty to commemorate the emperor's coming-of-age (*kampaku*) ceremony. Masakado, now fully pardoned, returned to Shimōsa the following summer, leaving the capital on the eleventh day of the fifth month of 937.[35]

Yoshikane's Revenge

Masakado had "not yet rested his legs from the journey and forty days had not yet passed" before he was forced back into the saddle to investigate rumors that Yoshikane was again on the march against him. On the sixth day of the eighth month, Yoshikane and a large army surrounded Masakado and his scouting party at Kogai Ford, near the border between Hitachi and Shimōsa (see the map on page 46). Outnumbered and unprepared for combat, Masakado and his men fled. While they attempted to regroup, Yoshikane raided homes and pasturelands around Masakado's home at Kamawa, leaving "ghostly ashes piled at every gate . . . while smoke in the distance shaded the sky like clouds, and fires dotted the earth like fallen stars."[36]

Masakado passed "a day or two" rethinking his tactics and gathering additional troops and arms. Nine days later, he and Yoshikane squared off once again at Horikoshi Ford, on the Kinu River a few kilometers northwest of Masakado's home. This battle was a shattering defeat for Masakado, who was struck by a sudden ailment in his legs and was unable to concentrate. His men broke and ran, while the enemy troops continued to raid and burn in the area.[37]

Yoshikane spent ten days raiding and hunting for Masakado before dispersing his men and returning to Kazusa. Masakado waited him out in hiding with his wife and children. On the nineteenth day of the eighth month, as Yoshikane was leaving Shimōsa, Masakado sent his family back to his Kamawa residence by boat. En route, however, they were intercepted and captured by some of Yoshikane's men who were acting on information provided by a spy.

Masakado's wife was carried off to Yoshikane's compound in Kazusa, leaving Masakado enraged and "although living in body, as if dead in soul." He spent three weeks devising plans to rescue her, but in the end he did not need to.

While Yoshikane attended to affairs at one of his other residences, in the Makabe district of Hitachi, his sons, Kimimasa, Kintsura, and Kimimoto, took pity on their sister and arranged her escape. *Shōmonki* reports that Masakado's wife quietly made her way back to Toyoda but says nothing further about what happened to the children who had been captured with her. Fukuda Toyohiko suggests that they may have been killed by

Yoshikane's men when their mother's escape was discovered, but it seems
unlikely that Masakado's wife would have left without her children or
that *Shōmonki*—which is not particularly sympathetic to Yoshikane or his
cause—would not have reported a dramatic outrage of that sort.[38]

In any event, with his family once again safe, Masakado set out almost
immediately in pursuit of Yoshikane, at the head of "over 1800 troops."
Faced for the first time with the prospect of confronting a fully prepared
Masakado, Yoshikane elected to retreat and evade rather than risk a decisive fight. Masakado burned Yoshikane's home and then spent a week
chasing him about the valleys and foothills between Mt. Tsukuba and
Mt. Kaba. However, unable to corner Yoshikane, Masakado eventually
returned to Shimōsa "empty-handed."[39]

Yoshikane's decision not to stand and fight may well have been the
wisest course of action open to him in light of his record to date, but it
proved an expensive choice of tactics. For Masakado had timed his campaign well: it was late autumn and the year's harvest was still in the fields.
Unable to engage his inimical father-in-law directly, he turned his
attention to burning and pillaging homes and crops belonging to
Yoshikane and his men, destroying "thousands of houses" and "tens of
thousands" of rice and grain fields.[40]

Nevertheless, Yoshikane was still not quite finished; nor had his distaste
for his nephew and son-in-law abated. He had, however, learned to
respect Masakado's military talents and began casting about for ways to
tip the odds in his own favor. His opportunity came when he learned
that a youth whom Masakado sometimes employed as a courier, Hasetsukabe Koharumaru, had been making frequent trips to visit relatives on
Ishida Estate in Hitachi, where Yoshikane was staying at the time.*
Yoshikane summoned the boy to his home and promised that if he
would help "devise a scheme to destroy Masakado, he would be relieved
of his grueling position as a porter, and made a mounted retainer," in

---

*Ishida (alternatively, Shida) Estate in the Makabe district of Hitachi was among the lands
administered by Minamoto Mamoru. Taira Kunika also appears to have had a residence and
a post there, which would probably have been taken over by Sadamori after his father's
death. Yoshikane was, therefore, probably in Ishida as a guest of his nephew or his father-
in-law.

addition to receiving "mounds of rice to bolster his courage, and robes to serve as trophies."[41]

For Koharumaru, this apparently represented an offer too good to pass up, Yoshikane's less-than-inspiring military record against Masakado notwithstanding. Koharumaru returned to his home in Okazaki village accompanied by a farmhand assigned by Yoshikane to assist him. The following morning, the two disguised themselves as charcoal carriers and set off for Masakado's Iwai residence, about 10 kilometers away. They spent "one or two days" there, assessing the layout of the compound, with special attention to the gates, the armory, the stables, and Masakado's sleeping quarters. The pair then returned to Ishida to report what they had learned to Yoshikane.[42]

On the night of the fourteenth day of the twelfth month of 937, Yoshikane slipped out of Ishida at the head of eighty-some horsemen and began the 30-kilometer journey to Iwai. They headed west, across the Kinu River into Shimōsa, "riding as swiftly as birds in flight." Around the hour of the boar (9 to 11 p.m.), they passed the Hōjōji temple complex, about 23 kilometers from Masakado's home, and turned south onto the main road. There they were spotted by one of Masakado's sentries, who slipped into their ranks and quietly rode along with them unnoticed as he worked his way toward the vanguard. When the column crossed the Kamo Bridge, near the border between the Sashima and Toyoda districts, he broke away and sped on ahead to warn Masakado of Yoshikane's approach.[43] After pausing for an hour or two to feed and rest his troops, Yoshikane surrounded Masakado's home just after dawn, at the hour of the hare (5 to 7 a.m.), catching Masakado inside with "fewer than ten warriors."[44]

Unlike the castles of later medieval warlords—protected by deep moats, wooden palisades, and earthworks—the warrior residences of Masakado's day were all but indistinguishable from those of other rural elites and differed only in size and opulence from the homes of nobles in the capital. They were large compounds, 150 meters square or more, constructed adjacent to the warrior's agricultural fields in or very near the alluvial lowlands of rivers. The main houses, stables, and other key buildings were surrounded by water-filled ditches a meter or so wide and about 30 centimeters deep, which were used to warm and store water, and by low—1- or 2-meter-high—fences or hedges constructed of wood, thatch, or natural vegetation (see the illustration on page 91). Residential compounds of this sort were economic centers—hubs of agricultural activities and trade—not military bases. Flammable, poorly fortified, and too expansive to be practically defended, they offered little protection against sieges.[45]

Night attacks—which usually involved setting fire to the enemy's home and shooting down any warriors, family members, or house servants who attempted to escape the flames—were an especially favored approach. A picture scroll depicting a night raid in 1141 on the home of Uruma Tokikuni, father of the future priest Hōnen, offers a riveting glimpse at the actions and ambience surrounding such fights: The armor-clad attackers have smashed open the screens of the Uruma home and storm across the veranda, overpowering the defenders who, taken unawares, fight only in casual robes and skirts. A severed arm, still clutching a sword, lies on the floor next to its dying owner. Women in an adjoining room dart about in panic, while the nine-year-old Hōnen (then called Seishi) brandishes a child-size bow and arrow in the doorway. Meanwhile, two warriors stand at the gates to the compound to prevent occupants of the house from escaping.[46]

Nevertheless, Yoshikane's plans did not work out quite as well as he had anticipated, for Masakado had not been taken by surprise. Thanks to the vigilance of his sentry, he had had ample time to arm himself and the men with him and to send for reinforcements. "With eyes wide and teeth gnashing," he seized the offensive, attacking before Yoshikane could. Thus it was Yoshikane's troops who were caught off guard. They may also have been struck from multiple directions, as more of Masakado's warriors and foot soldiers rushed to the compound.

Shōmonki indicates that Masakado killed more than forty men and drove off thirty-some more with only ten warriors, but this is unlikely. Not only are these odds a bit long to be believable—particularly since Masakado and his men would have been charging through one or two gates to his compound into a surrounding enemy—but Masakado had at least two or three hours' time in which to mobilize reinforcements from among the peasants and warriors living nearby. These relief troops may have arrived sporadically as the fighting began or Masakado may have positioned some of them out of sight with the intention of catching Yoshikane by surprise.

In any event, Masakado and his men easily—perhaps miraculously—drove them off, shooting down more than half of Yoshikane's warriors and scattering the rest "like mice scrambling for their holes," while Masakado's troops charged after them "like hawks after pheasants."

Koharumaru's role in setting up the battle was discovered—and repaid—almost immediately. Although he had not participated in the actual fighting, and went to ground as soon as he learned of the results, he was unable to run very far or for very long. Masakado caught up with him in less than two weeks and relieved him not only of his "grueling position as a porter" but of his head as well.

Yoshikane, in the meantime, slunk back to Kazusa and engaged in no further military actions against his nephew. A year and a half later, he died, rather anticlimactically, of an unidentified illness, bringing the first chapter in Masakado's saga to a close.[47]

Chapter 4

New Enemies and
New Friends

War is the child of pride, and pride the
daughter of riches.

—Jonathan Swift, *The Battle of the Books*

A man cannot be too careful in the
choice of his enemies.

—Oscar Wilde, *The Picture of Dorian Gray*

As the temple bells tolled in the new year of 938, Masakado's future
was looking very bright indeed. He had destroyed a good many of
his local rivals and had beaten the three main conspirators against
him—Yoshimasa, Yoshikane, and Sadamori—into inactivity. What's more,
he had accomplished all of this while remaining within the good graces
of the law.

To be sure, his retaliatory raids after the Nomoto battle had earned
him a trip to Kyoto to answer charges before the court. But the sympathetic ears of the officials handling the case allowed him to escape most
of the consequences for his actions, and the general amnesty of 937 freed
him of the rest. His battles with Yoshikane in the summer of 938 had
been defensive—and Masakado had even allowed Yoshikane to escape
rather than risk renewed government censure by pursuing him into the
Shimozuke provincial offices.

Better still, Masakado was now a man with a badge. In the eleventh
month of 937, the Council of State issued a warrant to the provinces of

Musashi, Awa, Kazusa, Hitachi, and Shimozuke declaring Yoshikane, Mamoru, Sadamori, and Yoshikane's sons Kimimasa and Kintsura outlaws and deputizing Masakado to apprehend them. The warrant may have been drafted in response to a countercomplaint Masakado made while he was in the capital answering Mamoru's charges, or it may have been the court's long-delayed answer to the charges Masakado filed after his battle with Yoshikane in Shimozuke. Either way, its impact on Masakado's status and prospects was enormous.[1]

While none of the alerted provincial governments made serious efforts to enforce the warrant—probably because at least three of the men it named were officers of these same provincial governments—it still vindicated Masakado and sanctioned—rationalized—any future military actions he might take against his relatives, placing the authority of the state behind his mobilization and command of troops.* This was of no small consequence, for even though privately armed, privately trained warriors had by this time acquired a near monopoly over the *means* of armed force, warrior autonomy in the *application* of force was yet centuries beyond the horizon. Indeed, the court still jealously guarded its exclusive right to approve the use of force, insisting that recourse to arms was acceptable when and only when it was sanctioned by the state.

Despite sweeping institutional changes, the underlying principles and the basic framework of Japan's military and police system remained much the same from the dawn of the *ritsuryō* era until well into the fourteenth century. The cardinal premise here was that final authority and formal control rested with the central government: all major officers continued to be appointed by the court; and all major crimes were reported upward, where the appropriate action was determined by the Council of State.

Under the law, district magistrates could dispose of most misdemeanors (that is, crimes punishable by light or heavy beatings) themselves.

---

*This warrant was, of course, promulgated *after* Masakado's hunt for Yoshikane in Hitachi, but it was drafted in response to a report filed by the Shimōsa provincial office after Yoshikane's attack on Masakado near the Shimozuke provincial capital in 936. As such, Masakado would likely have had little trouble using it to defend his Hitachi campaign had things come to that.

More serious offenses were reported to provincial governors, who could deal with minor felonies (crimes punishable by periods of labor service) on their own authority but were obliged to inform the Council of State of major felonies—armed robbery, murder, or rebellion—and await instructions.[2]

Only the central government could authorize the mobilization of troops to apprehend a felon or pass judgment on him following his capture. Court orders to arrest criminals or suppress rebellions were issued by the Council of State in the form of "Warrants of Pursuit and Capture" (*tsuibu kampu*), which gave the bearer legal rights to punish any troops who violated orders or failed to report for duty; authorized him to commandeer food and supplies as needed for his cause; and carried the promise of government rewards for any who aided in the campaign.[3]

It should, of course, be obvious from what we have already seen of Masakado and his enemies that a substantial gap separated legal principles from reality with regard to feuding and private warfare. In fact, the court's willingness to tolerate at least small-scale military activities conducted for enhancing or preserving personal profit grew at a pace just a few steps behind its dependence on private warriors for law enforcement.

Nevertheless, the court was remarkably successful at maintaining overall control, managing the samurai in much the same way that experienced parents or teachers handle rambunctious children. A certain amount of "boys will be boys" roughhousing was tolerated as long as it was not *too* disruptive. But there were clearly lines that could not be crossed without inviting disastrous consequences. Masakado and his contemporaries were well aware of those lines and took pains to remain within them.

As things worked out, however, Masakado—perhaps a bit too self-assured after his recent victories—began to press his luck. And although he managed to keep his legal nose clean for one more year, he also acquired dangerous enemies, and dangerous friends, through two incidents that began in the second month of 938. The first was set in motion by a combination of paranoia and overconfidence with regard to his cousin Sadamori; the second by an ill-fated attempt to intervene in a quarrel between provincial and district officials in Musashi.

The Feud with Sadamori

Sadamori had, as we have seen, initially been inclined to "join with Masakado, that amity might course from capital to countryside and spread harmony throughout the state," having reached the conclusion that his father's death had been an unfortunate result of getting mixed up with Minamoto Mamoru's family affairs, that "Masakado was not a true enemy," and that his own career prospects in the capital were more important than avenging his father.[4] Although Yoshimasa and Yoshikane persuaded him shortly thereafter to join their alliance—apparently convincing him that Masakado could just as easily be destroyed as appeased, with much the same results on Sadamori's freedom to pursue his career—his enthusiasm for the coalition and for filial vengeance waned rapidly in the face of Yoshikane's repeated failures.

What part, if any, Sadamori played in the battles between Yoshikane and Masakado is uncertain. *Shōmonki's* descriptions of events say nothing about his participation—they refer only to Yoshikane—but in a later passage the text does depict Masakado speaking of having defeated and discredited Sadamori as well. Sadamori's inclusion on Masakado's warrant also suggests his involvement in at least some of the fighting.[5]

In any event, Sadamori's real priorities changed little between the spring of 935 and the winter of 938. When he learned of his inclusion on the list of court "enemies in Hitachi" named in Masakado's warrant, Sadamori was quick to recognize the chilling effect this development could have on his career ambitions.

"There is," he mused, "no more egregious way to injure one's name or lose one's fortunes than to associate with iniquity. Even a man selfless and pure of heart will smell fishy if he dwells in a room filled with abalone. . . . If I roam about this evil region, I must acquire a wicked reputation." Eager to distance himself—literally as well as figuratively—from his erstwhile allies, he set out for Kyoto in the second month of 938.[6]

Masakado heard about this journey a week or so later and, no doubt recalling Sadamori's perfidy three years before, immediately became suspicious of what his cousin might be planning to tell the court. He called together a hundred or so horsemen—a substantial force for that era—and set off in hot pursuit, catching up with Sadamori in northern Shinano.

This was a bold and rather reckless move. Masakado was probably counting on the warrant he held (which named Sadamori) to provide the legal pretext he needed, but he was, by any reckoning, stretching the boundaries of his commission: He led a sizable body of armed men some 200 kilometers across four provinces, all but one of which lay beyond the jurisdiction of his warrant (see the map on page 66). Moreover, in order to cross into Shinano from Kōzuke on the Tōsandō road along which Sadamori was traveling, he would have needed to negotiate the surveillance checkpoint at Usui, presumably by leaving the road and swinging wide around it. Had he been caught, he would have had quite a time explaining himself.[7]

When he learned that Masakado was close on his trail, Sadamori elected to stand and fight rather than make a run for the capital. On the surface of things, this decision to risk combat seems puzzling. Sadamori was, after all, still under indictment, and killing the deputy sent to apprehend him would scarcely have helped clear his name or add weight to his contention that Masakado had been the real culprit in the troubles of the past few years.

In all likelihood, however, Sadamori felt he had little choice. He was traveling with packhorses, laden with provisions for a journey of several weeks, while Masakado had set off with a warband on a hunt. Sadamori's chances of reaching Kyoto before Masakado could run him down were therefore uncertain. By turning to face his pursuers, however, he could choose his ground. Then too, Sadamori would have known that he enjoyed a key logistical advantage over his cousin, for Sadamori's party had been trekking along unhurried, while Masakado and his men had been racing to catch them. And their mounts were not long on stamina.

Japanese warhorses were much smaller and much slower than the great chargers that carried European knights into the fray or even the thundering, graceful thoroughbreds ridden by samurai in movies and television programs. Most were the descendants of animals imported from China and Korea, interbred with broncos that had been in Japan since the Stone Age. Their bloodlines mingled wild ponies from the Mongolian steppes with Arabians brought to China by the second century C.E. and other horses that had diffused northward from southern China in prehistoric times.[8]

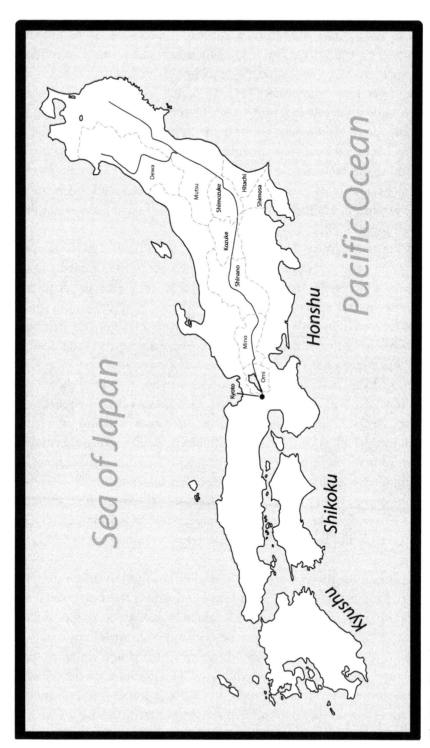

The Tōsandō road

The early samurai favored stallions raised in eastern Japan that were selected for their size and fierce temperament. These were stout, short-legged, shaggy, short-nosed beasts; tough, unruly, and difficult to control. They averaged around 130 centimeters at the shoulder in height—with the largest standing 140 centimeters—and about 280 kilograms in weight. (Modern thoroughbreds, by contrast, average 160 to 165 centimeters in height and weigh about 450 to 550 kilograms.)[9]

In general, a horse can carry only about a third of its own weight without severely compromising its running speed. A saddle, rider in full armor, and his weapons could easily exceed that limit for Japanese ponies. At full gallop, moreover, a horse places nearly eight times its normal weight on its hooves and cannot therefore sustain this effort for very long. Even modern racehorses can only run full out for 200 to 300 meters; and medieval ponies were unshod, compounding their difficulties.★

An intriguing experiment conducted in 1990 by NHK, the Japanese public television network, showcased the running prowess—or lack thereof—of medieval warhorses. A pony standing 130 centimeters tall and weighing 350 kilograms—larger than average for early medieval horses—was timed while carrying a 50-kilogram rider and bags of sand totaling 45 kilograms (to simulate the weight of armor and weapons). The poor beast dropped from a gallop to a trot almost immediately and never exceeded 9 kilometers per hour. After running for ten minutes, the horse was visibly exhausted. To put these numbers in perspective: riderless thoroughbreds can gallop at up to 60 kilometers per hour, whereas the standard that the modern Imperial Army prescribed for cavalry mounts carrying (unarmored) riders was 300 meters per minute—about 18 kilometers per hour.[10]

These factors explain Sadamori's choice of battlefield near the Shinano provincial temple (*kokubunji*) on the plain that runs along the Chikuma River. By waiting for Masakado on open ground rather than setting an ambush, his badly outnumbered but relatively well-rested

---

★Steel horseshoes were only introduced into Japan in modern times, but from the late Muromachi period, horses were sometimes fitted with straw sandals (*umagutsu*) very much like the *waraji* worn by humans to protect their feet during long marches. Kawai Yasushi, *Gempei kassen*, p. 53; Takahashi Masaaki, "Nihon chūsei no sentō," pp. 197–199; Kuroda Hideo, *Sugata to shigusa*, pp. 22–28; Sasama Yoshihiko, *Nihon no kassen bugu jiten*, p. 352.

horsemen had ample room to maneuver, maximizing their edge over Masakado's fatigued men and mounts.* This was to be an archetypal contest of mettle in "the way of bow and horse."

Early samurai skirmishes, particularly pitched battles on open ground, turned largely on the collective prowess of individual warriors rather than on the cunning of officers and generals, who fought in the ranks alongside their men and retained little tactical control once the fighting began. This was a consequence of the political structure of the day and the resultant composition of armies, which were patchwork affairs gathered for specific campaigns and disbanded immediately after the mission ended.

Warrior leaders knit together the forces they needed through complex networks, calling on a variety of relationships and forms of authority. Many of those who answered calls to arms brought with them followers and allies of their own, some of whom in turn had followers of their own. Commanders thus had no opportunities for drill and little hope of fielding disciplined, well-articulated armies.

Problems of command and control were further exacerbated by warrior temperament and self-interest. Heian samurai were privately equipped professionals whose vocations were defined and furthered by the skills they cultivated on their own using personal and family resources. Careers were determined by reputations built on individual prowess. Thus officers as well as warriors of lesser stature were, like modern professional athletes, more apt to think of themselves as highly talented individuals playing *for* a team than as component parts *of* a team. While the success of the group was always to the benefit of each of its members, a distinguishing individual performance could bring its own rewards—in the long term if not always the short term—even in the face of team failures.

Still it is easy—indeed, it is a well-entrenched mistake—to overstate the absence of cooperation and joint effort on early samurai battlefields. The warriors of the age seldom attempted large-scale tactical maneuver, but neither did they fight solely as individuals, independent of their

---

*Masakado was leading "a hundred or so" horsemen, a sizable force for his day, even if one assumes that this figure (reported in *Shōmonki*) is exaggerated. Extant sources give no numbers for Sadamori's party, but it is exceedingly unlikely to have been trudging to the capital with an entourage of more than a dozen or so warriors.

comrades. Rather, they tended to hang together in small teams of varying numbers and makeup. For while *armies* were temporary, irregular creatures, they were made up of smaller components: families and other groups that lived in close proximity to one another and that trained and fought together repeatedly. If the observations of their civilian contemporaries are to be believed, the members of these component organizations were able to coordinate, cooperate, and harmonize their actions with a positively uncanny degree of discipline and fluidity. Battles therefore tended to be aggregates of lesser combats: mêlées of duels and brawls between small groups, punctuated by general advances and retreats.[11]

Tactics and the face of battle were further shaped by the warriors' armor and weaponry. Japanese body armor was lamellar, constructed of rectangular scales of lacquered iron or leather laced into strips, which were then laced together vertically, each row overlapping the one above. This design, widely used across Asia and the Middle East, is more flexible, easier to move in, easier to store and transport, and requires less customization for fit than plate armor; and it offers better protection than chain mail. It also absorbs shock better than other types of armor by diffusing the energy of blows through the layers formed by the overlapping scales and lacings.[12]

The premier armor of the early medieval era, the *ōyoroi* ("great armor"; see the illustration on page 70), was just coming into fashion during Masakado's lifetime.[13] It featured a boxy, heavy cuirass that wrapped around the left, front, and back of the wearer's chest, while a separate piece, called the *waidate*, protected his right side. The front of the cuirass was often covered with a smooth deerskin or silk facing called a *tsuru-bashiri*, which kept the lamellae on the upper part of the chest from snagging the bowstring or the sleeves of the wearer's undergarment when he shot. A four-piece lamellar skirt hung from the cuirass, and the *waidate* protected the wearer's hips, abdomen, and thighs.[14]

In some earlier Japanese armors, the parts protecting the wearer's shoulders, neck, and torso were made all of one piece.[15] But this design restricted shoulder and arm movement, hindering easy use of the bow and arrow. To maximize freedom of motion for archers, the cuirass of the *ōyoroi* was cut around the shoulders and armpits, and the resulting gaps were covered by free-hanging accessory pieces (called *kyūbi no ita* and *sendan no ita*).

A mounted warrior in ōyoroi (*Mōko shūrai ekotoba*)

Large, flat, rectangular plates of lamellae, called *ōsode*, which were easily the most recognizable feature of early samurai armors, afforded protection for the shoulders and upper arms. About 30 centimeters square,
ōsode served mounted archers (who needed both hands to ride and
shoot) as substitutes for hand shields. They were fastened to the body of
the armor by cords so that they fell back and out of the archer's way
when he drew his bow but could be slung forward to cover most of his
face and upper body between shots.

Most warriors wore *ōsode* on both sides, but those of low status or
financial means sometimes wore only one—on the left, where they were
most likely to be struck when facing an adversary.[16] To protect his left
arm (which faced the enemy when shooting) and to keep the bowstring
from snagging on the sleeves of the warrior's under-robe, he wore a
close-fitting, armored over-sleeve (*kote*).

At around 30 kilograms, the *ōyoroi* was a good deal heavier than later
Japanese armors, but this was of small consequence, since it was intended
mainly for use on horseback. It fit loose and boxy at the waist so that it

could hang over the saddle without pushing up the plates of the skirt and exposing the wearer's thighs. The weight of the armor was thus borne by the saddle—or by the wearer's shoulders when he was on foot.

Early medieval helmets were slightly conical bowls of overlapping iron plates fitted with a shallow visor and augmented by a sweeping lamellae skirt that extended nearly to the wearer's shoulders. The front edges of the skirt were curled back to shield the face from arrows. Some helmets were decorated with a pair of flat metal antlers, called *kuwagata*, that resembled the antennae of large beetles.[17]

Kuwagata, tsuru-bashiri, and other decorations provided warriors with opportunities for individual or familial expression, as well as convenient tools for identifying one another. So, too, did the braided silk lacings that held the lamellar armor together. Both the color and the pattern of the lacings could be varied, making it possible to distinguish individuals even at quite some distance.

The bows of Masakado's day were of plain wood—usually catalpa, zelkova, sandalwood, or mulberry—made from the trunk of a single sapling of appropriate girth or from staves split from the trunks of larger trees and sometimes lacquered or wrapped with bark thongs. Simple wood bows of this sort will not bend very deeply without breaking and must therefore be long—sometimes 2 meters or more in the Japanese case.

This might have made them impossibly awkward to use from horseback but for their unique shape, with the grip placed a third of the way up from the bottom rather than in the middle in the manner of European longbows. Some historians have speculated that this unusual grip was adopted to facilitate the use of the weapon by mounted warriors, but there is evidence that the shape of the bow predates its use from horseback. Others argue that the lopsided proportions were adopted in order to balance the bending characteristics of the wood so that it would draw evenly without overstressing either end. Still others point out that this unusual grip appears to maximize the rebound power of the bow and minimize fatigue to the archer.[18]

Arrows were made of bamboo, with forged heads mounted into the shafts by long, slender tangs—in the same manner as swords were mounted into hilts. The arrowheads in use by Heian times assumed an enchanting variety of shapes and sizes, including narrow four-sided heads, flat leaf-shaped broadheads, forked heads, blunt wooden heads (used for practice), and whistling heads (used for signaling).

Warriors carried their shafts on their right hips in quivers (called *ebira*) that resembled small wicker chairs. The lower section of this device was box-shaped, with a grid of leather or bamboo strips across the top. Arrows were thrust through this grid and then bound by a loose cord to the top of an open-worked frame that rose from the back of the box.

Japanese archers used a thumb-grip draw of the sort popular across much of Asia and the Middle East: the right thumb was hooked over the string and locked in place with the right index and middle fingers; the string was then drawn and released by straightening the fingers, allowing the thumb to spring forward in an action similar to that used by children shooting marbles. On horseback the bow was drawn by raising both arms over the head and pulling downward; on foot the bow was simply held at chest level and the string drawn straight back with the right arm.

All but the lowliest warriors also carried swords, the weapon modern audiences mostly closely identify with the samurai. In fact, those who could afford it usually carried two: a long blade, called a *tachi*, and a shorter one, called a *katana*.

Tachi were slender, single-edged, and designed for cutting and slashing. The early history of this weapon is the subject of lively debate and speculation—but little consensus—spurred on by evidence that is not only incomplete, but equivocating.[19] Medieval *tachi* combine elements from several earlier types of sword, but the sequential relationship, if any, between these ancestral blades is far from clear. And efforts to put together a complete picture of sword evolution are further complicated by the dearth of surviving examples of swords from the early and middle Heian period. Nevertheless, it is clear that the elegantly curved weapons instantly recognizable today as "samurai swords" were just beginning to appear in the mid-tenth century, so the men who fought with Masakado and Sadamori probably carried a mixture of straight and curved blades. Both designs were carried blade down and slung from the belt.

Katana, also known as *sayamaki* ("wound case") because of the wrapped design of their scabbards, or *koshi-gatana* ("hip sword") because of the way they were carried thrust through the belt, were used in grappling and other very close combat, as well as for removing the heads from slain opponents and for committing suicide.

Audiences schooled in samurai movies and television are sometimes startled to learn that mystique and symbolic value notwithstanding, swords were never a key battlefield armament in Japan. They were supplementary weapons analogous to the handguns and knives carried by modern soldiers. While swords were certainly deployed in combat, they were far more important in street fights, robberies, assassinations, and other (off-battlefield) situations. This should scarcely be surprising, however, when one considers that early samurai were first and foremost mounted warriors, for *tachi* and *ōyoroi* were ill-suited to swordplay on horseback.

It would have been no easy task to close to sword range against adversaries, particularly mounted adversaries, armed with bows and arrows. Cutting or stabbing through *ōyoroi*—or even walloping an antagonist hard enough to unhorse him—presented an even more formidable challenge, particularly for a warrior whose balance, striking power, and freedom of movement were impeded by the rigid, boxy cuirass and loose-hanging shoulder plates of his own armor. Even expert swordsmen under optimal conditions cannot readily cut through Japanese armor. Sword techniques developed during the late medieval and early modern periods for use against armored opponents target gaps and weak spots in the armor, but this requires considerable precision and skill, even when fighting on foot and wielding the sword with both hands. It would have been doubly hard to accomplish one-handed on the back of a bouncing horse.

Simply knocking the opponent to the ground would not, moreover, have ended the contest, so the warrior would have had to dismount to finish him off with sword or dagger. But repeatedly jumping off and on his horse would have rapidly exhausted even the hardiest warrior, since his armor added nearly half again to his own body weight. It would also have given his horse ample opportunities to scamper off, converting him to an infantryman for the duration of the battle.

Encounters like the one between Sadamori and Masakado in Shinano were therefore decided by mounted archers, whose weak bows and heavy armor forced them to shoot only at very close range—usually 20 meters or less—and to target the gaps and weak points in the armor of specific opponents.[20] The result was a distinctive, somewhat peculiar form of light cavalry tactics that involved individuals and small groups circling and maneuvering around one another like dogfighting aviators.

In this sort of combat, horsemanship counted for as much as marksmanship. The angle at which warriors closed with opponents was crucial, because they could shoot comfortably only to their left side, along an arc of roughly 45 degrees, from the ten or eleven o'clock to about the nine o'clock position. Attempting to shoot at a sharper angle to the front would have resulted in either bumping the horse's neck with the bow or bowstring, or spooking the mount when the arrow was released and flew too close to its face. Attempting to shoot at a sharper angle to the rear would have twisted the archer right out of his saddle. And shooting the lengthy Japanese bow to the right of the horse's neck was awkward and difficult. Canny warriors, then, attempted to maneuver so as to approach the enemy on his right, where he could not easily shoot back, while keeping him on their own left.[21]

On the twenty-ninth day of the second month of 938, Sadamori tied his packhorses out of harm's way, donned his armor, and readied his weapons. Scattering his men about the field in small groups—taking care not to place any too close to the provincial temple and thereby draw the ire of the Shinano government—he had them dismount to rest and wait, partially concealed in the tall grass.

As Masakado's warband drew near, Sadamori and his horsemen rushed forward to meet them. In the ensuing mêlée, Sadamori's fresher troops were able to hold their own for a time and seriously wounded one of Masakado's lieutenants, Bun'ya Yoshitachi. But before long, Masakado's greater numbers began to tell. At length, one of Sadamori's key officers, Osada Maki, was killed, and determining that things were not going his way, Sadamori broke off, fleeing into the mountains, with a few of his remaining warriors close behind him.

By the time Masakado realized what was happening, it was too late to follow. Aware of the odds against running sadamori to ground in the wilderness, particularly with already tired troops unwilling to continue a pursuit so far from home, masakado turned back to Shimōsa empty-handed, "scratching his head a thousand times" in frustration as he rode.[22]

Sadamori, meanwhile, was experiencing some serious frustrations of his own. Now without provisions—having left his packhorses behind on the battlefield—and forced to travel off the roads to avoid Masakado, he "poured the tears of his barren journey upon the grass" and trudged onward toward the capital, "his exhausted horse licking the thin snow ... his hungry followers wrapped by the cold winds and lamenting."[23]

By the time his weary party limped into Kyoto, Sadamori's goals seem to have changed. No longer content merely to clear his name and take up his career again, he now focused on denouncing Masakado as he pleaded his case before the court. He was apparently just convincing enough to be absolved of culpability in the events of 936 but not quite enough to persuade the Council of State that it had been mistaken in its earlier assessment of Masakado. Nevertheless, it did issue a directive to Shimōsa to summon Masakado for further questioning.[24]

Masakado was outraged by the court's about-face in this matter: Sadamori was, after all, a criminal under indictment; he should have been arrested as soon as he set foot in the capital. Instead, he was not only granted an audience with the Council of State, he managed to clear himself and shift suspicion toward Masakado.[25]

Nevertheless, Masakado chose to downplay the summons, dealing with it as if it were merely a misunderstanding. Rather than report to the capital as directed, he met with the officer, Anaho Sumiyuki, who had delivered the order to Shimōsa, to explain himself. This apparently did not satisfy the Shimōsa provincial government, which continued to pester Masakado about coming in for interrogation. Nor did it entirely satisfy the court—or Sadamori. Sumiyuki's report was still a topic of conversation among the nobility in early 939, months after his return to the capital.[26]

In the sixth month of 939, Sadamori returned to Hitachi, bearing a copy of the directive summoning Masakado for questioning. To his chagrin, however, he soon discovered that his fellow provincial officials had little interest in badgering Masakado further, while Masakado himself, apparently acting on the premise that the 937 warrant against Sadamori was still in effect, was gathering men to hunt him down.

Determined to put some distance between himself and his dangerous cousin, Sadamori turned around and headed back toward Kyoto, riding west into Shimozuke to pick up the Tōsandō road. In the provincial capital there, he bumped into an old comrade from his days of service in the Imperial Stables, Taira Koresuke, who was passing through Shimozuke en route to taking up a new post as governor of Mutsu.[27] This chance meeting presented Sadamori with a new opportunity. He asked to accompany Koresuke to Mutsu, where he could avoid both Masakado's wrath and court gossip about his less-than-triumphant sojourn in Hitachi.

Koresuke readily agreed, but just as the two prepared to set off, Masakado stormed into Shimozuke and surrounded their camp, inspiring Sadamori to "slip away like the wind and disappear like a cloud." While Koresuke fussed, fretted, and then opted to abandon his erstwhile colleague and proceed to Mutsu alone, Masakado searched for his cousin, "hunting the mountains for his person and tramping the fields for his trail."[28]

Once again, however, Sadamori eluded him, this time hiding alone in the mountains of Hitachi, tormented by growing fears of bandits, as well as Masakado: "imagining the coughs of enemies when he heard the shrieks of wild birds, and startled by the approach of scouts whenever he saw the grass move."[29] As the days turned into weeks and then months, Sadamori's emotional state deteriorated:

> Looking to the skies, he pondered the turmoil of this world; lying upon the earth, he lamented the travail of protecting his life. First despairing and then in anguish, yet neither could he abandon his mortal coil.[30]

At length, following months of this self-imposed fugitive exile, Sadamori determined that he was no longer being hunted and slipped back into the Hitachi provincial capital and the shelter of the government compound.

The Quarrel in Musashi

About the same time that Masakado was stomping homeward from Shinano and Sadamori was hobbling into Kyoto, another figure who would soon feature prominently in Masakado's life, a certain Prince Okiyo, was taking up a new post as acting governor of Musashi.[31]

By the mid-tenth century, provincial governorships had, as we have seen, become highly lucrative posts, owing to a tax system that enabled officials to collect revenues beyond their assigned quotas and pocket the surplus. Acting governor appointments, which were usually made in tandem with regular gubernatorial postings, were most commonly sinecures for court nobles holding other positions in the capital, interval titles for otherwise qualified individuals awaiting regular gubernatorial jobs, or substitute assignments for situations in which the regular governor could not, for whatever reasons, carry out his duties. Okiyo appears to have been an example of the latter, dispatched to Musashi to serve out the remaining months of the term of Fujiwara Korechika, who left the post early to take up the assistant governorship of Hitachi.★

It seemed that Okiyo was eager to squeeze all he could from his post, acting in concert with the assistant governor, Minamoto Tsunemoto (introduced in chapter 2), "like a pair of chopsticks, winking at one another as they colluded to crack the bones [of taxpayers] and wring the oil from their flesh," while their followers "worked like swarming ants, single-mindedly plundering booty and spiriting it away."[32]

When the pair turned their attention on the Adachi district in the northeastern corner of the province, they met with adamant resistance from the district magistrate, Musashi Takeshiba. Takeshiba was, we are told, a man of impeccable reputation: "Year by year he diligently carried out his public duties, garnering much praise and no criticism. Indeed, so well did he oversee his district that his name was heard throughout the province, his measures for nurturing the people widely known."[33]

He was also a man to be reckoned with. His family, known as the Hasetsukabe until they adopted the Musashi surname in 767, had ruled this part of Musashi in the pre-*ritsuryō* era and had remained prominent in local affairs under the imperial state, serving as district magistrates in Adachi and as ad hoc functionaries in the provincial government office.[34] In principle, the imperial state subordinated provincial residents, including the old provincial nobility, to governing officers dispatched from the capital. We must, however, be careful not to equate principle with

---

★The prefix "acting" (*gon*) was originally added to titles when the individual holding the post lacked the formal credentials appropriate to the office. During the Heian period, however, "acting" posts (*gonkan*) were usually nominative supernumerary titles handed out when the regular post was already occupied. In this instance, Okiyo was apparently appointed as a kind of interim substitute for Korechika. Fukuda Toyohiko, *Taira Masakado no ran*, pp. 134–135.

practice, for in reality, elite local families like Takeshiba's were never far removed from power.[35]

To begin with, they monopolized the positions of district governments and staffed the dozens of lower-level offices that performed the day-to-day chores of provincial government administration. By the Heian period, they also began to acquire higher titles in the provincial bureaucracy, as the court retrenched its position in the countryside.

Under the original law, the four senior provincial officers had shared authority for most functions of government. During the ninth century, however, this arrangement began to unravel, with the court concentrating rights, powers, and responsibilities in the hands of the governor and awarding the increasingly hollow—but still prestigious—assistant governor, secretary, and inspector titles to influential gentry.[36]

Governors were thus obliged to work through provincial elites in order to carry out their orders. And while the governors' broader powers and authority generally gave them the upper hand in such negotiations, district magistrates and other locals did enjoy a few advantages over their superiors.

For one thing, they served longer, more secure terms of office. Candidates for district magisterial positions were nominated by the provincial governor and formally appointed by the Council of State. Unlike provincial offices, however, district posts were normally held for life and were de facto inheritable.

Lower-level functionaries in the provincial government (called *zōshikinin* in the eighth and ninth centuries, and *zaichō kanjin* from the tenth century onward) were appointed by the governor and, in principle, served at his pleasure. In practice, however, they were usually selected from a fairly small group of families with hereditary ties to the provincial office, and because they provided an essential—but otherwise missing—element of continuity and stability, they tended to retain their positions from administration to administration.[37]

District magistrates also received larger allotments of office lands than provincial officials. Moreover, as the people actually responsible (under the authority of the governor) for the oversight and registration of new paddy construction, district officials and their relatives were able to open fields or reclaim abandoned ones and keep them off the central government's books. They also practiced forced abandonment of fields, pushing peasant families and weaker rivals off their allotment lands and then reopening the fields themselves as private possessions. District magisterial families thus came to control sizable parcels of private and semi-private land.[38]

Their position at the grassroots end of the government's chain of command and their permanent presence on the land gave provincial elites an intimate familiarity with neighborhood affairs that no officer dispatched from the capital could hope to match. Provincial governors therefore found themselves dependent on local figures for many key functions of government, including tax collection, an arena in which the role of both governors and local elites widened and evolved during the eighth, ninth, and tenth centuries.

In Musashi, Takeshiba's family appears to have had a longstanding arrangement with successive provincial governors that permitted the family a relatively free hand in running Adachi and thus assessed taxes from the district at lower than expected rates. Okiyo and Tsunemoto, both imperial princes newly arrived in the province, were apparently unaware of these local precedents—or perhaps simply too arrogant to care about them. Accordingly, they viewed Adachi as a potential windfall and sent orders demanding payment of back taxes. Takeshiba vehemently protested this breach of protocol, but Okiyo and Tsunemoto remained undeterred.[39]

Their answer to Takeshiba's complaints was to call up troops, ride into Adachi, and strip clean several houses belonging to Takeshiba and his supporters. This action drew written protests even from their own subordinates in the provincial government offices. Nevertheless, rather than risk open conflict with public authority, Takeshiba went into hiding in the mountains, from whence he filed repeated appeals for the return of the confiscated property. But Okiyo and Tsunemoto merely stepped up their military posture, taking up secure positions in the mountains with their families.

Masakado heard of these events sometime early in 939 and took it into his head to offer his services as mediator to settle the conflict. Accordingly, he traveled to where Takeshiba was holed up in the mountains, and the two of them set out together for the Musashi provincial offices. When Okiyo got wind of this, he rushed back to the government compound to greet them, and the three warriors "tipped many a cup, opening a glorious relationship."[40]

It is anything but clear what Masakado thought he was up to, intervening in a quarrel between three men who were (as *Shōmonki* portrays him explaining to his followers) "neither family nor . . . brothers, nor blood."[41] He may simply have been acting out of an exaggerated sense of his own importance and responsibilities, or he may have smelled an opportunity to enhance his prestige and influence with both the government and the local population. In this context it is worth recalling that Masakado may have been attempting a similar mission of dispute arbitration when he rode into the ambush at Nomoto that touched off his conflict with Sadamori and his uncles (see chapter 3).

His decision to begin his involvement with a visit to Takeshiba rather than to Okiyo or Tsunemoto has led some scholars to conclude that he was less impartial than he let on—that his sympathies clearly lay with Takeshiba, the provincial, against the court and the governor's office, and that his intervention in Musashi was the first step in an escalating war with central authority.[42]

More likely, however, Masakado was simply exercising sound tactical judgment. By first seeking out Takeshiba and offering him a neutral flag, so to speak, under which to approach the provincial capital, he provided all three parties with a mechanism—and an excuse—for détente that did not require any one of them to back down or expose himself to undue risk. Okiyo's ready embrace of the opportunity to talk reinforces this interpretation.

Tsunemoto, however, remained in the field, perhaps in fear of or in disdain for Masakado, or perhaps simply because he was delayed for some logistical reason.[43] Whatever the motive underlying Tsunemoto's failure to return to the provincial capital, the decision to begin discussions—and celebrations—without him looked provocative in hindsight, and the conviviality of the negotiations was spoiled when "for no apparent reason" a group of Takeshiba's men surrounded Tsunemoto's camp, sending him and his men fleeing in panic.

This attack may well have been the product of miscommunication, with the Takeshiba partisans involved—identified in *Shōmonki* as "rear guards"—not even aware of what was happening in the government compound. Nevertheless, Tsunemoto became convinced that Okiyo had joined with Masakado and Takeshiba in a plot against him; he sped off to the capital, where he denounced Masakado and Okiyo, charging both with plotting rebellion against the state.

The *Konjaku monogatari shū* account of Masakado's story offers what may have been Tsunemoto's version of these events. It first describes Okiyo as having forced his way into his post by less than legal means and then accuses him of gratuitously punishing Takeshiba for protesting this action. It further notes that having observed these events and realizing that Okiyo and Masakado "were of a single heart," Tsunemoto dutifully raced to the capital to report the matter to the court. Ironically, this decision and the subsequent actions of the incoming provincial governor, Kudara Sadatsura, turned this hitherto imagined conspiracy into reality.[44]

Tsunemoto's charges threw the capital into an uproar. Fortunately for Masakado, however, his patron, Fujiwara Tadahira, was serving as chancellor (*daijōdaijin*) and regent (*sesshō*) at the time and could protect Masakado from immediate assumptions of guilt, even when his accuser was a provincial official and an imperial prince.

Tadahira first directed that Tsunemoto be interrogated by the Office of Imperial Police and ordered shrines and temples to offer prayers and conduct ceremonies to aid in the success of the investigation. He then sent Masakado instructions to answer Tsunemoto's charges.[45]

Masakado responded with a sworn statement, dated the second day of the fifth month of 939, supported by affidavits from the provincial governments of Hitachi, Shimōsa, Shimozuke, Musashi, and Kōzuke. In the interim, the court appointed a team of three envoys (*mommikkokushi*) to investigate matters in Musashi firsthand.[46]

As it worked out, these envoys never left the capital. On the third day of the tenth month of 939, they approached Fujiwara Arihira, the Left Middle Controller (*sachūben*), to ask that troops be assigned to accompany them on their mission. The request was turned down, but this judgment worried the investigators enough to make them seek an audience with Fujiwara Tadahira nineteen days later to persuade him to change his mind. On the fourth day of the twelfth month, they tried yet again. Fifteen days later, an exasperated Tadahira sent out orders that they must be off on their mission by the twenty-eighth day of that month. Finally, on the ninth day of the first month of 940, the officers were stripped of their commissions and censured. But they were pardoned and restored to new ranks and offices during the twelfth month of 941 after subsequent developments in the east provided retroactive validation for their timidity.[47]

In the meantime, on the ninth day of the sixth month of 939, the Office of Imperial Police reported on its inquiry into Tsunemoto's allegations, recommending that the erstwhile plaintiff be censured for bringing false charges. Tsunemoto was handed over to the Outer Palace Guard (*Saemonfu*) for incarceration.[48]

The Musashi incident offers up a revealing glimpse of the complex interplay between the law and force of arms in provincial governance during the mid-tenth century and a healthy corrective to the common image of the samurai as incipient feudal barons: Okiyo and Tsunemoto, the acting governor and assistant governor, eagerly resorted to bow and sword to press home their tax dispute with Takeshiba, the district magistrate. Takeshiba responded by putting warriors in the field as well, yet he also did his best to avoid an actual fight and concentrated instead on defending himself by filing legal briefs.

Masakado felt it necessary to arrive at the provincial capital under armed escort to ensure that he *would* arrive and to underline his right to be heard. Yet neither Okiyo nor the court interpreted this as necessarily indicative of criminal intent.

Tsunemoto fled to the capital rather than fight when Takeshiba's men confronted him. *Shōmonki* attributes this to Tsunemoto's inexperience in "the way of the warrior," but this is improbable. Tsunemoto was, after all, leading troops against Takeshiba when this whole episode started, was later involved in the military campaign against Masakado, and afterward served as commander of the Pacification Headquarters in Mutsu. Far from running scared, he simply recognized that his chances of success against (what appeared to him as) a tripartite alliance were better at court than on the battlefield.[49]

In any event, while Tsunemoto ranted and wailed before an increasingly skeptical court, his former ally Okiyo was experiencing troubles of his own with the incoming regular governor of Musashi, Kudara Sadatsura. Sadatsura, who arrived sometime during the sixth month of 939, was related to Okiyo by marriage, but the two did not get along. He seems to have been intent on squeezing his in-law out of any active role in provincial affairs and refused even to allow Okiyo to attend government hearings and meetings. Eventually this rebuff became too much for Okiyo, who stalked out of the province to seek shelter and support from his new chum, Masakado, in Shimōsa.[50]

Okiyo appears to have set his sights on becoming the sort of émigré court noble introduced in chapter 2. Having botched his acting governor assignment, particularly in his initial handling of Takeshiba, been accused of treason by Tsunemoto, and then snubbed by his in-law, Sadatsura, he must have seen the proverbial writing on the wall with regard to his career prospects at court. Consequently, he resolved to settle in the east and turned to Masakado for help.[51]

Masakado's willingness to take him in is both rueful and revealing. He must have known that embracing Okiyo risked reigniting and deepening court suspicions that the two of them had been plotting together all along. And he must also have been aware that harboring this persona non grata would not do his standing with the Musashi governor, Sadatsura, any good, either. Nevertheless, the prospect of having a follower of Okiyo's stature—and what that might do for his local prestige—apparently proved too much for Masakado to resist. Having argued his way out from under three successive charges of rebellion—with the support of his powerful patron and the various provincial governments that vouched for him—Masakado was feeling invulnerable. As he grew more confident in his local prowess and less awed by the court and the life he had once sought, he gave ever-freer rein to his ego and listened less to the good sense that had sustained him earlier in his career. Meanwhile, court perceptions of—and forbearance for—his escalating hubris were becoming colored by developments elsewhere.

Rainbows, Earthquakes, and Bandits

On the fifteenth day of the fourth month of 938, the first of a series of exceptionally destructive earthquakes struck the capital. The tremors and aftershocks continued for five days, forcing the cancellation of the Kamō Shrine Festival.

On the twentieth day of the fourth month, a divination conducted by the Bureau of Yin and Yang (*Ommyōryō*) attributed the cause to "warrior insurrections in the east and west." A month later, the Council of State attempted to remedy this "accumulation of ill fortune, earthquakes, and warrior disturbances" by changing the calendar era name from Jōhei ("Knowledge of Tranquility") to Tengyō ("Heaven Rejoices").[52]

The disturbances and insurrections cited in these reports included Masakado's scraps with his relatives, as well as Okiyo and Tsunemoto's quarrel with Takeshiba. But they also spoke of a much more pervasive problem, one that had been ongoing for nearly a century by this time: bands of armed marauders robbing individuals and tax shipments, raiding government offices and storehouses, and murdering provincial residents and officials. The activities of such bands were most visible in the east, but they were paralleled by the depredations of pirates operating on the Inland Sea.[53]

Bandit and pirate goings-on were coming to a violent boil in the late 930s, with Masakado and his cohort right in the thick of things. In the fifth month of 938, the court responded to complaints from Musashi about the "lawless activities" of Tachibana Chikayasu, a sometime ally of Masakado. In the eleventh month of 938, a petition from Izu lodged similar complaints against Masakado's younger brother Masatake and prompted the court to issue warrants for his arrest to Suruga, Kai, Izu, and Sagami. In the fourth month of 939, *emishi* in Mutsu and Dewa launched their first significant uprising in sixty years,★ and bandit gangs raided homes and government buildings in the capital. In the eighth month of 939, Fujiwara Tomomichi, the governor of Owari, was assassinated.[54]

At the hour of the sheep (1 to 3 p.m.) on the fifteenth day of the sixth month of 939, rainbows appeared in twenty places about the capital. At the hour of the cock (5 to 7 p.m.), there was a lunar eclipse. Divinations conducted in response revealed these awe-inspiring phenomena to have been "portents of military uprisings in the west and east," and fed court fears that events across the country might be spiraling out of control. The

---

★Until well into the ninth century, the northeastern third of Honshu remained outside the Japanese imperium as a hazy frontier zone inhabited by a people known to the court as the *emishi*. The *emishi* were politically, culturally, and linguistically distinct from the peoples of central and western Japan, but their ethnic identity remains a matter of debate.

government's reactions, however, remained, for the most part, measured. Emissaries were dispatched to shrines and temples across the country, "directing prayers to the gods and Buddhas for the protection of the country." An investigator was quietly posted to Owari. Troops were mustered in Mutsu and Dewa. And officers armed with arrest warrants were sent to Musashi, Kōzuke, Suruga, Kai, Izu, and Sagami.[55]

By the fall of 939, then, the mood in Kyoto was somber, tense, uneasy, and guarded, while Masakado was treading less and less gingerly down a dangerous path. Three times indicted and three times acquitted, he had to have been raising suspicions among courtiers wondering just how much smoke could be generated without at least a modicum of contributory fire. He had made two committed enemies in the persons of Sadamori and Tsunemoto and had taken on a liability-bound friend in Okiyo. These and other personal relationships would soon entangle him in serious legal trouble in Hitachi.

(1) The arrival of Masakado's head in the capital (*Tawara Tōda emaki*, aka *Tawara Tōda zōshi*)

(2) The arrival of Masakado's head in the capital (*Tawara Tōda emaki*)

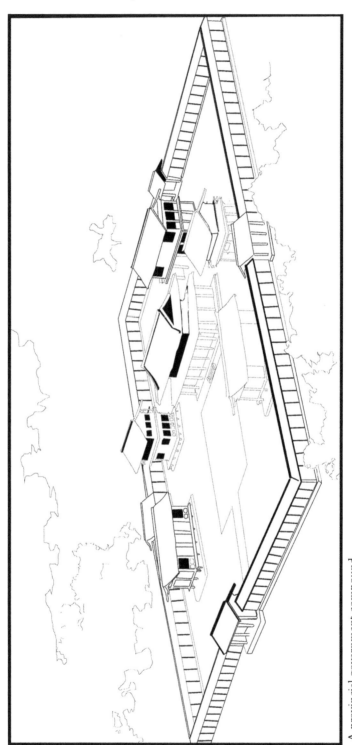

A provincial government compound

A provincial governor en route to his province of appointment (*Inaba dōengi emaki*)

An ambush (*Obusama Saburō ekotoba*)

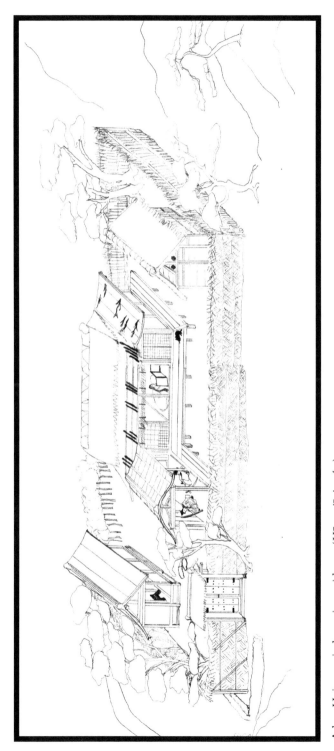

A late Heian period warrior residence (*Hōnen jōnin eden*)

Hidesato and Sadamori raid Masakado's home (*Hidesato zōshi*)

Sumitomo's final battle (*Rakuonji engi*)

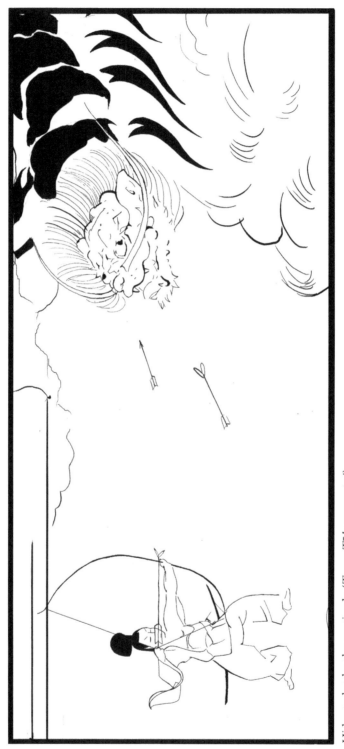

Hidesato battles the centipede (*Tawara Tōda monogatari*)

Chapter 5

Insurrection

Many victories have been and will be
suicidal to the victors.

—Plato, *Laws*

Never interrupt your enemy when he is
making a mistake.

—Napoleon Bonaparte

Masakado's hitherto scrupulous efforts to keep his legal nose clean
and remain on cordial terms with the authorities in the capital col-
lapsed abruptly in the winter of 939, when he swept into the Hitachi
provincial capital, occupied the government compound, and drove the
governor out of office by force. With this single dramatic act, Masakado
placed himself beyond the pale of the law. He was now a rebel against
the state, an unequivocal enemy of the court. But he did not stop there.

Within a month, he had captured the government headquarters of
eight other eastern provinces, replaced their governors with his own
family and followers, and was being feted among his entourage as the
New Emperor. Within three months, he was dead, and three months after
that, his head was hanging from a tree outside the East Market in Kyoto.

The circumstances and sequence of events that led to this abrupt turn-
around are puzzling, and Masakado's intentions have been analyzed and
debated for centuries. It is clear, however, that the story revolved around
the individuals serving in the Hitachi provincial government at the time.

The Incident at the Hitachi Capital

Early in 939, Fujiwara Korechika shifted from his post as governor of
Musashi to Hitachi, where he became the assistant governor. The reasons
behind this midterm change of office are unknown, but the move was
not the downward step for Korechika that it may appear. Hitachi was not
only wealthier than Musashi (and therefore offered choicer opportunities for skimming taxes and other revenue), but at the time of Korechika's
appointment it was (as noted in chapter 2) also one of three provinces
designated as *shinnō ninkoku*, or provinces whose gubernatorial posts
were reserved as sinecures for imperial princes, making the assistant governor for all intents and purposes the actual governor there. Korechika,
moreover, had family connections to Hitachi and probably held lands
there through his wife, a daughter of Taira Takamochi (and a sister to
Masakado's father, Yoshimochi, and to Sadamori's father, Kunika).[1]

In any case, his tenure in Hitachi was troubled from the start by the
activities of a warrior named Fujiwara Haruaki, who was (as *Shōmonki*
puts it) "from the first a disruptive man of the province and the bane of
its people." Haruaki appears to have spent a good bit of his time and
energy "willfully committing acts of ferocious evil," robbing travelers,
seizing crops, intimidating residents and officials, and evading taxes. The
last of these appears to have particularly riled Korechika, who sent him
repeated notices insisting on payment. When these produced no results,
Korechika compiled a list of Haruaki's various crimes and petitioned the
court for permission to have him arrested.[2]

Before he could be apprehended, however, Haruaki fled the province,
gathering up his wife, his children, and the rest of his household; and
trundling off to Shimōsa to seek refuge with Masakado. Along the way,
he paused to loot the government's emergency granaries in Namekata
and Kawachi, on the eastern and southern shores of Kasumigaura.[3]

Masakado not only took Haruaki in, he made him a client and placed
him under his protection. Thus when Korechika petitioned to extradite
the felon back to Hitachi, Masakado deflected all inquiries, insisting that
Haruaki had already left the area. Intriguingly, the Shimōsa provincial
government also declined to act on the Hitachi warrants, deferring to
Masakado's wishes—and to his local influence.[4]

At around this same time, it should be recalled, Prince Okiyo, whose power and perquisites as acting governor of Musashi had been seriously compromised by the arrival of the new regular governor, Kudara Sadatsura, also appeared on Masakado's doorstep. We have no direct evidence concerning the state of relations between Okiyo and Korechika—who had been governor of Musashi during the first part of Okiyo's stint as acting governor there—but they could not have been particularly friendly. Korechika had, after all, sat out Okiyo's and Tsunemoto's conflict with Musashi Takeshiba and left Okiyo to fend for himself when Masakado intervened in the quarrel.[5]

Thus, by the middle of 939, Masakado found himself with two new followers, both of whom nursed grudges against Korechika. In point of fact, Masakado himself had little reason to love his uncle, who had snubbed him during his visit to the Musashi capital on behalf of Takeshiba, and who appears to have sided with Yoshimasa and Yoshikane during Masakado's feud with them three years before. What is more, whatever Korechika's earlier allegiances might have been, by mid-939 he had clearly aligned himself with Masakado's most vexatious enemy, Sadamori.

Sadamori had returned to Hitachi from the capital in the summer of 939, but shortly thereafter Masakado had chased him into the mountains, where he hid out for "many days and months." We do not know precisely when this sojourn ended, but a letter from Masakado to his patron, Fujiwara Tadahira, indicates that Masakado believed his estranged kinsman—who still held the title of senior secretary of Hitachi—had once again taken up residence in the provincial government compound by late 939.[6]

"Collecting arms from all over the province, and mobilizing warriors even from beyond its borders," Masakado, Okiyo, and Haruaki assembled a substantial army—"more than a thousand men," if *Shōmonki* is to be believed. On the twenty-first day of the eleventh month of 939, they crossed into Hitachi. As they approached the provincial capital (located on what is now the site of Ishioka Elementary School and the Municipal Community Center in Ishioka City, Ibaraki prefecture), they found their path blocked by Sadamori and a host some three times the size of their own. Undaunted, Masakado announced his intention to present a formal petition demanding that the warrant against Haruaki be rescinded and that he be allowed to resettle in the province.[7]

Sadamori, whose battle record against Masakado to date had been anything but impressive, then made yet another colossal error in judgment. Confident that his overwhelming superiority in numbers would compel Masakado to back down, he rejected the petition and invited his cousin to fight instead. Masakado, however, called his bluff. He proceeded to deliver an object lesson in the dangers of naïve assumptions about relative advantage in combat.

Tenth-century armies were, as we have seen, patchwork assemblages based on relatively small core bands of fighting men organized under leading warriors in the provinces and the capital. The warriors belonging to these core entourages came from a variety of sources, including sons, other close relatives, and hired mercenaries. Most were direct economic dependents of the leaders, living in homes in or very nearby the leaders' compounds, where they could be at their more or less constant disposal.

Just *how* small these warbands were is difficult to ascertain, for few reliable sources record the numbers of followers under a given warrior's direct command, and those that do indicate substantial variation from one warrior to another. In general, however, it appears that the core units from which early samurai military forces were compiled averaged around a half-dozen or so mounted warriors, augmented by varying numbers of foot soldiers. Some were much smaller. But even the largest numbered only in the high teens or low twenties.[8]

For major campaigns, warriors also mobilized residents of the lands in and around the estates and districts they administered, enabling them to assemble armies numbering in the hundreds. Still larger armies had to be knit together through networks based on alliances of various sorts between warrior leaders or on the authority of calls-to-arms issued by the court and provincial governments.

All such alliances tended to be nebulous and short-lived; the larger the organization, the more ephemeral it was. This instability reflected the vague and fluid nature of the exchange of obligations underlying warrior partnerships, which were imprecise and lacked a firm base in law.[9]

Even the most powerful warriors of the age occupied only intermediate positions in the sociopolitical hierarchy and were dependent on connections with the higher echelons of the court to maintain their political and economic positions. Their autonomy in matters of governance and landholding was limited, and so, accordingly, were the forms of carrot or stick they could manipulate in order to recruit, maintain, and control followers.[10]

Nor were ideological constraints of much value in holding early samurai alliances together. Eloquent Confucian-inspired rhetoric notwithstanding, most warriors were remarkably practical men who viewed loyalty as a commodity predicated on adequate remuneration rather than as an obligation transcending self-interest. In the final analysis, therefore, the integrity of armies and military networks was only as strong as the members' perceptions that affiliation worked to their advantage. Warrior leaders could count on the services of their followers only to the extent that they were able to offer suitably attractive compensation.

The ability to reward depended on a number of factors. Some of these, such as possession of lands, government posts, or positions in the administrative structures of private estates, were relatively stable and could even be inherited. Others, such as personal military skills and reputation or connections at court, were more elusive. Similarly, the rewards offered could take many forms, including help in securing government posts or managerial positions on private estates, division of spoils from successful campaigns, and intercession with provincial governors or other higher authorities on behalf of one's followers.[11]

Sadamori's Hitachi army had been assembled through two overlapping chains of command: troops mobilized on the basis of personal—private—relationships and a much larger group called up under his authority as an officer of the provincial government. The vast majority of his troops were therefore considerably less than enthusiastic about risking their lives for their commander.

Thus when Masakado ordered the charge, the Shimōsa warriors swept forward, scattering and decimating the hastily assembled and poorly motivated Hitachi army. They then surrounded the government compound and blocked the exits. Korechika surrendered forthwith, offering Masakado a written apology. He also handed over his official seals of office and the keys to the government buildings and storehouses. Masakado placed him in confinement under guard—an act that may very well have saved his life.[12]

For by this time Masakado's men were raging out of control. They stormed through the compound looting, burning, and killing:

Prized twills and silks were doled out like wafting clouds; fine and rare treasures were scattered like divining sticks. Thousands of bolts of silk were seized . . . hundreds of hearthfires were obliterated, becoming smoke in a single instant.[13]

Those burning inside became confused by the smoke and were unable to get out. Those who did escape the flames were met with arrows and driven back in. The people and the wealth of the province were all destroyed.[14]

Still not sated, the army moved on to the provincial temple and convent at the northern end of the compound, and to the homes of resident clerks and officials surrounding it, the chaos and savagery building as they rode: [Beautiful women] were abruptly stripped naked and shamed; monks and laymen in the compound were thrust pitilessly into mortal peril. Saddles engraved with gold and silver, boxes inlaid in azure—how many thousands, how many tens of thousands?—the stores of untold numbers of homes, countless rarities, all plucked up by someone, all carried off by who knows whom. Lawful monks and nuns begged foot soldiers for their evanescent lives. The few officials and their ladies who survived experienced the cruelest humiliation of their existence.[15]

The looting and destruction went on for two days before the warriors' blood fever cooled and dissipated as abruptly as it had roiled forth. Korechika and other prisoners were led away in bonds, while clerks and other provincial functionaries "wailed for the dead amidst the ruins of the compound, and troops wandered about lost on the roadside."[16]

This astonishing turn of events seems acutely at odds with Masakado's erstwhile attempts to stay within the letter of the law. How is his occupation of the Hitachi provincial offices to be reconciled with his caution in confronting Yoshikane in Shimozuke three years earlier, his response to Tsunemoto's charges the previous year, or even his careful prevarication about Haruaki's whereabouts in the weeks leading up to the twenty-first?

Masakado himself later defended his actions as having been forced upon him: he had gone to Hitachi, he insisted, only to "inquire into the matter" of Haruaki's grievances with the governor and was reluctantly obliged to fight when challenged by "spirited warriors" assembled under his personal enemies.[17]

But even if we are to take this explanation at face value, it still begs the twin questions of why Masakado took the provocative step of entering Hitachi in force and why he took up Haruaki's cause at all. Nor does it explain why Haruaki sought Masakado's protection in the first place.

Shōmonki attributes Masakado's relationship with Haruaki to his general sympathies for underdogs, equating it with his championing of Takeshiba in Musashi. But this is less than convincing, for Haruaki was no Takeshiba. Takeshiba, an exemplary district magistrate, had been thrown into conflict with overzealous provincial officials in defense of longstanding agreements and of the people under his jurisdiction— precisely the sort of figure who ought to have inspired sympathy. Haruaki, in contrast, was a rapacious outlaw, fully deserving of the trouble in which he found himself.

Nor was Haruaki in Okiyo's league in terms of social status or political connections. Gaining Okiyo—an imperial prince and the acting governor of a province—as a follower enhanced Masakado's prestige and local influence. But his sheltering of Haruaki could only damage his relationship with Hitachi and risked tarnishing his general reputation as well.[18]

It would seem, then, that Masakado had little to gain and much to lose by taking up Haruaki's cause. A closer look at Haruaki's circumstances, however, suggests that Masakado's defense of this rather unsavory protégé may have been born from a combination of obligation and opportunity.

Masakado later described Haruaki as one of his "warrior followers" (*jūhyō*), and there is evidence that this relationship predated Haruaki's flight to Shimōsa.[19] Although we know nothing of Haruaki's ancestry or career other than what we can glean from *Shōmonki* and derivative texts, his surname marks him as descending either from emigrant court nobles—as Masakado was—or from some local elite house that had developed marriage or other close ties to a court family.

More intriguingly, his given name shares a common first character with that of Fujiwara Harumochi, the junior secretary (*shōjō*) of Hitachi at the time of the incident and one of Masakado's close associates. It was customary for court and elite provincial houses to compose names for male children by pairing one character from their father's name with another from a more-or-less standard list recycled within the family. The similarity of Haruaki's and Harumochi's names and the fact that both lived in Hitachi, then, strongly imply that the two may have been brothers or even father and son.[20] If that was the case, Haruaki's expectation of support from Masakado may have stemmed from Harumochi's relationship with him.

The possibility that Haruaki had a close relative in the Hitachi provincial government may also explain why Masakado believed he could pressure the assistant governor into pardoning him, without necessarily having to resort to violence. And it offers a further clue as to how Masakado was so easily able to trounce an army so much larger than his own: As a junior officer of the province, Harumochi would likely have been called—along with his men—to service in Sadamori's army. But once he discovered whom he had been mobilized to defend against, his personal relationship with Masakado—and the long-term prospects for personal gain it promised—would have eclipsed any obligations to Sadamori. Harumochi may therefore have begun the battle on the Hitachi side and shifted colors once the fighting started—exacerbating the confusion and further shaking the resolve of the Hitachi troops.

At any rate, we know from the fact that Haruaki owed taxes that he held lands in Hitachi. We also know that he held no government post, inasmuch as neither the *Shōmonki* authors nor Masakado cite any such title for him. The form of Korechika's communiqués to him—they were *ichō*, a documentary style used to address parties neither subordinate nor superior to oneself—suggests, moreover, that Korechika did not consider Haruaki to be entirely under his jurisdiction and hints at the existence of an influential patron outside the province. This raises yet another intriguing possibility: that Masakado's interest in Haruaki may have been in part an attempt to curry favor with this sponsor.

Haruaki was, however, more than just a friend of Masakado's friends. He was also an enemy of his enemies. Masakado's own accounting of events implies that Haruaki's legal troubles were in some measure the product of personal animosity on the part of Korechika's son, Tamenori. It further accuses Tamenori (who was on his mother's side yet another first cousin to both Masakado and Sadamori) of acting in concert with

Sadamori to raise troops, "willfully raid the provincial arsenal to appropriate weapons, equipment and shields, and challenge me [Masakado] to fight."[21]

Whether the acrimony between Tamenori and Haruaki or the collaboration between Tamenori and Sadamori was real, as alleged by Masakado, is less important than the additional light this belief sheds on Masakado's decision to travel in force to Hitachi to press Haruaki's case with the assistant governor. For it suggests that Masakado may have latched onto Haruaki's cause in part as an excuse to further browbeat Sadamori and discourage others—like Tamenori—from supporting him. It also explains why Masakado brought an army with him on what he later characterized as a juridical mission.

Masakado surely held his cousin in considerable contempt: Sadamori had cravenly declined to seek justice after his father's death in 936, had then betrayed Masakado by joining Yoshimasa and Yoshikane in the battle at the Shimozuke provincial offices, and had somehow talked his way out of arrest and raised court suspicions about Masakado the previous year. He had, moreover, run from the field and gone into hiding on each of the three occasions he faced Masakado in battle. Yet he still possessed a directive authorizing him to detain Masakado for questioning—and even though Masakado believed that this warrant had already been answered, he would also have known that Sadamori could use it as a pretext to attack him.

Under the circumstances, traveling with a large force was the best way for Masakado to ensure that he would *not* have to fight. That is, Masakado viewed his army as a deterrent rather than a provocation to a challenge from Sadamori, Korechika, or Tamenori.[22]

Lord of the Kantō

Whatever his original intentions when he entered Hitachi, Masakado, having raided and burned a provincial government office, was now a state criminal. Unsettled by this turn of events and well aware that he would soon be confronting court armies deputized to apprehend or destroy him, he lingered in Hitachi just long enough to regain control of his troops and then withdrew to his base in Shimōsa, arriving in

Kamawa, with Korechika and other prisoners in tow, on the twenty-ninth.[23] He did, in other words, precisely what he had done in the after-math of each of his earlier victories: fall back to his base to contemplate his next moves.[24]

He passed just a week and a half weighing his options and then took the field once more. This time he rode north, into Shimozuke "astride a fierce and fiery mount and leading followers as numerous as clouds, raising their whips and pressing their stirrups as if to traverse ten thou-sand leagues of mountains."[25]

On the eleventh day of the twelfth month of 939, he crossed the bor-der and drew up his army outside the Shimozuke provincial government headquarters. Terrified and inexplicably caught unprepared without suf-ficient troops to defend the compound, the newly appointed governor, Fujiwara Hiromasa, and the out-going governor, Ōnakatomi Matayuki, surrendered immediately. Masakado took possession of the compound, confiscated the seals and keys of office, and appropriated the governor's stipend and operating funds. He then sent Hiromasa and Matayuki, their families, and a handful of their key retainers back to Kyoto under guard, much to the consternation of those deported:

> Children and ladies usually sheltered indoors behind blinds aban-doned their carts and walked the frost-covered roads; retainers accustomed to dwelling beside the compound gates left their horses and saddles and trudged toward the snowy hills. . . . Officials and subjects of the province knit their brows and shed tears of anguish; gentlemen and ladies beyond the provincial borders raised their voices in pity and compassion.[26]

Four days later, he moved on to Kōzuke and took over the provincial government offices from the assistant governor, Fujiwara Hisanori. Shortly thereafter, he sent Hisanori back to the capital under armed escort.[27]

As the news of Masakado's victories spread, the governors of other eastern provinces abandoned their posts and "startled like fish, flying like birds, ascended to the capital in haste." On the nineteenth, Masakado announced the appointments of his brothers and senior liegemen to replace the absconded officials in Shimozuke, Kōzuke, Hitachi, Kazusa,

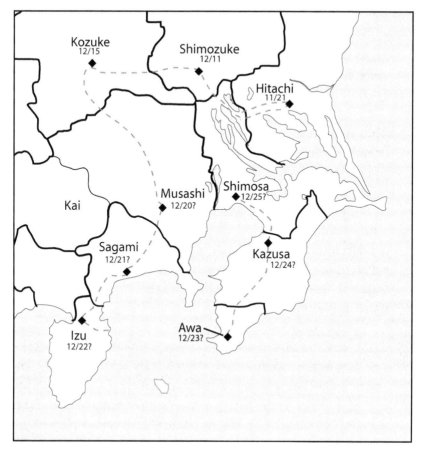

Masakado's provincial conquests

Awa, Sagami, Izu, and Shimōsa; and set off on a quick tour of the east, confiscating the seals of office and keys to the government buildings in each province he visited but instructing those officials who had not already fled to remain at their posts and continue their normal duties.[28]

The Court's Response

The first news of the Hitachi incident reached the court on the second day of the twelfth month of 939. On the twenty-seventh, a corroborating report came in from Shinano; and on the morning of the twenty-ninth, a second messenger from Shinano brought word that Masakado had also overrun the provincial government compounds in Kōzuke and Shimozuke and that the deposed officials from those provinces were en route to the capital, shepherded by some of Masakado's troops. That evening, the governor of Musashi, Kudara Sadatsura, arrived in Kyoto and was urgently debriefed by the Council of State.[29]

> Thus officials in the capital were greatly surprised and there was turmoil throughout the palace. . . . The emperor lowered himself and placed his palms together above his forehead [in supplication to the Buddhas] while a hundred officials performed ritual ablutions and offered a thousand prayers to shrines and temples. What is more, ranking clergy of the [temples] on Mt. Hiei and Mt. Kōya conducted exorcisms while attendants at various shrines performed rituals of sudden death and destruction. . . . The names of evil ones were burned on altars, and effigies of the rebels were hung from thorn and maple trees.[30]

The court also undertook some more mundane steps in response to the news. On the twenty-ninth day of the twelfth month, it ordered troops mobilized in Shinano and sent special envoys (*keikokushi*) to take charge of defenses at the barriers guarding the entrances to the capital region. On New Year's Day of 940, music performances were suspended, and special military commanders (*tsuibushi*, literally, "Envoys for Pursuit and Capture") were deputized for the Tōkai, Tōsan, and San'yō circuits. On the ninth, the court determined Tsunemoto, whose accusations against Masakado seven months earlier had landed him in jail, to have been vindicated by subsequent developments, released him, and promoted him in rank.[31]

On the eleventh, the Council of State issued a special directive to "the governors of the various provinces of the Tōkai and San'yō circuits":

> Persons who have previously earned special merit shall be selected and given irregular rewards.
>   Taira Masakado has engaged in accumulated evils and secretly acted out long-nurtured violence. He chaotically attracts untidy broods, and habitually behaves like a wild wolf. He prevaricates with provincial officials and robs them of their seals of office. He

seizes public lands and plunders them. Crafty bands and foolish followers join him, some seeking of their own accord to escape the censure of the Court; many others, hoping to temporarily extend their lives, are extorted into joining.

Masakado does not reflect on his rightful low status, forgets the majesty of the Court, and willfully gives rein to his rebellious intentions. Moreover, he embraces opportunistic plots. But even if he has ten thousand thousand men in armor, what paper flower can he assail? Even if he has hundreds of stalwarts, what rope band of a fortress can he overcome with them? He stands alone, [like the frog who] knows the breadth of the well bottom, but forgetting to safeguard against what lies beyond the sea.

Since creation this Court has seen many insurrections, but none that compare to this. Now and again there have been those who yearn with treasonous spirit, but all have met with calamitous obliteration. The Heavenly Sovereign alone visits upon them the punishments of Heaven. What sort of sacred warriors shall the gods call forth this time? Is all under Heaven not the sovereign's realm? Are there any in the nine provinces who are not imperial subjects? When the sovereign's armies were bewildered, were there no patriots? Among the tillers and swains, were there no subjects who acted selflessly?

Thus the Minister of the Left petitions the throne for an edict commanding, "Let he who slays the bandit leader be granted, under imperial seal, titles to his lands that shall pass to his progeny in perpetuity. Let he who cuts down the bandit's henchmen, be rewarded with rank and office."

Let the various provinces heed this, enacted by imperial decree. Spread the word near and far, and let all know of it.[32]

In the event, the forces sent into the field against Masakado embodied a hybrid of old and new arrangements, reflecting a military and police system in flux. In 940 the court was still groping and experimenting its way toward a workable organizational framework within which it could efficiently control and direct the private military resources germinating and ripening in the capital and the countryside.

Thus, on the eighteenth day of the first month, the Council of State designated a lineup of officers to take charge of the campaign. Fujiwara Tadabumi was named Field Marshal for the Pacification of the East (*seitō taishōgun*), with his younger brother Tadanobu, Fujiwara Kunimoto, Taira Kiyomoto, and Minamoto Tsunemoto as his lieutenant generals (*fukushōgun*); and Taira Kintsura and Fujiwara Tōshikata as his major generals (*gungen*). On the eighth day of the second month of 940, Tadabumi received his formal commission, along with the ceremonial sword (*settō*, literally, "scepter sword") that symbolized it, and departed for Shimōsa with a flourish, cheered on by crowds "bunched together with sleeves overlapping and hems joined . . . and not a gap to be found along the roadway."[33]

These appointments followed the provisions of the *ritsuryō* codes for assembling wartime armies. As noted in chapter 1, the imperial state had never maintained a standing army for large-scale offensive or defensive campaigns. Instead, it knit together wartime expeditionary forces from temporarily mobilized provincial regiments under staff officers holding short-term commissions. At the close of the campaign, the officers' commissions expired, the armies were dissolved, and the troops returned to their homes.

Expeditionary forces were composed of one or more armies (*gun*), each numbering between three thousand and twelve thousand men. Each army was commanded by a general (*shōgun*), assisted by varying numbers of lieutenant generals, major generals, brigadier generals (*gunsō*), and majors (*rokuji*), depending on the size of the army. When three such armies were assembled, a field marshal (*taishōgun*) was designated to command the entire expeditionary force.[34]

Thus the command structure represented by Tadabumi and his staff was a relic of the *ritsuryō* military institutions. At the same time, the appointed individuals represented the new realities of power and governance evolving during the early Heian period. Tadabumi himself was exactly the sort of figure who had hitherto served as a general or field marshal for imperial armies: a ranking aristocrat who also held other (civil) posts in the central government.[35] The others, however, were warriors and career provincial officials. At least three were simultaneously named to provincial government posts in the eastern provinces controlled by Masakado. Kintsura was the son of Masakado's old enemy, Yoshikane. Both he and his elder brother, Kimimasa (who was also appointed secretary of one of the eastern provinces), had been included on the arrest warrant given to Masakado in 937. And Tsunemoto was, of course, the assistant governor of Musashi who clashed with Masakado, Okiyo, and Takeshiba in the early part of 939.[36]

By appointing Masakado's peers and personal enemies to government posts in the "rebel" provinces and as commanders of the troops called up against him, the court sought to co-opt private interests and resources to its cause. This policy served as the mainstay of the government's efforts to deal with Masakado and henceforth became fundamental to its strategic thinking. In the decades surrounding Masakado's uprising, the court introduced a series of new-fangled military titles as the cornerstone of its military and police apparatus. Appointment to such posts, which included both standing and ad hoc commissions, carried the promise of lucrative rewards for meritorious performance.

All in all, this system, working in tandem with other centripetal social and political forces, did a remarkably good job of keeping the emerging warrior caste in hand. In essence, it played warriors against one another—setting thieves to catch thieves. By deputizing powerful warrior leaders, the court gave them incentive to compete on behalf of the system rather than against it. For nearly three hundred years, the result was that whenever powerful warriors like Masakado seemed to challenge the central government's authority, there were always peers and rivals like Sadamori who could readily be persuaded that cooperation with the state offered a more dependable path to success.

"Insurrections East and West"

Masakado had gone from a man who "enjoyed official favor from sea to sea and whose influence spread through the provinces around him" to public enemy number one in the space of less than a month.[37] As it happened, he could not have picked a worse time to fall off the legal wagon, for his was not the only major military problem the court had to cope with in 940.

The *emishi* uprising in the northeast that had begun seven months earlier was still ongoing, as were outbreaks of lawlessness and organized violence all over the country. On the twelfth day of the first month, Suruga reported trouble with bandits in and about the province. On the twenty-fifth, a rapid messenger arrived from Tōtomi with the news that an imperial envoy had been captured by bandits in Suruga and that the Kukigasaki barrier in the province had been "attacked and destroyed by bandits, while warriors came, surrounded the provincial temple, carried off goods, and shot people to death." On the fifth day of the second month, Awaji reported that bandits had plundered weapons and other goods from public and private storehouses in the province.[38] But the most serious problem of all (next to the one posed by Masakado) was in the west, where a provincial official turned pirate named Fujiwara Sumitomo was rapidly getting completely out of hand.

Unlike Masakado's east, by the tenth century western Japan had long since ceased to be a wild and woolly frontier zone. The court seems, in fact, to have recognized no essential differences between the western provinces—even those on the distant islands of Kyushu and Shikoku—and those surrounding the capital. And while transportation to and from—and in and around—the east depended mainly on horseback, the west was tied together primarily by sea routes. Tax goods were being hauled to Kyoto by ship as early as 746, and by 806 even officials journeying to their provinces of appointment had forsaken the San'yōdō, Nankaidō, and Saikaidō highways for the greater speed and comfort of sea travel.[39]

As movement between Kyushu and the capital became more and more focused on sea routes, specialist boatmen began to appear all about the Inland Sea region. Their leaders came from similar backgrounds (and fostered similar ambitions) to those of Masakado and his peers in the east: men descended from the provincial chieftains of the pre-*ritsuryō* era or from court houses that had settled in the provinces. But unlike their eastern counterparts, local elites in the west rarely built their fortunes by accumulating lands or overseeing agriculture. Instead they focused on organizing followers in bands—just like their eastern counterparts—and earning a living through monopolizing water transport of goods and people. On the side, many also robbed these same shipments.[40]

Pirate activities in and around the Inland Sea began to attract court attention in the mid-ninth century and became a serious nuisance by the second quarter of the tenth. Suppressing them posed a thorny problem, inasmuch as the pirates presented a fluid threat, conducting a kind of guerilla warfare from hidden bases on islands and inlet rivers. Widespread and operating in complete disregard for provincial borders, they "drifted north and south like floating grasses, committed only to profit and yearning naught for their homes. Like birds, they scattered when pursued and regathered when given respite."[41]

Sumitomo seems to have exploited a combination of local connections and illustrious pedigree to make an already difficult situation far worse. Born into an elite family of Iyo province on the southwestern coast of Shikoku, he was adopted by Fujiwara Yoshinori, a former governor of Chikuzen and assistant governor-general (*shōni*) of the *Dazaifu* (a supraprovincial government office in Kyushu), making him heir to a court lineage of high to intermediate rank. After a brief stint as a provincial secretary in Iyo, Sumitomo elected to abandon his government career and concentrate his energies on organizing the seamen of his

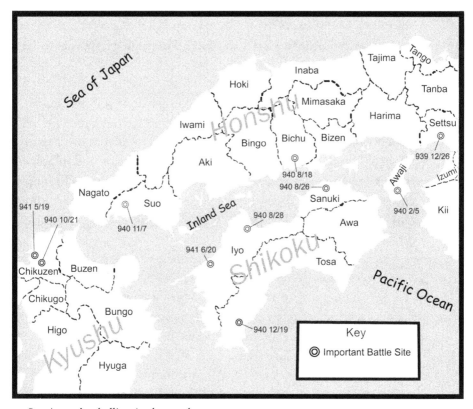

Sumitomo's rebellion in the southwest

home region into a coalition under his leadership. At the peak of his power, he virtually controlled the entire Inland Sea (see map on the previous page).[42]

Making his base on Hiburi Island, off Iyo, Sumitomo caught the court's attention for the first time in early 936. By the middle of that year, he had assembled more than a thousand boats and crews, which he directed in raids up and down the coasts of Honshu and Shikoku, "robbing government property, killing people" and generally disrupting the "comings and goings of the high and the low."[43]

The government responded by attempting to co-opt the pirate leadership, beginning by deputizing Sumitomo himself to "pursue and capture the pirates" under his own command. It followed up by appointing Ki Yoshito governor of Iyo and simultaneously commissioning him as "envoy to pursue and capture in the Nankai Circuit" (*tsuibu Nankaidō shi*). Yoshito, a career provincial official who had held several military posts in the capital, also pursued his mission through the application of carrot rather than stick, offering amnesty and the means for a fresh start to any pirates who surrendered to him.[44] The strategy appears to have worked remarkably well:

> The pirates, upon hearing of his compassion and tolerance, repented their errors and more than 2500 surrendered. Pirate leaders Ono Ujihiko, Ki Akishige, Tsu Tokinari—all told more than 30 men—bound their hands, offered their name cards, and submitted. At this Yoshito showed them all leniency, gave them clothing and food, assigned them fields, provided them with seed, and taught them to farm. The people's troubles were at last quieted; the provinces and districts restored."[45]

Three years later, however, Sumitomo had become restless and was once more "attempting to gather warriors and set out on the sea." Unlike Masakado, who seems to have stumbled into open rebellion, Sumitomo appears to have very deliberately chosen to challenge the court. He began with a terrorist campaign aimed at disrupting life in the capital, sending agents into the city to set fire to homes and public buildings. The fires continued night after night, "forcing men to the rooftops . . . and women to hoard water in their homes." Unsure who or what was

causing these blazes, the population rapidly grew anxious. In the meantime, as reports of new outrages in the provinces began trickling into the
capital, the court dispatched messengers to Kyushu and Shikoku, with
orders summoning Sumitomo to Kyoto for questioning.[46]

In the twelfth month of 939, the assistant governors of Bizen and
Harima, Fujiwara Kotaka and Fujiwara Koremiki, heard rumors that
Sumitomo was behind the nightly fires in the capital and set out to
report this to the court. Unfortunately for them, Sumitomo had spies of
his own and raced off to intercept. He caught up with Kotaka and
Koremiki near the Ashiya postal station in Settsu (now Ashiya City in
Hyogo prefecture) in the wee hours of the morning on the twenty-sixth
day of that month. Sumitomo's men fell upon Kotaka and his party "at
the hour of the tiger (3 to 5 a.m.), loosing arrows that fell like rain." Surrounded and badly outnumbered, Kotaka's men fought back briefly but
were quickly forced to surrender. Kotaka was captured and bound. His
wife was raped and murdered. Koremiki, Kotaka's son, and the other
members of his entourage were also put to the sword. Kotaka was thereafter released, but not before the pirates had "severed his ears and cut off
his nose" as a warning to other provincial officials. He staggered into
Kyoto a few days later to be greeted by a shocked and horrified court.[47]

The close timing of all these events with Masakado's insurrection in
the east produced a reaction at court that bordered on paranoia, leading
to all sorts of wild speculation about Masakado's plans and motives.
Rumors that Masakado was about to invade the capital—perhaps fueled
by the report from Shinano that he had troops escorting the deposed
officials from Kōzuke and Shimozuke to Kyoto—arose almost immediately. In response, the Council of State ordered the entrance points to
the city fortified. More intriguingly, the streets of Kyoto were also soon
abuzz with suspicions of collusion between Masakado and Sumitomo,
reflected in a Council of State discussion following the Fujiwara Kotaka
incident that concluded, "It appears that Sumitomo has plotted with
Taira Masakado in this activity."[48]

While there is no reliable evidence that Masakado and Sumitomo ever
actually met, much less that they coordinated any plans, the speculation
that Sumitomo unilaterally and opportunistically "heard of Masakado's
treason and thereupon contrived a rebellion" of his own—as one mid-
eleventh–century account put it—is certainly plausible. Sumitomo

clearly had an intelligence network of some sort, and his uncle Yoshinori had been the assistant governor of Kazusa when Masakado captured the provincial government there and sent its senior officers packing. It is unlikely therefore that Sumitomo was *not* aware of what was brewing in the east, and it is eminently reasonable to suppose that he might have deliberately moved to seize the moment, exploiting the court's preoccupation and consternation to further his own agenda.[49]

In any event, once planted, the notion that Masakado and Sumitomo were in cahoots took firm root in the imaginations of both contemporary and later observers. By the early twelfth century, historical narratives were reporting that "the pair pledged to work together so that one of them could run the government as he pleased while the other enjoyed an Emperor's life."[50] And by the late medieval period, the legend had grown to include a meeting in 936 to formulate this plan:

> On the nineteenth day of the eighth month of that year, the pair, Sōma Masakado and Fujiwara Sumitomo, climbed Mt. Hiei. There they gazed down upon [Kyoto] and plotted treason together. "To state our intentions plainly," they agreed, "Masakado is of imperial descent and should become sovereign; Sumitomo is a Fujiwara and should become Regent." After that both returned to their own provinces.[51]

The enduring hold of this anecdote is attested to by the fact that tourists today can still visit the point on Mt. Hiei known as "Masakado's Crag."[52]

All of which raises the key question of what Masakado's plans really were. If, as suggested earlier, his capture of the Hitachi provincial offices was not premeditated—the inadvertent by-product of an attempt to further humble Sadamori—why did he go on to seize the other eastern capitals? What was he *thinking*?

Chapter 6

Apotheosis

Go with your fate, but not beyond.
Beyond leads to dark places.
—Mary Renault, *The Bull from the Sea*

The successful revolutionary is a statesman,
the unsuccessful one a criminal.
—Erich Fromm, *Escape from Freedom*

Although 940 would be the last new year Masakado would welcome in, he did begin it well, as the overlord of eight provinces. It is, however (as one Chinese dynastic founder was famously reminded), one thing to seize a kingdom from horseback and quite another to rule it—or even to *want* to rule it. And the question of what Masakado wanted—what sort of thinking promoted his actions in the eleventh and twelfth months of 939—is both intriguing and critical to understanding Masakado and his world. I have already argued that he rode into Hitachi to remonstrate—by intimidation, if need be—not to conquer. So what schemes and goals carried him on to Shimozuke, Kōzuke, Kazusa, Shimōsa, Awa, Sagami, and Izu?

The traditional view of things casts Masakado's takeover of the east as the first step in a campaign to make himself ruler of the entire country. *Shōmonki* contends that this ambition was born shortly after his return to Shimōsa from Hitachi.

It portrays Prince Okiyo approaching Masakado in Kamawa with a bold proposal: having already made himself an outlaw by "striking down one province," Masakado, he argues, might as well annex the rest of the east and see where that leads. Without missing a beat, Masakado replies that this is exactly what he had been thinking and declares his intention to "begin with the eight provinces" of the east and then move on to capture the capital and the rest of the country. After all, he suggests, this is a perfectly reasonable aspiration for "a third generation offshoot" of the imperial line such as himself.[1]

Having thereby outlined his agenda, Masakado sets forth on his blitzkrieg through Shimozuke and Kōzuke; collects the keys and seals of office from Kazusa, Awa, Sagami, Izu, and Shimōsa; and holds a ceremony in the Kōzuke provincial capital appointing new officials to replace the governors and assistant governors who have fled or been deposed. These proceedings are, however, dramatically interrupted by an entertainer who steps forward and declares herself to be "an oracle of the Great Bodhisattva Hachiman." Slipping into a trance, she intones, "We confer imperial rank upon our child Taira Masakado. . . . The Great Bodhisattva Hachiman calls forth an army of eighty thousand and bestows this rank upon him."[2] At this:

> Masakado proffered his neck, twice bowing in obeisance. The four companies guarding the proceedings stood and cheered, while many thousands prostrated themselves. . . . The Acting Governor of Musashi [Prince Okiyo] and the Hitachi Secretary, Fujiwara Harumochi—at the time, Masakado's chief deputies—displayed joy like paupers become wealthy, and smiles like lotus blossoms in full bloom. Thereupon they offered Masakado a title of their own making, calling him "the New Emperor."[3]

Reassured by this supernatural affirmation of his newfound destiny, Masakado goes on to appoint his own court and bureaucracy, prepare seals for the emperor and Council of state, and lay plans for building a new imperial palace in Shimōsa.[4] More poignantly, he rejects warnings from a page and from his younger brother Masahira that he might be in the throes of impractical hubris. "The imperial dignity," argues Masahira, "is not something one can contend for by means of wisdom, nor can it be contested for by might. From ancient times until now, sovereigns who rule Heaven and Earth, kings who have inherited their position, have done so by the grace of Heaven. How can you scheme with such certitude? Surely this will be vilified by future generations!"

"Nonsense," scoffs Masakado in reply,

> The arts of arms and bow have abetted the courts in both China and Japan. Success at returning arrows has lengthened many a short life. Whatever else I may be, I have extolled my name as a warrior throughout the East, flourishing in battles from the capital to the hinterlands. The people of this world will always anoint their sovereigns through victory in combat. Even if there is no precedent for this in our country, there is in all other lands. . . . What realm cannot be taken by force? What is more, in addition to the power of numbers, I have long and successful experience in plotting strategy. My heart is undaunted as it would cross mountains; my strength is unflagging as it would crush rocky cliffs.[5]

Shōmonki's recounting of these events makes for compelling drama and neatly justifies the narrator's abrupt shift of attitude toward Masakado for the remainder of the tale. Hitherto portrayed as the righteous hero of an unsought feud with his uncles and cousins, Masakado is treated thereafter as the villain of a scandalous rebellion against the divinely ordained order of the emperor's realm. And although he may have been brought to the brink of this démarche largely through the unintended consequences of well-meaning actions, he leaps into the abyss eagerly, seduced by success, opportunity, and supernatural portents.

It is, nonetheless, difficult to take much of this seriously, for *Shōmonki*'s account not only burdens Masakado with the sudden onset of a vainglory and arrogance dramatically at odds with his behavior before and after these incidents, it also turns on events not recorded in any other source and on anecdotes fraught with anachronisms. The title of New Emperor, the oracle proclaiming Masakado's ascension, the building of a new imperial palace, and the naming of new central government officials appear only in *Shōmonki* and texts derived from it. These are exceedingly odd omissions in light of the frenzy and paranoia that gripped the court in 940. Had Masakado really done these things—or if he was even *believed* to have been doing any of these things at the time—surely government documents and court diaries would have recorded (and censored) them.

This section of *Shōmonki* is, moreover, rife with suspiciously strange phrasings and other errors. Masakado's conversations with Masahira and the page are, for example, sprinkled with classical allusions and mixtures of contemporary and classical language, much of it taken verbatim from Chinese texts no provincial warrior would have been likely to have read, much less to quote.[6]

The oracle incident is even more captivating—and suspicious. *Shōmonki* describes the mysterious woman who delivers the message as a *shōgi* or, in an alternative version, a *kamunagi*. Both terms describe entertainers who performed at shrines for the benefit of the divinities celebrated there, as well as at more secular functions. She identifies herself as a messenger from Hachiman, one of the most important figures in the Shintō pantheon, enshrined first at Usa in Buzen province, on the northeast coast of Kyushu and later at the Iwashimizu Hachiman Grand Shrine in Kyoto (built in 859) and the Tsurugaoka Hachiman Grand Shrine (founded in 1063) in Kamakura.

Originating in an amalgamation of deities worshipped by several clans in northeastern Kyushu, by the mid-eighth century, Hachiman had become associated with Ōjin, the fifteenth or sixteenth emperor (depending on whether one counts his mother, Jingū, as an empress regnant or simply as a regent) in the traditional reckoning (according to which he reigned from 270 to 310). In keeping with these (belatedly discovered) regal origins, he assumed the role of guardian to the imperial house, called upon to make pronouncements concerning succession.* In 809 he was officially declared to be (in addition to his Shintō identity) a bodhisattva—that is, a Buddhist divinity who has achieved nearperfect enlightenment and virtue but who renounces entrance into Nirvana out of compassion for—and in order to render help to—other sentient beings.[7]

---

*His most famous such verdict occurred in 769, when an oracle from his shrine in Usa called for the enthronement of Dōkyō, a Buddhist priest and the alleged lover of the Empress Regnant Shōtoku. A subsequent oracle, however, rescinded the first and ended Dōkyō's hitherto meteoric political career.

Hachiman was therefore a natural choice for the role he plays in Masakado's saga—at least from the perspective of the courtiers who formed the audience for *Shōmonki*. The problem here, however, is that the Hachiman cult did not spread to eastern Japan until the late eleventh century. In Masakado's day, no one outside the court in Kyoto—certainly no resident of the east—would have invoked an oracle from Hachiman to advance claims to the throne, because the backing of this deity would have meant little to the local audience he was attempting to win over.[8]

Shōmonki's contention that Masakado's followers "offered him a title of their own, calling him 'the New Emperor,'" is also problematic—albeit not completely far-fetched. This sobriquet either never came to the court's attention at all until decades after the fact or it was never regarded as a cause for alarm, since no contemporary court records— indeed, *no* records compiled before *Shōmonki*—mention it. And the title itself ("*Shinnō*"), essentially a pun on the legal designation for princes of the blood (also pronounced "*shinnō*" but written with different charac- ters), has no history of usage in Japan before or after this time. Thus while it is possible that Masakado's men really did nickname him the New Emperor in celebration of his successful takeover of the east, there is no reason to believe they meant this appellation to be taken literally—and even less reason to believe that Masakado did.

The gist of Masakado's alleged conversation with Prince Okiyo is, however, cogent and consistent with his behavior elsewhere.[9] Intrigu- ingly, some court records cite Okiyo alongside Masakado as a principal in the insurrection.[10] This may be the result of the animosity between Okiyo and Kudara Sadatsura, who, it should be recalled, was the gover- nor that replaced Okiyo and the man who drove him out of Musashi to take shelter with Masakado. He was also the first of the absconded provincial officials to arrive in the capital after the insurrection began. His debriefing therefore represented the earliest firsthand account of the affair heard in Kyoto. The court's perception of Okiyo as something akin to a coconspirator may also explain why it determined Minamoto Tsunemoto to have been vindicated and released him from jail. Other- wise there is really no direct relationship between Tsunemoto's accusa- tions earlier in the year and the events that unfolded from the eleventh month onward.

In any event, whether or not Okiyo was the first to raise the issue,

Masakado's "as well hanged for a sheep as a lamb" assessment of his situation after the debacle in the Hitachi provincial capital offers a plausible rationale for his subsequent actions. But it does not, in and of itself, tell us what his long-term plans and goals were.

The Letter to Fujiwara Tadahira

Among the most important—and underappreciated—bits of evidence we have for sorting out this question is Masakado's letter to his patron, Fujiwara Tadahira, dated the fifteenth day of the twelfth month of 939—the same day Masakado captured the provincial capital in Kōzuke. Although this document, quoted in full in *Shōmonki*, is not mentioned in any other source—not even Tadahira's diary, *Teishin kōki*—it is by and large believed to be genuine. As such, it represents the *only* source we have that tells us Masakado's side of the story.[11]

In it, Masakado pleads his lack of guile, the extent to which he has been unjustly maligned and defamed by his enemies, and his fidelity to the law. He repeatedly asks for Tadahira's "august indulgence" (*kōsatsu*), "conjecture and sympathy" (*suisatsu*), and his "consideration" (*sasshi*). And he emphasizes that he is a victim of circumstances rather than a willful rebel against court authority:

> Masakado humbly addresses you.
>
> I have now seen many frosts and many cycles of the stars without receiving your gracious instruction. I deeply desire an audience with you, and scarcely know how to explain the rush of recent events. I would be profoundly grateful for your august indulgence.
>
> A few years ago, I was summoned to answer a grievance filed by Minamoto Mamoru and others. When, in awe of this warrant, I hastened to the capital and presented myself, I was informed that I had already been pardoned, and could therefore return home immediately. I went back to my village. Thereafter I forgot about military affairs, henceforth living peacefully, with loosened bowstrings.
>
> But during that time, the former secretary of Shimōsa, Taira Yoshikane, roused thousands of warriors and attacked me. I could

not very well turn my back and run. While I defended myself, many people were killed or injured, and much property stolen, by Yoshikane. All this was conveyed to the court in a report from the Shimōsa provincial government. The court then issued a warrant ordering various provinces to work together to pursue and capture Yoshikane and the rest.

Nevertheless, I received another messenger, summoning Masakado and others to court. Because I was uneasy with this, however, I did not, at length, go to the capital. Instead, I sent a detailed explanation with the government's emissary, Anaho Sumiyuki.

Then, this summer, while I fretted and awaited news in response, Taira Sadamori arrived in Hitachi bearing a warrant summoning me. The provincial officials repeatedly sent me notices of this warrant. This is the same Sadamori who, [having been named in the warrant issued against Yoshikane,] had eluded capture and slipped back into the capital. The nobles ought to have arrested and interrogated him then. That, on the contrary, they issued him a warrant endorsing his charges is the height of hypocrisy!

Later, the Right Lesser Controller, Minamoto Sukenori, came bearing a document that conveyed your wishes. It stated that it had been decided, on the basis of charges made by Musashi Assistant Governor Tsunemoto, that I should be interrogated.* While I waited for the arrival of the investigators, Tamenori, the son of Hitachi Assistant Governor Fujiwara Korechika, was intently abusing public authority, and delighting in making false accusations.

---

*Masakado appears to have jumped to the wrong conclusion concerning this summons. Tadahira's diary and other court records indicate that he sent an agent to question Masakado on the twelfth day of the second month of 939—three weeks *before* Tsunemoto arrived in Kyoto with his allegations. While special investigators (*mommikkokushi*) were appointed to investigate Tsunemoto's charges, they never actually left the capital—and were subsequently sacked and punished. In the meantime, Tadahira apparently assigned an investigator of his own to look into Tsunemoto's accusations, but his diary names the man as Tadaaki (surname unknown). Minamoto Sukenori must therefore have been dispatched in conjunction with Sadamori's warrant. See *Teishin kōki* 939 2/12, 3/3, 6/7, 6/9; *Honchō seiki* 939 6/7.

At this time, having received an appeal from one of my warrior followers, Fujiwara Haruaki, I set off to Hitachi to investigate. But Tamenori was of one mind with Sadamori. Leading three thousand spirited warriors, they willfully appropriated weapons, equipment and shields from the government armory and challenged me to fight. At this I encouraged my men and aroused their spirits. Thus we struck down Tamenori's warriors.

I do not know how many souls perished in my subsequent occupation of the province, only that those subjects who lived through it all became my prisoners. The assistant governor, Korechika, presented me with a letter of apology stating that it was his failure to educate his son Tamenori that had allowed this matter to escalate to armed rebellion.

While it was not my original intention, having struck down one province, the crime was not light and might as well have extended to a hundred territories. Thus, while inquiring into the court's judgment, I seized the other Bandō provinces.

I respectfully remind you that I am a fifth-generation descendant of the Kashiwabara emperor [posthumously know as Kammu]. Even, [therefore,] if I were to take permanent possession of half the country, could it be said that it was not my destiny? Men who, in ancient times, seized the realm with a flourish of military might can be seen in every history book. I possess Heavenly-endowed military skill. Ruminating on this, can any among my peers compare to me? And yet the nobility grant me no commendations, but time and again hand down admonishments. Reflecting on this, there is much shame, but what honor is there? I would be most grateful if you would consider and understand this.

Many decades have now passed since that day in my youth when I first registered in your service. And now I have unexpectedly delivered this affair to a world in which you are Chancellor and Regent! Needless to say, my regret is extreme. Although I harbor plans to overthrow provinces, could I have forgotten you, my master of old? If you will but ponder this for a while, I would be most joyful. I seek to convey much with little.[12]

Respectfully,
Masakado

All in all, the letter conveys the impression that Masakado had not—at least not yet—resigned himself to rending all ties with the central authorities. The final paragraph is particularly suggestive in this regard. The letter is obviously self-serving, and as such, needs to be read with a certain amount of skepticism. But at the same time, one wonders why Masakado would have bothered to write it at all had his intention really been to overthrow the emperor and the court.

There are two possible answers to this question: The first is that Masakado had a change of heart after he sent the letter and in the end resolved to give free rein to dreams and ambitions he had hitherto scarcely known he possessed. But this only begs the question of what he had hoped to accomplish *before* he changed his mind. The second possibility is that he had something different in mind all along.

If we assume—as most scholars have—that the *Shōmonki* account of Masakado's claims to imperial dignities was nurtured from some germ of underlying truth, the simplest verdict would be that while Masakado was probably not expecting to seize the whole country, he *was* bent on establishing a new independent kingdom in the east.[13] In the absence of any corroborating evidence, there is, however, no particular reason to make this assumption. It is just as likely that the *Shōmonki* author stitched together much of this section of the tale entirely from whole cloth, in order to further demonize Masakado and add drama to the narrative. If this was indeed the case, then a closer look at Masakado's letter to Tadahira reinforces a tantalizing alternative hypothesis.

Most of this document is, as already noted, apologetic and propitiatory in tone. But the final section of the letter—the two paragraphs following Masakado's explication of how he came to capture the Hitachi provincial offices and why he did not stop there—stands out from the rest. While there are a number of phrases and clauses in this section that are open to multiple interpretations, the underlying tenor of rationalization, suppliance, and negotiation is clear. When considered in its full context—alongside the apologia of the first part of the letter, Masakado's fervent efforts over the preceding four years to keep his legal record clean, and his theretofore nearly unblemished record of success in dealing with his local rivals—the impression of a man unwilling or unable to reconcile himself to an existence fully independent of the court and its realm seems unmistakable.

Masakado's list of gubernatorial appointments reflects the same conservative attitude. These appointments are not corroborated in other records (other than those derived from *Shōmonki*), and the entire incident therefore very well may be—like the anecdotes concerning the oracle, the appointments of new court ministers, and the plans to build a new imperial capital—simply a fabrication by the *Shōmonki* author. Even so, Masakado's choices here follow an intriguing pattern, one that is at odds with the rest of the picture *Shōmonki* paints of Masakado during this period.

Four of the eight billets went to Masakado's brothers, indicating his strong familial loyalty, but all eight appointees were former provincial officials or men from émigré court families whose members had customarily served as provincial officials—that is, they were all duly qualified for their offices under the precedents of the imperial state system. Masakado's appointments of assistant governors rather than governors to Hitachi and Kazusa, moreover, also preserved the *shinnō ninkoku* tradition (whereby the governorships of these provinces were reserved as sinecures for imperial princes). All in all, Masakado's choices here reflect exceedingly odd sensibilities for a rebel allegedly bent on displacing the emperor or breaking the eastern provinces free from court rule.[14]

Rebellion or Redemption?

Masakado's purpose in writing to Tadahira may simply have been to bemoan his fate or expostulate for the record, but he may well have been seeking to haggle. In fact, the letter reads very much like an attempt to establish a negotiating position: Masakado first exculpates or extenuates his actions up to and including the occupation of the Hitachi provincial government compound and then acknowledges his guilt in seizing control of the rest of the eastern provincial offices. Next, he "respectfully reminds" his patron that his pedigree (which is, in fact, more illustrious than Tadahira's own) and talents justify his usurpation of power and complains, like an ancient Rodney Dangerfield, that the court has not accorded him due respect. In the final paragraph, he recalls his long association with Tadahira, reassures him that his own feelings and sense of obligation stemming from this relationship have not changed, and beseeches the regent to consider his words and actions carefully, ending with an apology, a plea for understanding, and a cryptic suggestion that all is not what it at first seems.

It is, moreover, significant that Masakado's one and only communication with the court took the form of a personal letter to his patron. Had he truly been intent on making a "new emperor" of himself—even if only in the east—it would have been more appropriate for him to have delivered his message in the form of a royal proclamation, a dispatch from the (new and rightful) sovereign to his minister, or even a peer-to-peer communiqué from one sovereign to another. The respectful, even obsequious, tone the letter takes toward Tadahira is particularly out of place in an epistle from a man who would be emperor.

Far from being focused on revolution or secession, Masakado seems to have been intent on restoring himself to good graces within the established social and political fold, calling on his powerful patron to intercede on his behalf. This casts a very different light on his actions in the wake of the Hitachi debacle, suggesting that he may have ridden into Shimozuke and Kōzuke as a step toward reconciliation with—not separation from—central authority. That is, well aware that he had committed an offense too serious to be overlooked, he determined that his best hope was to make himself too prodigious to be dealt with like an ordinary criminal. Unable to retreat, he sought to surge forward, establish a disheartening position of strength, and take advantage of the chaotic situation the court was facing at the time to negotiate some form of pardon.

If this scenario seems far-fetched, we need only recall that Minamoto Yoritomo did something very similar two hundred forty years later. More to the point: so did Masakado's kinsman Taira Koreyoshi, some fifty years later.[15]

Yoritomo, a dispossessed heir to a leading samurai house, adeptly parlayed his own pedigree, the localized ambitions of provincial warriors, and a series of upheavals within the imperial court into the creation of a new institution—called the shogunate, or *bakufu*, by historians—in the eastern village of Kamakura. The saga began in 1159, when Yoritomo's father, Yoshitomo, joined a clumsy attempt to seize control of the court. In the resulting Heiji Incident (named for the calendar era in which it occurred), Yoshitomo was defeated by his longtime rival Taira Kiyomori, who then gleefully executed Yoshitomo's allies and relatives and exiled his sons—including Yoritomo, who was thirteen at the time.

For the next two decades, Kiyomori's prestige and influence at court grew steadily. In 1171 he arranged to marry his daughter Tokuko to the emperor. In 1179 he staged a coup d'état, seizing virtual control of the court. Kiyomori reached the height of his power in 1180, when his grandson (by Tokuko) ascended the throne as Emperor Antoku. That same year, however, a frustrated claimant to the throne, Prince Mochihito, provided Yoritomo with an opportunity for revenge. Twice passed over for succession—the second time in favor of Antoku—Mochihito sent out an appeal for someone to rescue the court from Kiyomori.

The man who answered it, Yoritomo was, by any reckoning, an unlikely champion for Mochihito: in 1180 he had even less going for him than typical warrior leaders of his age. His father's misadventure two decades before had cost him the career as a government official and warrior noble he would otherwise have enjoyed, and doomed him instead to an obscure life as a minor provincial warrior. He held no government posts, led no warband of his own, and controlled no lands. His one and only asset was a shaky claim to leadership among his surviving relatives. And so, being unable to work within the system, Yoritomo hit on an ingenious end run around it.

He used Mochihito's call to arms as a pretext to issue one of his own, declaring a martial law under himself across the eastern provinces. In essence, Yoritomo was proclaiming the existence of an independent state in the east, a polity run by warriors for warriors. But he took pains to portray himself as a righteous outlaw, a champion of true justice breaking the law in order to rescue the institutions it was meant to serve. This touched off a groundswell of support, as well as a countrywide series of feuds and civil wars loosely justified by Yoritomo's crusade against Kiyomori and his heirs. These conflicts are collectively remembered as the Gempei War, named for the alternative readings for the Minamoto (Genji) and Taira (Heike) houses.

Yoritomo had his first—and last—taste of combat in the ninth month of 1180 at the Battle of Ishibashiyama in Sagami province, where his army was routed and very nearly destroyed. He managed to escape, but for the rest of his life he left the fighting to subordinates and focused on managing events from behind the lines in his capital at Kamakura. Things went better for the Minamoto forces two months later, when they met and defeated a Taira army at Fujigawa in Suruga province. A combination of floods and droughts ruined the harvests for 1180 and 1181 and were followed by plagues and famines, forcing both sides to turn their attentions elsewhere for about a year and a half. Yoritomo used the time to consolidate his position in the east. In the meantime, Kiyomori died of fever in the third month of 1181, cursing Yoritomo on his deathbed.

When the fighting resumed in 1182, Yoritomo's cousin, Kisō Yoshinaka, emerged as the leading general for the Minamoto, while Kiyomori's sons, Munemori, Tomomori, and Shigehira, carried on the fight in his name. In the seventh month of 1183, Yoshinaka captured and occupied Kyoto, forcing the Taira to flee, along with the infant Emperor Antoku. At this point, a retired emperor, Go-Shirakawa, stepped back into the political picture.

Yoshinaka and Yoritomo had, from the start, been rivals and uneasy allies at best. Go-Shirakawa, who was well aware of this, now attempted to take advantage of their rivalry in order to eliminate Yoritomo and regain control of the east. He named Yoshinaka protector of the court and gave him warrants to pursue and destroy not just the remaining Taira leaders but Yoritomo—who was, nominally at least, Yoshinaka's overlord—as well.

Unfortunately for Go-Shirakawa and the court, Yoshinaka and his men proved to be even more obnoxious, troublesome, and overbearing than Kiyomori and his sons had been. Within a month, Yoshinaka was imposing his own dictatorship on the capital, forcing a frustrated Go-Shirakawa to change directions once again and appeal to Yoritomo for help.

By the end of 1183, Yoritomo and Go-Shirakawa had negotiated an agreement that legally recognized many of the powers Yoritomo had seized over the east and extended some of them over the rest of the country, in exchange for Yoritomo's promise to restore peace and order countrywide and to keep the tax and estate revenues flowing to Kyoto. Armed with this new legitimacy for his regime, Yoritomo dispatched an army under his youngest brother, Yoshitsune, who defeated and killed Yoshinaka in the Battle of Ujigawa in the first month of 1184. From there Yoshitsune took up the job of tracking down and eliminating Kiyomori's sons. In a series of daring encounters, climaxing with the Battle of Dannoura in the third month of 1185, Yoshitsune did just that. The Gempei War was over, and Yoritomo had secured a permanent status for his new warrior-led regime in Kamakura.

Taira Koreyoshi's story is smaller in scale, less dramatic, and far less well known than Yoritomo's, but it, too, featured a pardon negotiated through extortion and bribery. In fact, its early chapters followed a pattern similar to those of Masakado's saga. The grandson of Sadamori's brother, Shigemori, and the son of a one-time assistant governor of Kazusa, Kanetada, Koreyoshi burned and raided the provincial government offices in Shimōsa in the first month of 1003. We know little about this incident beyond its immediate result: the court's dispatch of an officer to "pursue and strike down" Koreyoshi. This, however, proved easier ordered than done. Koreyoshi evaded capture for at least eight months, while his insurrection spread across Kazusa and Musashi, as well as Shimōsa. At length, he appears to have fled north to Echigo, where he hid out for several years. In the meantime, he sent repeated appeals to his patron, the powerful regent Fujiwara Michinaga, to intercede on his behalf. By 1012, Koreyoshi had managed to achieve some sort of amnesty for his crimes, and was serving as commander of the Pacification Headquarters in Mutsu. He held this post until 1018, when he was forced to resign after a dispute with the provincial governor. He died four years later, in 1022, apparently still in the good graces of the court.[16]

Yoritomo and Koreyoshi both crossed the line into rebellion against state authority and were able to navigate their way back to the court's favor. So, for that matter, were Masakado's contemporaries and rivals, Taira Sadamori and Fujiwara Hidesato. Masakado might have succeeded as well, had his winning streak continued a bit longer.

Miscreancy and Misfire in Hitachi

The final round of the insurrection began in the middle of the first month of 940, when Masakado led an enormous army—some five thousand men, according to *Shōmonki*—into Hitachi to track down Sadamori, Tamenori, and the remainder of his enemies. His first move was to rendezvous with local allies in northern Hitachi, who threw him a lavish banquet and then passed on reports from their spies warning that Sadamori and his entourage "had been fluttering hither and yon like clouds, their lodgings undetermined."[17]

Masakado thereupon divided his forces and sent them fanning out across the province. Ten days of searching turned up nothing on Sadamori or Tamenori, but one company did happen upon Sadamori's wife traveling or residing, for reasons now lost to posterity, with the widow of Minamoto Tasuku, the warrior who ambushed Masakado at Nomoto in 935.[18] Two of Masakado's captains, Taji Tsuneaki and Sakanoue Katsutaka, reported this to Masakado, who immediately issued orders that the women "not be shamed." By this time, however, his troops had already captured them, robbed them of their clothing, and raped them.[19]

This incident provides yet another reminder that the rules of war in Masakado's day offered scant protection for what we would today call noncombatants. Women, children, and others in the proximity of raids, sieges, and other battles faced indiscriminate slaughter along with the warriors. Women who somehow survived—even women of status, like the wives of Sadamori and Tasuku—might still be handed over to victorious troops to be robbed or raped. Those who wished to avoid this fate sometimes committed suicide.[20]

Such grim realities testify to the extent to which the face of war is shaped by time and place, for Masakado and his contemporaries were no more savage than warriors and soldiers elsewhere; they simply followed a code of conduct that evolved under a specific set of social and political circumstances.

Modern Western notions of who can and cannot be a morally acceptable target of military action have their roots in two pots: the medieval European Church's efforts to establish immunity for its property and its personnel; and knightly condescension, born of pride of class, which dictated that knights should defend rather than simply rule the weak and innocent. The social and political structure of Heian Japan, however, produced no parallels to either of these sources.[21]

To begin with, tenth-century warriors could scarcely have looked upon all nonwarriors as inferiors in need of mercy and protection. Defined more by craft than by pedigree, and drawn from lower and middle ranks of the court nobility and the upper tiers of rural society, they were servants and officers of the powers-that-were, not a ruling order unto themselves.

Similarly, the Japanese religious establishment lacked a unified voice through which to dictate military ethics to warriors; and was insufficiently separate from the secular realm to make compelling claims that its lands and its clergy deserved immunity and shelter from warrior activities. In contrast to the monolithic doctrinal presence of the Church in Europe, religious authority in Japan was fragmented between a half-dozen or so autonomous Buddhist and Shintō institutions representing different schools and sects. The great temples and shrines, moreover, not only competed with one another for patrons and followers, they also contended for secular power with the elite noble houses of the court. Some of the larger religious institutions even maintained private military forces to police their lands, defend the grounds and personnel of the main temple, and enhance their political clout within the capital.[22]

The absence of compelling reasons for defining protected classes of noncombatants gave birth to a culture of warfare that viewed anyone and everyone in the path of a warband on the march as "collateral damage" (to borrow a phrase from modern military analysts), with the predictable result that warrior treatment of those not directly involved in a particular fight came to be shaped largely by needs and priorities of the moment. Except under unusual circumstances, therefore, warriors were seldom prone to worry about noncombatants.

Nevertheless, when Masakado learned of what had happened to Sadamori's wife and her companions, he was aghast. In an effort to make amends, he sent Sadamori's wife, who was, *Shōmonki* relates, "of no common countenance," a set of fine robes together with a short poem composed "in order to ascertain her true heart":

'Though elsewhere,
I send messages on the wind to inquire,
Where the flower separated from its branch now dwells.

She responded with a poem of her own:

'Though elsewhere,
The scent of the flower scatters and comes to me
And I do not feel myself to be alone.[23]

The somewhat incongruous image of a hard-nosed warrior like Masakado exchanging verse with the wife of his enemy notwithstanding, poetry served as a crucial means of communication for the aristocracy, and those who aspired to that status, of the Heian period. Poems were the chosen medium for relaying any but the most businesslike messages, particularly those that required delicate tact or subtlety. They also represented an essential social ritual. Significant occasions or encounters demanded an appropriate verse, composed in the cliché-ridden thirty-one-syllable *waka* format, to mark them. Receipt of such poems demanded that one respond in kind, preferably using the same imagery.

In this incident, Masakado couched a touchy—and, under the circumstances, rather insensitive—question in vaguely flirtatious terms. "Where," he inquired, "is your husband, Sadamori?"[24]

Alas, for Masakado, Sadamori's wife's "true heart" harbored no intentions of betraying her spouse, even at the risk of reprising the treatment she had just experienced. The elegant conventions of poetic communication, however, allowed her a graceful means of deflecting Masakado's interrogation with a reply that could also be read as thanking him for his gesture of sympathy.

Tasuku's widow was, however, less impressed with Masakado's charity and less inclined to maintain any pretense of accepting his apology. Instead, she bitterly threw his own words and images back at him:

Like flowers fallen and scattered
There is nothing left for me.
Like the blowing wind,
My heart has become barren.[25]

Chastened and unable—or perhaps simply unwilling—to pry further information out of the captured women, Masakado returned to his hunt for Sadamori and Tamenori. But after "many days" of fruitless searching, he was compelled to demobilize the majority of his troops and head for home with a much reduced force.[26] This was exactly the opportunity for which Sadamori had been waiting. Gathering up his own troops, he came out of hiding and rushed off in pursuit. In the meantime, he had acquired a valuable new ally: a soon-to-be-legendary warrior from Shimozuke named Fujiwara Hidesato.

Fujiwara Hidesato

Hidesato, whom we met in chapter 1, was a man of similar background and aspirations to Masakado and Sadamori. His family was a branch of the same Fujiwara lineage from which the Regents' House (*Sekkanke*) emerged, descended from Fujiwara Uona (721–783), a great-grandson of Kamatari, the first man to bear the Fujiwara surname. A prominent courtier in his day, Uona climbed to the senior second rank and held the office of Minister of the Left until a scandal sparked by his own malfeasance cost him this position and got him exiled to a post at the *Dazaifu* in Kyushu. None of his sons climbed higher than the fifth rank.[27]

The warrior branch of this line began with Uona's fourth son, Fujinari, a career provincial official who rose to junior fourth rank, lower grade, and served as secretary or assistant governor of Shimozuke, assistant governor of Harima, and governor of Ise and Harima before dying young—at the age of thirty-seven—in 822. During his tenure in Shimozuke, sometime around the first decade of the ninth century, Fujinari married a daughter of Totori Naritoshi, the patriarch of a prominent local house, and established a base for himself and his descendants there. Hidesato's ancestors thus arrived in the east a half century before Masakado's.[28]

Fujinari's eldest son, Toyozawa, appears to have been raised in his mother's home, while his father moved on to other posts elsewhere. Unlike Fujinari, however, Toyozawa displayed minimal ambitions toward a career in the capital and focused instead on exploiting his maternal family's connections in order to establish himself as a local magnate. Eventually he even married into his mother's house, essentially merging the Totori into the Fujiwara, and obtained appointments first as secretary and then as acting governor of Shimozuke. His son Murao married into another prominent local family, the Kashima, and held a number of provincial offices, including secretary of Shimozuke and governor of Kawachi.[29]

By the time Hidesato was born, around the end of the ninth century, his family had been in Shimozuke for three generations, wedding local gentry each time.[30] They had therefore become thoroughly provincialized, maintaining several homes—which Hidesato inherited—in and around what is now Sano City, in Gumma prefecture.[31]

At the same time, they maintained close connections to the court and the capital, and continued to seek appointment to provincial governorships about the country. Hidesato appears to have spent some time during his youth serving in the capital, where he became a client of Minamoto Takaaki, the seventeenth son of Emperor Daigo.[32] Like Masakado, he was, however, apparently unable to obtain court posts, even with the aid of such an exalted patron, and returned to the east to seek his fortune there instead.

Although some medieval texts make claims of military offices for Toyozawa and Murao, Hidesato was the first of his family who can be identified as a warrior in contemporaneous sources. His principal occupation prior to his involvement in the Masakado affair appears to have been the advancement of his personal wealth and power by whatever means, fair or foul.

While he is not known to have held any regular government office during this part of his career, he did manage to get himself into trouble early on, prompting the governor of Shimozuke to request his banishment in 916. He returned to the province shortly thereafter, only to be censored once again, when the governor complained to the court of his "lawless activities" in 929. Sometime between this date and 940, however, he must have managed to redeem himself enough to secure appointment as the *ōryōshi* of Shimozuke.[33]

Ōryōshi ("envoy to subdue the territory") was one of the most venerable—and most sought after—of the new military titles the court developed for co-opting private warrior resources in the provinces. It originated during the late eighth century as a designation for officers deputized to lead *ritsuryō* provincial regiments to duty stations outside their home provinces. By the 930s, however, *ōryōshi* had evolved into an ongoing position comparable in spirit and function to sheriffs or marshals on the nineteenth-century American frontier. *Ōryōshi* had jurisdiction over a whole province and were involved in all aspects of peacekeeping, from investigation to apprehension and even punishment. Most were local warrior leaders serving in their home provinces, although on occasion, provincial governors or assistant governors requested the *ōryōshi* title for themselves.[34]

Unlike the *tsuibushi* ("envoy to pursue and capture") commission utilized for the warriors sent against Fujiwara Sumitomo, Hidesato's *ōryōshi* post signified a standing office that was not specifically tied to a single mission.[35] And it did not expressly require Hidesato to get involved with the forces arrayed against Masakado.

His motivation for joining this effort may have been at least in part personal: Hisanori, the assistant governor of Kōzuke whom Masakado deposed and ushered back to the capital, was his uncle. More likely, however, he simply smelled an opportunity for bountiful rewards.

In this context it is noteworthy that when Masakado laid siege to the Shimozuke provincial capital in the twelfth month of 939, Hidesato, who must have been in the province and was almost certainly already *ōryōshi* at the time, did nothing. His decision not to move during this incident speaks volumes about his loyalties and priorities. So does his decision to join Sadamori in 940.[36]

Blunder, Mishap, and Rout

After the incident with Sadamori's wife, Masakado's companies groped about Hitachi for another week without laying hands on their quarry. While it is unlikely that Sadamori could have eluded them indefinitely, he did not really need to, for time was now working against his hunters. Winter was rapidly giving way to spring—it was already mid-March by our modern calendar—and the onset of the agricultural season. Masakado's troops, who had by this time been campaigning with him for three months, could ill-afford to remain away from their lands much longer.[37]

This is precisely why Masakado had returned to the offensive, attempting to take the fight to Sadamori rather than simply preparing his defenses. He was keenly aware that if he waited, the beginning of the spring planting would dramatically complicate troop recruitment and mobilization, and that the vulnerability of newly sown fields would severely circumscribe his tactical options. Nevertheless, he also knew that he could not hold his army together and keep it dashing ineffectively about Hitachi much longer. Stymied, he demobilized most of his men and headed for home.

Sadamori and Hidesato, of course, faced the same seasonal recruiting problems as Masakado. Unlike Masakado, however, they had an imperial warrant backing their conscription efforts, enabling them to pose as the vanguard of a government army and to take advantage of the promise for rewards that status implied. Furthermore, their warriors had not already spent the past three months in the saddle. In addition, Sadamori and Hidesato could promise their recruits a short campaign of subjugation rather than the lengthy war of endurance and resistance to which Masakado's men could look forward.

On the first day of the second month of 940, Masakado's scouts reported Hidesato and Sadamori leading troops toward Kamawa, advancing along much the same route that Yoshikane had taken three years earlier. He hastily reassembled his warband, divided it into two companies under himself and Fujiwara Harumochi, and rode into Shimozuke to meet them.

This was a much sounder decision than it may at first appear. Taking the offensive broadened Masakado's tactical options and mitigated his growing disadvantage in numbers, particularly if he could catch his enemies unprepared in camp or on the march.[38] It also held forth the

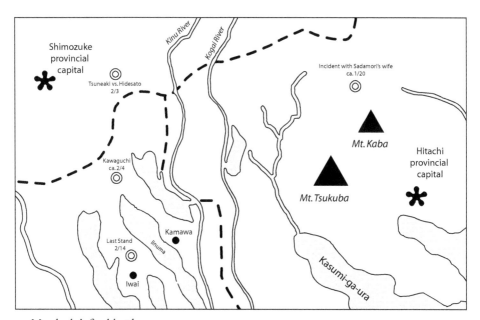

Masakado's final battles

possibility of a quick victory, which would have enhanced his reputation and standing with both the court and his own followers—strengthening his bargaining position and reducing the danger of desertions and disaffection. In addition, moving the fight to Shimozuke protected his base (including the homes of his men) and left him the option of retreat.

His intelligence appears, however, to have been faulty, or perhaps the invaders unexpectedly changed their route, for Masakado's main force missed them completely. While the vanguard groped about, detachments from Harumochi's company under Taji Tsuneaki and Sakanoue Katsutaka—the same captains who had discovered Sadamori's wife—stumbled across Hidesato's camp. After observing for a while from the top of a nearby mountain, Tsuneaki, who was, we are told, "renowned as a man worth a thousand," made the bold—and, as things turned out, imprudent—decision to engage rather than risk letting the enemy slip away while he alerted Masakado. But when Tsuneaki rode down upon him, Hidesato, although presumably caught by surprise, was able to rally his troops and use his numerical superiority to first repel and then anni-hilate the attackers. Tsuneaki's company "scattered to the fields in all directions, those who knew the roads shooting away as if from a bow-string, and those who did not yet know the way reeling about like wheels."[39]

Tsuneaki and his surviving men fell back to Shimōsa, where they reconnected with Masakado and the rest of the army. Sadamori and Hidesato pursued, catching them at Kawaguchi, on the northern tip of Iinuma, northwest of Masakado's Kamawa residence (see the map on page 135). This time Masakado appears to have held his own. Although the "public liegemen" at length forced his outnumbered "private ban-dits" into retreat, they were unable to strike a decisive blow. With night-fall approaching and uncertain how many reinforcements Masakado might yet bring to bear against them, Sadamori and Hidesato broke off and withdrew to Shimozuke to regroup.[40]

The Final Reckoning

His enemies' conservatism earned Masakado a brief respite but not one that availed him much. As he retreated from Kawaguchi, most of his remaining captains broke off and returned to their own homes to tend to their own affairs. By the time he reached Kamawa, he was escorted by little more than a handful of men from his core entourage.

While Hidesato and Sadamori stumped about Shimozuke and Hitachi "gathering crowds, charming them with words, raising warriors, and doubling their numbers," Masakado slipped into hiding in the marshes around Sashima. These were the same wetlands in which he had hidden from Yoshikane three years before. They were extensive and could be navigated in many places only by boat.[41] In the fall of 937, they had enabled Masakado to elude his pursuers until Yoshikane's men tired of the hunt and compelled him to withdraw.

But this was neither fall nor 937. Masakado's circumstances—and with them, his strategic imperatives—had changed fundamentally. No longer just a warrior squabbling with a personal enemy, he was now a state criminal whose survival depended on not merely outlasting a single opponent but on remaining powerful enough to force the court to compromise with him. And this strength turned on his credibility with his men, which was already fading in the wake of his recent defeats and his enemies' swelling numbers. The onset of the planting season rendered a lengthy war of escape and evasion suicidal for Masakado's followers, who could not afford to let the fields they managed lie fallow—or see them torn up by rampaging enemies.

Every day he remained on the run, moreover, diminished Masakado's stature and made it seem less likely that joining him might bring greater rewards than forsaking him. If he was to prevail, he needed to turn things around very quickly. And so, as Sadamori and Hidesato rode into Shimōsa at the head of their newly reinforced army on the thirteenth day of the second month of 940, Masakado issued what was to be his final call to arms, summoning any and all who still followed him to a rendezvous point near his Iwai residence.

Time was, however, also beginning to work against Hidesato and Sadamori. On the eighth day of the second month of 940, the government's formal command staff, headed by Fujiwara Tadabumi, had departed the capital, raising troops as they traveled eastward. On the ninth and tenth, the court sent edicts to the various provinces along their route, ordering them to mobilize warriors to join the advancing army.[42]

With the formally commissioned imperial army on its way, Sadamori and Hidesato now faced a rapidly closing window of opportunity.

Unless they could destroy Masakado before the government army arrived, they would have to surrender much of the credit—and the attendant rewards—for the victory to Tadabumi and his officers. Delay might also mean desertions as their recruits slipped away to return to their planting or to enlist under Tadabumi instead. Unable, therefore, to wait or to waste time searching about the marshes for Masakado, they sought to force him out of hiding by raiding and burning homes about his base, beginning with Masakado's own compound at Kamawa.[43] (See the illustration on page 92.)

This was, as Fukuda Toyohiko has observed, a risky tactic, one that might well have backfired, enraging warriors all about Shimōsa and galvanizing them to Masakado's cause. In the event, however, it had the opposite effect—at least if we are to believe *Shōmonki*, which insists that the people of the province "did not grieve over what they had lost at the hands of the Hitachi [army]; rather they lamented Masakado's political missteps."[44]

On the morning of the fourteenth, Masakado arrived at the meeting place he had designated. To his dismay, he found only a handful of stalwarts waiting for him. *Shōmonki* explains that his "usual army of more than 8000 men had not yet assembled," but, as Kitayama Shigeo notes, both this number and the expression "not yet" are absurd.[45] While Masakado must, at his peak, have been drawing men from all over the Kantō, he had also long commanded the resources of most of the warriors in Shimōsa, none of whom should have had any difficulty reaching him in time. By now, however, news of the approaching imperial army had worked its way across the east, and Masakado's prospects for success no longer seemed plausible to any but the most diehard wishful thinkers. The vast majority of the eastern warriors who had once followed him—including, it would seem, Prince Okiyo, Fujiwara Haruaki, and Fujiwara Harumochi, who had brought him into insurrection in the first place—chose to stay home or go into hiding rather than risk annihilation at Masakado's side.

The figure of the erstwhile New Emperor reviewing the "just over four hundred men" assembled on his behalf that windy March morning recalls images of Richard III contemplating his future as the sun rose on Bosworth Field five and half centuries later. Masakado had not, insofar as we know, passed the night entertaining a parade of spectral visitors promising him death on the morrow; nevertheless, he must have felt his last hopes of wresting a pardon, and undoing the debacle he had set in motion in Hitachi three months earlier, evaporating with the morning mist. Unlike Shakespeare's Richard, however, Masakado appears to have resigned himself to his fate, choosing a glorious end over further escape and evasion. He led his men to the flatlands north of the Tone River, near his Iwai residence, positioned them with their backs to a protective hillside, and waited for Sadamori, Hidesato, and Tamenori.★ They found him that afternoon, late in the hour of the sheep (1 to 3 p.m.).

Masakado had selected his battle site well. A violent wind gusted from the south, "howling through the branches [of nearby trees], echoing across the ground and carrying clods of earth" into the faces of his advancing enemies.[46] The gale toppled over the shields on both sides of the field, but this impaired Hidesato and Sadamori far more than it did Masakado. Outnumbered as badly as he was, Masakado could not have lasted long in a defensive posture, anyway. His enemies, by contrast, could, under more favorable conditions, have remained behind their shield lines and pelted Masakado's men with volleys of arrows. But they could not easily shoot into the wind, and the dirt blowing at their eyes put the Hitachi and Shimozuke warriors at a further disadvantage as Masakado's horsemen rode toward them with the blast at their backs.

Sadamori's center fell back to regroup and counterattack, but Masakado was not about to cede the offensive. His warriors charged into the breach as it opened, shooting down more than eighty men. Most of the rest broke and ran, leaving behind "just over 300 spirited warriors, who lost their bearings and dashed about aimlessly."[47]

With an astounding upset victory all but within his grasp, however, Masakado made a lethal blunder. As he chased the fleeing "government" troops from the field, he "forgot the march of the wind," and when he wheeled about to return to his main body, he found himself downwind

---

★ *Shōmonki* places this final battle in "Kitayama in the Sashima district," while *Fusō ryakki* assigns it to "Shimahiroyama" and *Konjaku monogatari shū* names the spot "Yamakita." There are numerous theories—and little consensus—concerning these place names, but most scholars do agree that the battle site must have been somewhere near what is now Iwai City, in southwestern Ibaraki prefecture. As Hayashi Rokurō observes (*Shijitsu Taira Masakado*, p. 196), there is nothing in the vicinity even vaguely worthy of the name "mountain" (*yama*), making all these place names a bit puzzling.

and cut off from his original position by Hidesato, Sadamori, and their remaining warriors. "At that time, the punishment of Heaven revealed itself."[48]

There is a remarkable difference of opinion among the various accounts of this battle as to exactly how Masakado met his end. While *Shōmonki* maintains that he was "struck by a divine arrow, shot blindly," another narrative is less specific about the origins of the shaft—noting only that "struck by an arrow, he perished alone on the field"—but adds that "Sadamori, Hidesato and the others rejoiced, and had a ferocious warrior cut off his head." A twelfth-century account, however, credits Sadamori with the kill and introduces a rivalry between the two commanders, relating that "Masakado was struck by one of Sadamori's arrows and tumbled from his horse. But Hidesato galloped to the spot, cut off Masakado's head, and entrusted it to one of his troops; whereupon Sadamori dismounted to confront him." The text offers no further details about the ensuing quarrel, but as we saw in chapter 1, Hidesato must have persevered. For he not only received the greater part of the court's recognition for the victory, he came to be regarded by medieval times as the one who shot Masakado after cajoling the secret of Masakado's single vulnerable point from his mistress.[49]

Nearly half the warriors who had stood with Masakado at the start of the day—197 men—perished with him. The Hitachi and Shimozuke warriors collected their heads, along with 300 shields, 199 bows and quivers, 51 swords, and a cache of "treasonous documents," which may have included a copy of Masakado's letter to Fujiwara Tadahira.[50]

The rest of Masakado's men scattered, many, as noted previously, before the battle. Masakado's brother Masayori and Fujiwara Harumochi had fled to Sagami, where they were tracked down and killed a few days later. Prince Okiyo was discovered and executed in Kazusa on the nineteenth day of the second month. Shortly thereafter, Fujiwara Haruaki and Sakanoue Katsutaka were cut down in Hitachi.[51]

On the eighth day of the fourth month, Fujiwara Tadanobu (Tadabumi's younger brother) and Taira Kintsura began a hunt through Shimōsa for the rest of Masakado's brothers and his remaining captains. They did not succeed in capturing anyone important, but they did frighten several of Masakado's brothers into shaving their heads, taking

Buddhist vows, and stealing away into the mountains, while the others simply "abandoned their wives and children, each losing himself in the wilds."[52]

This action brought the military campaign to an end. On the sixteenth day of the second month, the court had issued a general amnesty pardoning any of Masakado's followers who surrendered to the proper authorities. Word of this offer spread rapidly in the wake of Tadabumi's arrival in the east and sent the survivors significant enough to be bothered with scurrying to turn themselves in.[53]

"And so," *Shōmonki* intones, Masakado's

> wives and children wandered about the roads in [unbearable] shame while his brothers lost their homes and positions and had no place even to hide. His followers, once as numerous as the clouds, scattered in the dark sky, beyond the mists. Those who had held to him like shadows perished meaninglessly in mid-flight. Others survived, but combed the mountains and streams calling for lost parents or offspring. Still others lamenting separation from husbands or wives, searched about the province and inquired beyond.[54]

In the end, it warned, Masakado's story is a tragedy, the tale of a good man brought low by corrupt underlings—Okiyo and Haruaki—and by a failure of foresight and self-control:

> [Confucius's *Analects* caution,] "Think naught of things far off, and sorrow will be close by." . . . Thus did Masakado accumulate a superb record of service at court; his loyalty and reliability course through the ages. But he focused his life's calling on ferocity and recklessness, doing battle each year, each month. Accordingly, he paid no heed to scholars, taking pleasure only in the military arts. And so he crossed shields with his relatives, earning rebuke over his affection for wickedness. His evil deeds accrued until they clung to him; admonishments for his iniquity were heard throughout the eight provinces [of the east]. In the end, he was destroyed . . . and bequeathed to posterity the name of a rebel.[55]

Epilogue

How could you be a Great Man if history brought
you no Great Events, or brought you to them
at the wrong time, too young, too old?

—Lois McMaster Bujold, *Memory*

Poetry comes nearer to vital truth than history.

—Plato

The Council of State received the news of Masakado's death on the twenty-fifth day of the second month of 940, when a messenger from Shinano arrived in the capital. Celebration was cut short the following morning, when a rapid messenger appeared with a report that Masakado was poised to invade Mutsu and Dewa at the head of some thirteen thousand troops. Having been thus assured that Masakado was either dead or stronger than ever and expanding to the northeast, the residents of Kyoto spent the next ten days exchanging rumors and alternating between alarm that the renegade warrior might soon be at their doorstep and relief that, if not dead, he was at least marching in the opposite direction from the capital. Then on the fifth day of the third month, posts from Hidesato and provincial officers in Kai arrived, confirming Masakado's demise.[1]

Two weeks later, the court learned that Taira Kimimasa had captured and executed Prince Okiyo in Kazusa, and two weeks after that, a messenger from Musashi brought the news that Okiyo's remaining men had been killed there. On the eighth day of the fourth month, Fujiwara Tadanobu and Taira Kintsura began hunting down the rest of Masakado's brothers and allies in Shimōsa.[2]

Masakado's head arrived in the capital, where it was hung for display outside the East Market on the tenth day of the fifth month. Three days later, Tadanobu returned to Kyoto and formally surrendered his commission as Field Marshal for the Pacification of the East.[3]

The Masakado insurrection was over, but it would be more than a year before the court could truly relax, for Fujiwara Sumitomo was still at large and still terrorizing the Inland Sea region.

Seeking Sumitomo

As 939 gave way to 940, Sumitomo's insurrection had, in fact, been gaining momentum. His arson campaign in the capital continued for at least three more months, prompting the Council of State to post additional guards to the gates of the city and to order the Office of Imperial Police and the Outer Palace Guard to step up night patrols of the streets. In the meantime, Sumitomo's fleet attacked Bizen province on the twentieth day of the first month, scattering government military forces there. Two weeks later, pirates raided the government arsenal in Awaji.[4]

Although concerned that it might be facing challenges to its sovereignty from both the east (where Masakado was—at least insofar as anyone in Kyoto was yet aware—at the apex of his powers) and the west, the court nevertheless recognized a qualitative distinction between the two threats. In the east, it had identified Masakado himself as the source of the trouble and correctly calculated that once he and his key henchmen had been eliminated, life in the region would quickly return to an all-things-considered amenable status quo ante. The pirate problem in and around the Inland Sea had, however, been fermenting for decades; Sumitomo's coalition building had simply exacerbated the situation.

Accordingly, the court adopted a two-layered strategy. First, it attempted to decapitate the alliance by buying off Sumitomo with a promotion to junior fifth rank, lower grade. Second, it commissioned "Envoys to Pursue and Capture the Pirates of the Southern Sea" (*Tsuibu Nankai kyōzoku shi*) and issued arrest warrants for "Sumitomo's evil followers."[5]

The government was hoping that it could tilt Sumitomo's ambitions back toward the center and away from his local allies (thus its citation of Sumitomo's *followers*, rather than Sumitomo himself, on the warrants). In the face of this second invitation to return to the imperial fold, however, Sumitomo chose not to "play a sanctimonious part with a pirate head and a pirate heart," agreeing instead with Gilbert and Sullivan that "it is, it is a glorious thing to be a pirate king."[6]

On the eighteenth day of the eighth month of 940, just six months after acknowledging receipt of his promotion, Sumitomo led a fleet of some four hundred vessels in a raid on Iyo (see the map on page 111). After pillaging the government compound there, he moved on to burn and loot the provincial capital in Sanuki on the northeastern coast of Shikoku, pausing en route to burn "more than a hundred warships" in Bitchū and Bizen across the Inland Sea on Honshu.[7]

The court responded by sending troops to reinforce the provincial capital of Awa, on the eastern tip of Shikoku; ordering shrines and temples in the capital and the Inland Sea region to pray for victory; and commissioning yet another officer, Ono Yoshifuru, to "pursue and capture" pirates in the southwest. Yoshifuru sped at once to Harima, accompanied by Masakado's old adversary Minamoto Tsunemoto as his second-in-command. There they built "more than 200 ships," which they set sailing for Iyo. Meanwhile, Fujiwara Kunikaze, the assistant governor of Sanuki, had been "summoning and assembling brave men" on the island province of Awaji after being chased from Sanuki during Sumitomo's raid there. He returned to Shikoku in the tenth month of 940 "to await the arrival of the government army."[8]

A few weeks later, pirates routed government forces in Kyushu. A fortnight after that, they captured a government official in Suo, on the southwestern tip of Honshu, and burned him alive. Then in the twelfth month of 940, pirates raided and burned the Hata district in Tosa, on the southern coast of Shikoku. And so things continued well into the early months of 941.[9]

By this time, Sumitomo claimed to command some fifteen hundred ships and several thousand freebooters. Nevertheless, he was about to receive a sharp reminder of just how tenuous the military allegiances of his age could be.

Early in the second month of 941, one of his captains, Fujiwara

Tsunetoshi, learned that Yoshifuru and the government fleet were headed his way. After a quick reassessment of his options, Tsunetoshi "abandoned his troops and fled secretly" to Fujiwara Kunikaze. Eager to take advantage of Tsunetoshi's detailed knowledge concerning the pirates' homes and hideouts, and of the lands and sea lanes in and around Shikoku, Kunikaze enthusiastically accepted his services. With Tsunetoshi to guide and advise him, Kunikaze went on the offensive, scattering the pirate fleet "like leaves floating about the sea surface."[10]

But while this victory—the government's first noteworthy military success against Sumitomo—no doubt buoyed court morale, it proved far from decisive. In the fifth month of 941, Ono Yoshifuru's fleet sighted Sumitomo's main force and gave chase but was unable to catch it, "owing to heavy winds and waves." While the government ships were searching for them, the pirates landed in Chikuzen and attacked the *Dazaifu*. After quickly overwhelming the troops stationed there, Sumitomo's men stormed into the government compound, looting it of "the treasures of generations" and then setting it aflame, burning it completely to the ground.[11]

Word of this disaster reached Kyoto on the nineteenth day of the fifth month. In response, the court commissioned Fujiwara Tadabumi—who had returned to the capital from his eastern campaign only a week earlier—as Field Marshal to Pacify the West (*Seisei taishōgun*). As things worked out, however, Sumitomo's fate was sealed before Tadabumi and his subalterns could even set sail for the theater of combat, making this appointment even more superfluous than Tadabumi's commission to subdue Masakado had been.[12]

On the twentieth day of the fifth month, Ono Yoshifuru found Sumitomo and his freebooters still anchored in Hakata Bay, off the coast of the now-razed *Dazaifu* compound. After positioning most of his fleet at the entrance to the bay, Yoshifuru led a sizable detachment ashore. Then he fell on the pirates from both land and sea (see the illustration on page 93).[13]

Sumitomo had, in fact, been expecting this attack, and welcomed it as an opportunity to crush Yoshifuru's force and "determine life or death with a single blow." But the government troops proved considerably more formidable than he had expected.

Yoshifuru's warriors pelted the freebooters with arrows, killing dozens and sending the rest scrambling back to their ships, only to run straight into Yoshifuru's waiting armada, which made short work of them. Some eight hundred pirate ships were captured, and scores more were put to the torch. Hundreds of pirates were killed or wounded, and "countless men and women" drowned while attempting to escape. "The pirate leadership was utterly scattered: some dead, some surrendered, some dispersed like clouds."[14]

Sumitomo's coalition had been shattered, the captains and crews who comprised it had been decimated, and the menace of piracy on the Inland Sea had been largely curtailed. Sumitomo himself, however, managed to slip away—albeit not for long. A fortnight later, he and his son Shigetamaru were captured in their native Iyo.[15] Their heads were shipped to the capital, arriving on the seventh day of the seventh month, just in time to add to the celebrations surrounding the Tanabata star festival.★

And to the Victors . . .

The lion's share of the credit for destroying Masakado went to Fujiwara Hidesato, which was probably appropriate, inasmuch as his confederates, Sadamori and Tamenori, had seen nothing but failure until he joined them. Even more importantly from the court's perspective, Hidesato was the only one of the three who was actually deputized to act on its behalf and the only one likely to have done otherwise.

To control men like Masakado, the government needed the support of others like him; that is, of other warrior leaders in the provinces. This support was, in turn, dependent on the court's ability to convince such men that it was in their own best interest to support the state rather than join forces with the Masakados. This could be accomplished only by offering the warriors a stake in the survival of the polity—by

---

★The Tanabata (literally, "Seventh Night") festival celebrates a Chinese legend concerning two celestial lovers: the weaver maid Orihime and the herdsman Hikoboshi. Condemned to dwell on opposite sides of the Milky Way, the pair—better known today as the stars Vega and Altair—were allowed to meet for only one night a year, on the seventh day of the seventh month.

making them a part of it and thus linking their personal fortunes to its success.[16]

Hidesato's title as *ōryōshi* of Shimozuke rendered his private military resources public and represented one of the most important devices the court used to attract provincial warrior leaders to its service. There were added rewards in the form of rank, office, and land granted for meritorious performance of assigned or assumed tasks.

It was necessary to reward a man like Hidesato with juicier plums than needed to be offered to someone like Sadamori, whose involvement in the conflict was personally motivated and whose interests were already inexorably bound up with those of the court. Accordingly, Hidesato was raised to junior fourth rank, lower grade, given lucrative governorships in Shimozuke and Musashi, and allotted merit lands (*kōden*) "to be transmitted to his progeny forever"; Sadamori was awarded only junior fifth rank, lower grade, and the much less profitable assistant directorship of the Right Imperial Stables (*uma no suke*), in addition to retaining his post as secretary in Hitachi.[17]

No source mentions any reward at all for Tamenori, but Tsunemoto fared curiously well. *Shōmonki* explains that "although his charges were originally but empty words, in the end they became true," thus earning him a promotion to junior fifth rank, lower grade, an appointment as assistant governor-general (*shōni*) of the *Dazaifu*, and—shortly thereafter—a commission as Ono Yoshifuru's deputy commander, to proceed against Sumitomo.[18]

On the twenty-fifth day of the third month, Fujiwara Shigemochi was dismissed from his post as assistant governor of Kazusa, "owing to his having been robbed of his provincial seal during Masakado's insurrection." Incongruously, Fujiwara Korechika had been allowed to quietly resume his duties in Hitachi a few days after Masakado's death. We have no information on the court's disposition of the other provincial officials who capitulated to Masakado.[19]

Posterity

The reputations they established through their service against Masakado propelled all three of his principal enemies—Fujiwara Hidesato, Taira

Sadamori, and Minamoto Tsunemoto—on to stellar careers as warriors and government officials. And all three sired illustrious warrior lineages: the Bandō Fujiwara, the Ise Heishi, and the Seiwa Genji.★ Indeed, the majority of the leading samurai houses of medieval Japan claimed descent from one of these lines.

Tsunemoto's family's star burned brightest of all. One genealogy credits him with having been "an expert with bow and horse, and skilled in the martial arts," although he would seem to have come by this talent rather late in life: *Shōmonki* informs us that in 939 when Masakado forced him to flee from his post in Musashi, he was "not yet practiced in the ways of the warrior." Military credentials notwithstanding, however, Tsunemoto became an archetypical career provincial official, serving as assistant governor of Shimozuke and Kazusa; as assistant governor-general of the *Dazaifu*; as governor of Chikuzen, Shinano, Mino, Tajima, Izu, and Musashi; as commander of the Pacification Headquarters in Mutsu; and in numerous central court posts. He also fathered nine sons, at least three of whom became warriors of some reputation.[20]

The most important of these was his eldest son, Mitsunaka, born in 912 and raised primarily in the capital. Like his father before him, Mitsunaka served as commander of the Pacification Headquarters, as governor or assistant governor of at least ten provinces, and in half a dozen or more posts at court. Ironically, our first record of his involvement in military activities is from 960, when he and several other warriors were ordered to investigate rumors that one of Masakado's sons was abroad in the capital. In 969 he brought his military resources to the support of imperial Regent Fujiwara Morotada's efforts to eliminate his chief court rival, Minamoto Takaakira. Morotada's success in this affair (known to historians as the Anna Incident, after the calendar era in which it occurred) left him virtually unchallenged at court, and this

---

★As I noted in chapter 2, "Genji" and "Heishi" represent alternative (Sino-Japanese) readings for the Minamoto and Taira houses. The Seiwa Genji were the branch of Minamoto descended from Emperor Seiwa (r. 858–876), and the Ise Heishi were a branch of the Kammu Heishi descended from Emperor Kammu (r. 781–806). The name Bandō Fujiwara designates the line of Fujiwara that established itself in eastern Japan (the Bandō, cf. chapter 2). This lineage is also known as the Hidesato-ryū ("Hidesato line") Fujiwara, a good indication of Hidesato's prominence within it.

cooperation between Mitsunaka and Morotada marked the beginning of a patron-client bond between Mitsunaka's line of the Seiwa Genji and the Fujiwara Regents' House (*Sekkanke*) that endured for two centuries. Mitsunaka's seventh-generation descendant Minamoto Yoritomo (introduced in chapter 6) founded the Kamakura Shogunate, an event that marks the dawn of the medieval era.[21]

Fujiwara Hidesato achieved no further advances in court rank after 940, but he did manage to obtain a steady sequence of appointments to provincial government posts. The weightiest among these was his tenure as commander of the Pacification Headquarters, an office that both Tsunemoto and Sadamori held before him but that Hidesato's descendants were able to monopolize for more than a century thereafter. Hidesato's final appearance in the historical record was in the late spring of 947, when his patron, Minamoto Takaakira, petitioned on his behalf for merit fields to be granted in reward for his having struck down some of "the late Masakado's brothers." According to family tradition, he died late in the second month of 958.[22]

Both Hidesato's title as commander of the Pacification Headquarters and his patron-client relationship with Takaakira passed along to his eldest son, Chiharu. Chiharu's career began well, with a series of minor posts in the capital and the provinces, including a stint as acting assistant governor of Sagami, but it ended badly—and early. In 967, following the death of Emperor Murakami (r. 946–967), he and Minamoto Mitsunaka were designated to take command of the Suzuka Barrier in Ise. The assignment was prestigious and largely ceremonial; nevertheless, both warriors declined to accept it. Mitsunaka pleaded illness; Chiharu's reasons are lost to a lacuna in the only source that records the event, but they must have seemed spurious, for the court accepted Mitsunaka's excuse and censored Chiharu for his refusal. Two years later, during the Anna Incident, Chiharu led troops in support of his hereditary patron, Takaakira, who was at the time Minister of the Left. When Fujiwara Morotada and Mitsunaka prevailed, Chiharu was stripped of his rank and exiled to the island of Oki, off the coast of western Honshu.[23]

Chiharu's disgrace did not, however, end his family's fortunes. Hidesato's descendants can be identified as martial servants of the nobility and holders of central court military posts down to the end of the Heian period. Nevertheless, the eastern Fujiwara enjoyed their greatest measure of suc-

cess as provincial rather than capital military figures. Over the remainder
of the tenth and eleventh centuries, Hidesato's descendants served in a cat-
alog full of provincial offices across the north and east, becoming major
powers in Shimozuke, Sagami, Musashi, and Mutsu.[24]

The most spectacular success story here began with Hidesato's great-
great-great-grandson Tsunekiyo and his heirs, who on the strength of
marriage ties to powerful northern warrior houses, managed to establish
what came near to being an autonomous kingdom in Mutsu between
the late eleventh and the late twelfth centuries. Tsunekiyo married a
daughter of Abe Yoritoki, a warrior chieftain of *emishi* descent. Both
Tsunekiyo and Yoritoki were killed in the so-called Former Nine Years'
War of 1055–1062, and in the aftermath, Tsunekiyo's widow married the
son of another prominent *emishi* chieftain, Kiyowara Takenori.

Takenori had played a Hidesato-like role in this conflict, distinguishing himself on behalf of the government in suppressing the rebel Yoritoki. As a reward, he was given most of the property interests formerly
held by Yoritoki. Added to his own lands, this made him a truly formidable power in northeastern Japan. But not so formidable as Tsunekiyo's
son Kiyohira was to become.

Kiyohira inherited most of Takenori's holdings, as well as what remained
of those of his father and his maternal grandfather, Yoritoki. He turned this
into an empire that endured until 1189, when it was destroyed, along with
his great-grandson Yasuhira, by Minamoto Yoritomo.[25]

This was, however, scarcely the end of Hidesato's legacy. His
descendants—including the Satō, the Ōtomo, the Mutō, the Iga, the
Hatano, the Matsuda, the Oyama, the Shimokabe, and the Sano—
represent some of the most illustrious provincial warrior houses of the
medieval era.

More colorfully, by the end of the Heian period, Hidesato had come
to be regarded as having been a master of mounted archery and the pro-
genitor of a family tradition of instruction in this art, particularly the ritualized competitive form known as *yabusame*. Warriors claiming to have
"learned and passed on the secret methods of Hidesato" were very much
in demand at the hunts and other archery contests staged by Minamoto
Yoritomo during the early days of the Kamakura shogunate.[26]

Taira Sadamori all but disappeared from the historical record after his
brief appearance there during his feud with Masakado. We know little

about the rest of his life, save that he went on to serve terms as governor of Tamba and Mutsu, and as commander of the Pacification Headquarters. We know a great deal more about his progeny.

The decades that followed Masakado's defeat witnessed an intensification of rivalries in both the capital and the countryside between three competing Taira lineages. The most prominent of these descended from Sadamori and his brother Shigemori, many of whose sons and grandsons Sadamori adopted. A second major lineage derived from Masakado's original enemy, Yoshikane, through his son Kimimasa. Kimimasa and his brother Kintsura, it may be recalled, obtained appointments as provincial secretaries in Kazusa and Shimōsa during the Masakado affair. And after his thrashing of Prince Okiyo, Kimimasa was rewarded with the governorship of Awa. Later he also served as governor of Musashi. His descendants maintained base lands in Kazusa and Shimōsa, as did a third lineage, descended from Yoshikane's brother Yoshifumi. The Yoshikane and Yoshifumi lines were related by marriage, through Masakado, whose wife was Kimimasa's sister and whose daughter married Yoshifumi's son Tadayori (see the genealogical chart on page 36). Neither house got along well with Sadamori's line. Kimimasa's son Masayori even came to blows with Sadamori's son Korehira in 998, prompting court intervention and censure.[27]

All four of Sadamori's natural sons—Korenobu, Koremasa, Koretoshi, and Korehira—enjoyed careers as governors and assistant governors in a succession of provinces. But like their father, they directed their ambitions primarily toward the capital, where they built formidable reputations as martial servants of the court and the nobles who comprised it. Koremasa, his son Koretoki, and his grandson Naokata were particularly successful in this pursuit.[28]

Koretoki, a much-celebrated warrior, served Fujiwara Michinaga, under whom the Fujiwara Regents' House reached the crest of its power and prosperity. Naokata became a client of Michinaga's son Yorimichi and, in 1024, established himself as a leading central warrior-noble when he disposed of some bandits who had taken hostages in the capital.[29]

In 1028 Taira Tadatsune, a maternal grandson of Masakado, attacked and ravaged the provincial government compound in Awa. After three days of heated debate and considerable pressure from Fujiwara Yorimichi, the court commissioned Naokata as *tsuitōshi* ("envoy to pursue and strike down") to bring him in, following essentially the same strategy of co-opting private grudges and using a troublemaker's personal enemies and rivals against him that it had successfully employed against Masakado three-quarters of a century earlier.

By 1030, however, two years of fighting had produced nothing but widespread destruction across Awa, Kazusa, and Shimōsa, as Tadatsune stubbornly refused to negotiate terms with a hereditary family enemy, and Naokata proved unable to force him to surrender. Naokata's reputation evaporated quickly when an exasperated court sacked him and replaced him with Minamoto Yorinobu, a grandson of Tsunetomo.[30]

Naokata's failure to bring Tadatsune to justice wrought irreparable damage on his house, while success in the same venture boosted the standing of the Seiwa Genji under Yorinobu and his heirs. At the same time, the spotlight within the Taira shifted from Koremasa's line to that of Sadamori's youngest son, Korehira.

Korehira served briefly as governor of Ise and established a landed base there for himself and his heirs, who accordingly came to be known as the Ise Heishi. During the late 1090s, his great-grandson Masamori forged for himself and his family a patron-client relationship with successive retired emperors that endured for three generations. Between 1160 and 1179, Masamori's grandson Kiyomori rode this relationship to hitherto unimagined heights of power—achieving appointment as prime minister (daijōdaijin), marrying a daughter to the emperor, and ultimately staging a coup d'état that left him in virtual control of the court—only to be pulled down again by Minamoto Yoritomo and his kinsmen.[31]

And then there were the legends.

As we saw in chapter 1, tales about Masakado himself were soon being related all over Japan—entire books have, in fact, been devoted to this subject.[32] The stories range from accounts of what happened to his head, to fanciful notions that he was more than human—a giant, the offspring of a serpent, a man with seven bodies or with one who had but a single vulnerable point—to apocryphal yarns about encounters with Sumitomo, Sadamori, and Hidesato.

Neither Hidesato nor Sadamori achieved this level of notoriety. Nevertheless, while neither made more than fleeting appearances in *reliable* historical sources, both enjoyed vivid afterlives in folklore.

Sadamori's legacy ran closer to infamy than glory. Clearly he does not come off well in *Shōmonki*, which portrays him prevaricating, running, hiding, losing repeatedly, backstabbing, and whining. He fares only a little better in other accounts of the Masakado affair. The twelfth-century tale collection *Konjaku monogatari shū*, for example, depicts him "casting away his public duties and rushing down from the capital" to avenge his father in 936, only to conclude upon his arrival in Hitachi that he "could not contend with Masakado's power and spirit. And so he remained in hiding in the province, unable to pursue his true intentions."[33]

Another tale in the same collection paints an even less flattering portrait. This story, set in the early 970s while Sadamori was serving as governor of Tamba, depicts a callous brute—and a fool:[34]

In this yarn, said to have been related by a daughter of Sadamori's number one retainer, Tate Morotada, Sadamori finds himself suffering from an infected wound, and sends for a renowned physician from Kyoto. After examining the injury, the doctor informs Sadamori:

> This wound calls for extreme care. It must be treated with a medicine called Dried Infant. This drug is not known to many people, and with the passage of days, even it becomes less effective. You must obtain it quickly.★
>
> The doctor then departs, whereupon Sadamori summons his son Korenobu and reports the diagnosis, adding, "In any case, I have heard that your wife is pregnant. Get that fetus for me!"[35]

Korenobu is properly horrified at his father's order, but he is also unsure how to refuse it. Nevertheless, rather than making funeral arrangements as Sadamori instructed, he visits the physician and tearfully explains what is happening. The doctor is also shocked by Sadamori's proposal and promises to help.

He confronts Sadamori, who cheerfully confirms that he is indeed

---

★Dried infant (*chigo hoshi* in this account, but also known as *hoshi chigo*, *hoshi ko*, or *oroshi-taruko*) was prepared from a male fetus, usually one that had been aborted or miscarried. A fifteenth-century medical text, *Kinsō hiden jō*, describes it as "the absolute best medicine for mending bone, muscle, brain and viscera that have been cut." For a detailed discussion of this wonder drug—including a translation of *Kinsō hiden jō*'s step-by-step instructions for preparing and applying it—see Andrew E. Goble, "War and Injury," pp. 321–324.

planning to fashion the drug he needs from his own unborn grandson. At this, the physician rejoins that "a blood relative cannot become medicine. Find another in all haste."

Thus frustrated, Sadamori makes inquiries about other sources for fetuses. Learning that one of his kitchen maids is six months' pregnant, he orders the fetus brought to him immediately. But "when they open her belly to look," they discover that the fetus is female and therefore unusable, so they discard it. "Nevertheless," the text matter-of-factly informs us, "another fetus was found elsewhere, and the Governor survived."

Once assured of recovery, Sadamori rewards the physician with a horse and several other gifts and sends him off to prepare for his return to Kyoto. He then calls Korenobu to his side and confides that he fears for his reputation should the physician spread rumors about this incident in the capital—as he is likely to do. Intriguingly, his concern lies not with his murder of the innocent women who provided the medicine he needed, or even with his intended murder of his daughter-in-law, but with the fact that he was suffering from a battle wound. "In the capital," he explains, "I have a reputation of being dependable. Thus it is likely that I will soon be posted to Mutsu to deal with the *emishi* uprising there. But would it not be egregious if people began to gossip about my having been shot by someone or other?"

Rather than risk this, Sadamori orders Korenobu to kill the doctor. Korenobu coolly replies that he can do this rather easily by posing as a bandit and waylaying him during his trip back to Kyoto. He then takes his leave, ostensibly to prepare for his mission.

Instead, however, he goes straight to the doctor and tells him about Sadamori's orders. Reassuring the now-terrified physician that he has not forgotten the man's kindness in saving his wife and child, Korenobu instructs him to dismount and walk as he crosses a certain mountain, while letting the officer assigned to accompany him ride in his place. The doctor does as he is told, and sure enough, as the pair reaches the pass, a "bandit" appears and shoots down the man on the horse.

When Korenobu reports back to Sadamori that he has killed the doctor but that the officer with him escaped, Sadamori is "delighted" by the news. Later, however, he discovers that the physician is still alive and calls Korenobu to account.

In response to his father's inquiries, Korenobu shrugs disingenuously and answers, "How could I have known that the doctor would travel on foot like a servant? I assumed the deputy on the horse to be the master, and shot him to death." Unable to refute this logic, Sadamori relents.

The text concludes, "That Sadamori thought to open the belly of his pregnant daughter-in-law to take out the fetus reveals his cruel and shameless heart." One might wonder why the narrator expresses no similar indignation over Sadamori's completely pointless slaughter of the kitchen maid or of the unfortunate young woman who actually provided him with the fetus he wanted—or, for that matter, over Korenobu's casual murder of the physician's bodyguard. In this light, the yarn reveals as much about the sensibilities of Heian nobles toward their servants as it does about Sadamori's reputation in posterity.

The latter was, in any event, at least somewhat less despicable than the foregoing might suggest. Another apologue, titled "How Taira Sadamori Shot Down Robbers in the Home of a Priest," casts Sadamori more heroically.[36] This incident is supposed to have taken place around the beginning of 979, while Sadamori was en route homeward following his posting as governor and commander of the Pacification Headquarters in Mutsu.

Arriving in the southern part of Kyoto late in the evening, Sadamori calls on the home of an old friend, "a certain wealthy priest," asking to be allowed to spend the night, as it is already too late to reach his own residence at a reasonable hour. The priest initially refuses to see him, explaining through a servant that a diviner has warned that he must spend the night in strict seclusion, silence, and fasting, lest he be "robbed of his life by bandits."

But Sadamori is persistent, reminding his friend that a warrior guest might actually prove useful in the event that robbers really did appear. At length, the priest relents, breaks his cloister, and invites Sadamori in. He does, however, insist that Sadamori alone is welcome; his retainers and servants must remain outside. Sadamori agrees and sends his men on ahead without him.

Sure enough, in the middle of the night, Sadamori is awakened by noises coming from the gates of the house. Snatching up his bow and arrows, he slips stealthily into the carriage house and crouches in the dark. From this vantage point, he discovers a band of robbers—about ten men, all told—breaking through the gate and scurrying into the courtyard.

Sadamori responds with a cunning combination of stealth, deception, and misdirection worthy of a master ninja. Slipping into the pack and pretending to be one of them, he first directs the robbers toward a part of the mansion that holds nothing of value. Then while the thieves work their way from empty room to empty room, Sadamori begins to pick them off, one by one. He shoots the first in the back, drags the body out of sight, and then shoots a second robber in the chest and stashes him next to his comrade. In the meantime, he shouts alarms from the shadows that "someone" is shooting at "us" and that "we" had best run for "our" lives.

As the bandits scramble to escape, Sadamori shoots down one after another, using whistling arrows (*kaburaya*) that stoke their panic. He kills three or four near the gate and wounds at least one more. The next morning, one of those who got away is found lying in a ditch a short distance from the house with an arrow in his hip. Under interrogation, the man gives up the rest of his cronies.

Perhaps the most striking thing about Sadamori's legacy in folklore is its mundane secularity. His coldhearted brutality in the account of his quest for a fetus to treat his battle wound is all the more unsettling because it represents entirely human—and entirely believable—behavior. His defeat of the robbers—who outnumber him ten to one—is similarly bereft of otherworldly overtones. He wins by clever tactics and archery skills. Indeed, the moral of the story would seem to be that the virtue of moderation extends even to divination and prophecy. As the *Konjaku monogatari shū* puts it: "Thus this wise priest was well-met with Sadamori, and his life was saved. Had he been too strict in his cloister, and not admitted Sadamori, he would surely have been killed."[37]

Masakado, by contrast, rapidly evolved into a supernatural hero. So, too, did Fujiwara Hidesato. Curiously, however, legends about Hidesato, which appear in various medieval war tales, focus on his life before and during the Masakado Insurrection. They have almost nothing to say about what happened to him thereafter.[38]

In his literary afterlife, Hidesato became known as "Tawara Tōda," a sobriquet that appears for the first time in a *Konjaku monogatari shū* tale about a feud between Hidesato's grandson Morotō and Taira Koremochi, Sadamori's grand-nephew and adopted son. *Tōda* means "Fujiwara first-born," marking his status as his father's eldest son. *Tawara*, as rendered in its earliest appearances, refers to his home in the Tawara district of Shimozuke; but as Hidesato's legend evolved, it came to be written with a character meaning "straw sack" and said to derive from a magical reward he received for one of his exploits.[39]

This adventure supposedly began sometime in the early 930s on the Seta Bridge, near the mouth of the Seta River at the southern tip of Lake Biwa, east of Kyoto.

One fine day—so goes the tale—Hidesato was crossing this overpass, which marked the entrance to the capital region from the east, and found his way blocked by a gigantic serpent lying across the roadway. Clearly no ordinary snake, the beast was over 60 meters long, "with two glittering eyes like twin suns hanging in the heavens, and two horns standing high, like the treetops of a winter-ravaged forest. Its iron teeth grew up and down, its crimson tongue seemed to spit flames." It was not, however, sufficiently horrific to intimidate Hidesato, who blithely steps on and over the monster, to continue along his way.[40]

A short distance down the road, he glances down to discover a short, odd-looking man standing before him. "I have," the man announces, "been living under that bridge for more than 2000 years now, watching the comings and goings of the high and the low. But until today, I had not seen a man of your fortitude. In my homeland we have long battled an enemy, and have been tormented by him. Would that you could somehow strike him down for me!"*

Hidesato thereby accompanies the man back to Lake Biwa, where the waves part before them to reveal a miraculous road and a magnificent palace about 5 kilometers ahead. Inside the palace, Hidesato is directed to a seat of honor at a sumptuous banquet attended by beautiful young women. They drink and dine for many hours, "far into the night," until cries of alarm announce that "the enemy" is approaching.

Hidesato snatches up his bow, which "required five ordinary men to string, and had never once left his side," and rushes outside, with the wind howling and the lightning crashing around him. A short while later, he spots what appears to be an island, flanked by two or three thousand

---

*In an alternative version of this story, Hidesato is visited the evening after his encounter with the serpent by a beautiful young woman, who reveals herself to have been the serpent and implores Hidesato to rescue her people (*Tawara Tōda monogatari*, pp. 90–93).

torches, approaching the palace. Upon closer inspection, however, he realizes that "the enemy" is in fact a gigantic centipede (see the illustration on page 94). He draws an arrow, waits until the beast is within range, holds his breath, and shoots, aiming right between the creature's eyes. But the arrow bounces off, "echoing as if it struck iron." Startled, Hidesato tries a second arrow, aiming at the same spot, but this too bounces off harmlessly.

With but a single arrow remaining (having, for reasons now lost to posterity, brought only three with him), Hidesato thinks frantically—and then inspiration strikes. Recalling that human saliva is toxic to centipedes, he spits on the tip of his last arrow and launches it at the same target toward which he sent the first two shafts. This time, "whether because it was poisoned or because it struck the same spot for the third time," the arrow buries itself deep between the monster's eyes, piercing all the way through the creature's throat. At this, "what had appeared to be two or three thousand flaming torches flicker out; what had seemed a great island topples to the ground with an echoing crash."

Hidesato's host, who has by now revealed himself to be the Dragon King, the ruler of all the oceans and waterways, rewards him with a bolt of fine silk, a suit of armor, a sword, a gold-copper bell, and a rice straw sack (*tawara*). Upon returning home with his bounty, Hidesato discovers that the cloth and the sack are—of course—magical. The silk bolt can never be exhausted, no matter how much cloth is cut from it; and the sack can never be emptied of anything placed in it, no matter how much one draws out. "Hence," we are told, "he was thereafter called 'Tawara Tōda.'"

Another Hidesato legend relates his first encounter with Masakado and makes clear that but for the grace of a poor first impression, the court very nearly had Hidesato as an enemy rather than its champion. According to this account, when Hidesato first learned of Masakado's uprising and his self-declaration of imperial status, his first inclination was to join him. After all, he reasons, "this Masakado is not only a formidable stalwart, he leads a ferocious retinue. We are of the same mind; should we not each rule half of Japan?"[41]

But when he journeys to Shimōsa to introduce himself to Masakado, things do not go well. The would-be emperor greets him casually, wearing only a white under-robe and without bothering even to comb his hair. Later, as the two dine, Masakado spills food on his lap and simply brushes it from his pants onto the floor. Appalled, Hidesato, who "has always had a good eye for men's characters," determines that a man like this can never be emperor and departs as hurriedly as he can.[42]

Somewhat ironically, in light of the martial prowess and the assessment of Masakado he displays in the foregoing yarns, Hidesato's romantic legacy also embraced a belief that he needed cunning, deception, and supernatural assistance to defeat Masakado. Then again, perhaps this was only fair, since as Hidesato supposedly discovered in his first battle with him (and as attentive readers will recall from chapter 1), Masakado himself "stood over seven feet tall, his corporeal form was all of iron, and he had two pupils in his left eye." What is more, he was accompanied on the field by six other warriors of identical appearance, "and no one could discern which was the real Masakado."[43]

As the story goes, a much-chagrined Hidesato, convinced that "even if the whole nation of Japan came together to fight, there can be no way to contest with this man," determines instead to call on Masakado a second time to offer his services—which Masakado gleefully accepts.[44] Shortly after taking up residence with his new master, however, he chances to meet and fall in love with one of Masakado's concubines, Kozaishō.

One evening, as the lovers engage in a stolen moment of chitchat, Hidesato asks Kozaishō about Masakado's seven apparent bodies. She replies that he has only one true form, the others being but reflections. When Hidesato then inquires whether there is any way to tell which is the real Masakado and which are the reflections, she answers that only his true form casts a shadow. For good measure, she also tells him about Masakado's single vulnerable point. At this, Hidesato excitedly realizes that his affair has been no chance encounter after all—that he has been led to this moment and to this piece of information by divine providence.

Thus armed with the knowledge he needs to defeat Masakado, Hidesato begins sneaking a bow and arrow with him on his nightly visits to Kozaishō and waiting afterward in the darkness for Masakado to visit her. At length, his patience is rewarded, and while Masakado and Kozaishō converse, Hidesato spies on them through a crack in the door. Watching carefully, he confirms that only one of the seven Masakados before him casts a shadow in the lamplight. He draws an arrow, aiming at the spot (just below Masakado's ear, in this version of the story) Kozaishō identified, and shoots. As the shaft strikes home, the six shadow

Masakados vanish "like the flash of lightning or the flicker of a lamp flame," and the real one slumps to the floor. Hidesato then collects his head and returns to his troops—and to his destiny.[45]

Assessing Masakado

Even reduced to a body of flesh and bone, and trimmed down to a more believable stature of five or six feet tall, Taira Masakado was, by any measure, a giant of his world. He was a skillful warrior, born of a prestigious line; a charismatic leader who drew followers from all across the east; and a powerful local magnate, respected and influential in the governments of four provinces—even before his insurrection made him the overlord of eight. He threw the imperial court into an uproar, capturing and holding the attention of the nobility for months. And he has been remembered, celebrated, and castigated for more than a millennium. There is, in short, little about him that smacks of average or typical.

And yet he was also *of* his world, inescapably a product of his times and circumstances. Masakado may have been superlative, but he was scarcely unique. His values, his ambitions, and his methods were those of his class and his peers. He was far more like the men he fought—those he conquered and those who conquered him—than his contemporaries (and their progeny) among the high nobility dared admit. Had events unfolded only a little differently, Masakado might easily have been Yoshikane, Sadamori, Hidesato, or Tsunemoto. More to the point, any of these men could have been Masakado.

The warriors of medieval Japan embraced Masakado as one of their own, the first samurai to rear up and challenge the court-centered polity. So, too, did many generations of historians in their wake. Masakado's insurrection has long been invoked as a portent of decay in the imperial state structure and of a feudal world soon to come.

Scholars today, however, discuss the political, social, and economic order of the Heian period in terms of interplay between rural and urban elites, and balance between centrifugal and centripetal forces. In Masakado's day, the court was rapidly fashioning a new working arrangement with the elite residents of the countryside, one that relied heavily on personal relationships and private resources, and offered provincial administrators expanded freedom of action and opportunities for profit—yet maintained the basic social, political, and economic hierarchies of the imperial state. Far from signaling the imminent collapse of court rule, these accommodations preserved, prolonged, and in many ways enhanced it by co-opting provincial ambitions to serve the center.

Once we understand this system, it is easy to see that far from being the incipient provincial warlords chafing under courtier domination that they were once envisioned to have been, Masakado, his allies, and his enemies were men with one foot in the countryside and the other firmly planted in Kyoto—"bridging figures," in the words of the late Jeffrey Mass.[46] Their aspirations pointed toward service to, rather than freedom from, the court.

The civil nobility was able to maintain tight constraints on the autonomy of even the most powerful warriors in matters of governance and landholding throughout the Heian period. Freedom of local action was not the same as independence or even autonomy for the simple reason that the warriors themselves did not yet think in those terms.

Indeed, a careful examination of Masakado's life and career suggests that it remains an open question whether the Heian era witnessed any true provincial warrior "rebellions" prior to Minamoto Yoritomo's transient declaration of independence for the east in the 1180s. Before that, whenever powerful warriors stepped too far out of line and posed a challenge to central authority, the court was always able to find peers and rivals more conservative in their ambitions and assessments of the odds against successful rebellion to subdue them.

Even celebrated "rebels" like Masakado and Taira Tadatsune were more like unruly adolescents testing the limits of state patience than revolutionaries seeking to overthrow the state. Neither was willfully in defiance of central government authority—at least not initially. Their quarrels were local, not national; their insurgencies aimed at specific provincial officials and their subordinates and policies, not the national polity. And even after their actions rendered them state criminals, their first—and most enduring—instincts were to seek reconciliation with the state through the offices of patrons in the capital.

Masakado's life and career made legends of himself and his rivals, but they neither transformed his world nor signaled epoch-making changes soon to come. They outline and exemplify his age, but they did not define it. In the end, Masakado's world went on much as he had found it.

NOTES

Chapter 1. Masakado and His Legacy

1. *Nihon kiryaku* 940 2/25, 3/5; *Teishin kōki* 940 3/5.
2. *Fusō ryakki* 940 2/8; *Kojidan* p. 312; *Teishin kōki* 940 3/5, 3/18, 3/25, 4/2; *Nihon kiryaku* 940 3/25.
3. *Ryō no gige*, p. 191.
4. For more on the practice of collecting heads, see Karl Friday, *Samurai, Warfare and the State*, pp. 152–155; Kuroda Hideo, "Kubi o kakeru"; Suzuki Masaya, *Katana to kubi-tori*; Thomas Donald Conlan, *State of War*, pp. 21–25.
5. *Tawara Tōda emaki* (reproduced in Noguchi Minoru, *Densetsu no shogun: Fujiwara Hidesato*, pp. 40–41); *Teishin kōki* 940 5/15; *Chōshūki* 1094 3/8; *Chūyūki* 1097 3/8, 1110 1/29.
6. See *Taiheiki* (*Keichōbon*) 16 *kan* "Nihon chōteki no koto," vol. 3, pp. 89–90. A virtually identical account appears in *Tawara Tōda monogatari*, p. 136.
7. Kajiwara Masaaki and Yashiro Kazuo, *Masakado densetsu*, p. 58; Murakami Haruki, *Taira Masakado densetsu*, pp. 43–44.
8. Kajiwara and Yashiro, *Masakado densetsu*, pp. 58–62; Aoki Shigekazu, *Taira Masakado: sōgen no nobi*, pp. 253–254; Murakami Haruki, *Taira Masakado densetsu*, pp. 44–45.
9. Oda Kan'e, *Taira Masakado koseki kō*.
10. Judith N. Rabinovitch, *Shōmonki*, p. 3.
11. Aoki Shigekazu, *Taira Masakado*, pp. 254–255; *Taira Masakado ni matsuwaru densetsu*.
12. Denki densetsu kenkyūjo, *Taira Masakado no ran to kanren denshō*.
13. Aoki Shigekazu, *Taira Masakado*, p. 255; Rabinovitch, *Shōmonki*, p. 34; Murakami Haruki, *Taira Masakado densetsu*, pp. 45-46; "Denki densetsu kenkyūjo," *Taira Masakado*.
14. *The Hour of the Ox: A Trip into the Japanese World of the Supernatural*; Charles Whipple, *Masakado's Revenge*.
15. Kajiwara and Yashiro, *Masakado densetsu*, pp. 61–65; Aoki Shigekazu, *Taira Masakado*, p. 252. Iwai-shi shihennsan iinkai, *Taira Masakado shiryōshū*,

pp. 168–235. Includes a nearly comprehensive collection of literary references to Masakado.

16. Quotations from *Shōmon ryakki*, reproduced in Iwai-shi shihennsan iinkai, *Taira Masakado shiryōshū*, p. 72. Kashiwabara is more commonly known as Kammu, the fiftieth emperor in the traditional reckoning, reigning from 781 to 806.

17. *Honchō monzui* 940 1/11 Daijōkanpu.

18. *Shōmonki*, pp. 139–141.

19. Rabinovitch, *Shōmonki*, pp. 33–52.

20. *Tawara Tōda monogatari*, pp. 126–127.

21. Murakami Haruki, *Taira Masakado densetsu*, pp. 49–52; Denki densetsu kenkyūjō, *Taira Masakado*.

22. The following account of the origins of the samurai is condensed from Karl Friday, *Hired Swords*. For an alternative view, see Wm. Wayne Farris, *Heavenly Warriors*.

23. For more on the political structure and the events of this period, see Bruce Batten, "Foreign Threat and Domestic Reform"; Batten, "State and Frontier in Early Japan"; Cornelius J. Kiley, "State and Dynasty in Archaic Yamato"; Inoue Mitsusada with Delmer Brown, "The Century of Reform"; Joan R. Piggott, *The Emergence of Japanese Kingship*.

24. Batten, "Foreign Threat and Domestic Reform," pp. 10–14.

25. See, for example, the forces described in *Nihon shoki* 591 11/4 and 602 2/1.

26. *Ryō no gige*, p. 192.

27. *Shōmonki*, p. 101.

28. Stephen Turnbull, *The Samurai: A Military History*, pp. 14, 16.

Chapter 2. Masakado's World

1. See John W. Hall, "Kyoto as Historical Background," or William H. McCullough, "The Heian Court," for more on Kyoto and its history.

2. Paul Wheatley and Thomas See, *From Court to Capital*; Ronald P. Toby, "Why Leave Nara?"

3. Hall, "Kyoto as Historical Background," pp. 6–7. McCullough, "Heian Court," pp. 20–25.

4. Hayashi Rokurō, *Kodai makki no hunran*, pp. 26–35.

5. The *Engi shiki*, a tenth-century legal compendium, gives travel distances between the capital and Shimōsa of fifteen days out and thirty days returning (*Engi shiki*, p. 607). I have estimated the time that rapid messengers required from the time that elapsed between the dispatch and arrival of messengers reporting news on Masakado's death in 940. See *Fusō ryakki* 940 2/8 and *Nihon kiryaku* 940 2/25.

6. Fukuda Toyohiko, *Taira Masakado no ran*, pp. 68–72; Dana Robert Morris, "Land and Society," pp. 195–198; Wm. Wayne Farris, *Population, Disease, and Land in Early Japan*, 645–900, pp. 118–140.

7. Bruce L. Batten, "State and Frontier in Early Japan," p. 53.

8. Dana Robert Morris, "Peasant Economy," 35, pp. 44–45.

9. Morris, "Land and Society," pp. 216–217.

10. Morris, "Peasant Economy," pp. 45–52, 165–175 Cornelius J. Kiley, "Provincial Administration and Land Tenure," pp. 266–268; Morita Tei, *Zuryō*, pp. 37–39.

11. Iyanaga Teizō, "Ritsuryōseiteki tōchi shōyū," pp. 37–39.

12. For an extensive and detailed elaboration on this point, see Mikael Adolphson, Edward Kamens, and Stacie Matsumoto, eds., *Heian Japan: Centers and Peripheries*.

13. Kiley explores this central idea in detail in "Provincial Administration."

14. Yoneda Yūsuke, *Kodai kokka*, pp. 115–118. Yoshie Akio, "Shōki chūsei sonraku no keisei," pp. 112–114.

15. Morris, "Peasant Economy," pp. 163–205. Yoneda Yūsuke, *Kodai kokka*, pp. 145–146.

16. Morita Tei, *Zuryō*, pp. 136–138.

17. *Heian ibun* doc. 339.

18. Morita Tei, *Zuryō*, pp. 50–52, 107–117.

19. *Ruijū sandai kyaku* 2:606 (896 4/2 daijōkanpu); 2:623–224 (835 10/18 daijōkanpu, quoted in 867 12/20 daijōkanpu; 894 7/16 daijōkanpu).

20. Ishimoda Shō, *Kodai makki seijishi jōsetsu*, pp. 43–44. *Ruijū kokushi* 798 2/1; *Shoku Nihon kōki* 838 2/9, 2/10, 2/12, 839 4/2, 850 2/3, 857 3/18; *Ruijū sandai kyaku* 2:614 (840 2/25 daijōkanpu), 2:620–621 (891 9/11 daijōkanpu), 2:623–624 (867 12/20 daijōkanpu), 2:640–641 (867 3/24 daijōkanpu), 2:565 (Kōzuke no kuni ge, quoted in 899 9/19 daijōkanpu); *Nihon Montoku tennō jitsuroku* 857 3/16, 858 2/22; *Nihon sandai jitsuroku* 861 11/6, 862 5/20, 866 4/11, 870 12/2. Ishimoda also cites the cases of a district magistrate in Tsushima who led 300 men in an attack on the governor in 857, and two district magistrates in Iwami who led 270 peasants in revolt against the "misrule" of the governor.

21. *Chōya gunsai*, 525; *Heian ibun* doc. 339; *Konjaku monogatari shū* 19.4, 28.2. Friday, *Hired Swords*, pp. 82–85.

22. Cornelius J. Kiley, "Estate and Property in the Late Heian Period," pp. 110–111.

23. For more on this phenomenon, see Takahashi Masaaki, *Bushi no seiritsu*, pp. 13–20; or Hall, *Government and Local Power*, pp. 116–128.

24. G. Cameron Hurst III, *Insei*, pp. 19–35, discusses this system in detail.

25. *Ruijū sandai kyaku* 2:617–618 (905 8/25 daijōkanpu); 2:638 (Settsu no kuni ge, quoted in 860 9/20 daijōkanpu).

26. Kitayama Shigeo, *Taira Masakado*, pp. 23–28.

27. *Ruijū sandai kyaku* 2:619–621 (797 4/29 daijōkanpu, quoted in 891 9/11 daijōkanpu; 842 8/15 daijōkanpu, quoted in 895 11/7 daijōkanpu). The court issued repeated prohibitions against *zuryō* establishing residential bases

in their provinces, in areas as far apart as Kyushu and Kazusa. See, for example, *Ruijū sandai kyaku* 2:619–621 (891 9/11 daijōkanpu; 895 11/17 daijōkanpu); *Nihon sandai jitsuroku* 884 8/4.

28. Kiley, "Provincial Administration," p. 335.

29. Hodate Michihisa, "Kodai makki no tōgoku to ryūjū kizoku," pp. 7–12; Takahashi Masaaki, *Kiyomori izen*, p. 14.

30. *Ruijū sandai kyaku* 1:302 (744 10/14 *kyaku*); 1:303 (868 6/28 *kyaku*).

31. Fukuda Toyohiko, "Ōchō gunsei kikō to nairan," pp. 87–88; Uwayokote Masataka, *Nihon chūsei seiji-shi kenkyū*, pp. 271–273; Haruda Takayoshi, "Taira Masakado no ran no buryoku," pp. 249–250.

32. Fukuda Toyohiko, *Tōgoku heiran to mononofu-tachi*, pp. 6–7; Wm. Wayne Farris, *Heavenly Warriors*, pp. 188–189; Morris, "Land and Society," pp. 198–199; Kiley, "Provincial Administration," p. 281. For more on Heian marriages and family structure, see William McCullough, "Japanese Marriage Institutions in the Heian Period"; Peter Nickerson, "The Meaning of Matrilocality"; Ivan Morris, "Marriage in the World of Genji"; Wakita Haruko, "Marriage and Property in Premodern Japan from the Perspective of Women's History"; Hattō Sanae, "Kodai ni okeru kazoku to kyōdōtai"; Hattō Sanae, "Sekkanki ni okeru zuryō no ie to kazoku keitai"; Sekiguchi Hiroko, "Kodai kazoku to kon'in keitai"; Tabata Yasuko, "Kodai, chūsei no 'ie' to kazoku: yōshi o chūshin to shite."

33. Oboroya Hisashi, *Seiwa Genji*, pp. 21–27.

34. *Sompi bummyaku*, vols. 3 and 4.

35. *Sompi bummyaku* 4:1–4. Some scholars have questioned whether the warrior Taira are truly an offshoot of the Kammu Heishi. They note that the principal source for believing that they were is the Heishi genealogy in the *Sompi bummyaku*, which contains numerous errors and is generally considered to be the least reliable section of the work. Yet, as Yasuda Motohisa has observed, we have no means by which to correct most of these errors and therefore have little choice but to accept the general outline of the genealogy. See Yasuda Motohisa, *Bushi sekai no jōmaku*, pp. 68–69; Takahashi Masaaki, "Masakado no ran no hyōka o megutte," p. 26; or Morita Tei, *Zuryō*, pp. 139–140. The definitive study of the early Heishi is Takahashi Masaaki, *Kiyomori izen*.

36. *Sompi bummyaku* 4:11–38. Kitayama Shigeo, *Taira Masakado*, p. 55.

37. Kitayama Shigeo, *Taira Masakado*, pp. 52–53.

38. Kitayama Shigeo, *Taira Masakado*, p. 54.

39. *Sompi bummyaku* 4:11. *Shōmonki, Konjaku monogatari shū* #25.1, and *Fusō ryakki* (939 11/21) give Masakado's father's name as Yoshimochi, whereas *Sompi bummyaku* lists it as Yoshimasa and identifies Takamochi's seventh son as Yoshimochi (4:14) but describes "Yoshimasa" as the man who once served as *Chinjufu shōgun*. Historians are divided on the issue of which name was correct. Those favoring *Yoshimochi* generally argue that the older

sources should rightly be presumed more reliable here. (See, for example, Rabinovitch, *Shōmonki*, 73n.) The case for *Yoshimasa*, however, rests primarily on the fact that the names of Masakado and all his siblings use the character "masa." (See Giuliana Stramigioli, "Preliminary Notes on the Masakadoki and Taira No Masakado Story," 270n. Aoki Shigekazu, *Taira Masakado: sōgen no nobi*, p. 42.)

In light of the fact that Takamochi's firstborn was also originally called Yoshimochi and later changed his name to Kunika, it seems likely that Masakado's father changed his name from Yoshimasa to Yoshimochi at some point in his life, presumably after his sons reached adulthood, and they received adult names featuring the "masa" character from their father's original given name. I have, in any event, chosen to use *Yoshimochi* in this book, in part to minimize confusion with Masakado's cousin (or uncle, see chapter 3) and adversary, also called Taira Yoshimasa.

40. Aoki Shigekazu, *Taira Masakado*, pp. 42–43; Kitayama Shigeo, *Taira Masakado*, pp. 57–60.

41. Aoki Shigekazu, *Taira Masakado*, pp. 46–48; Fukuda Toyohiko, *Taira Masakado no ran*, pp. 68–72.

42. Nishioka Toranosuke, "Bushi kaikyū kessei no ichiyoin to shite no 'maku' no hatten," pp. 305–380; Aoki Shigekazu, *Taira Masakado*, 46–48.

43. For more on horses as political gifts, see Hurst, "*Kugyō* and *Zuryō*," pp. 80, 88–89.

44. Fukuda Toyohiko, *Taira Masakado no ran*, pp. 54–67.

45. Fukuda Toyohiko, *Taira Masakado no ran*, pp. 67–68.

46. *Sompi bummyaku* 4:11.

47. *Ōnin-ki*, a literary account of the Ōnin War of 1467–1477, gives Masakado's birth year as 889, which would make him fifty-two at the time of his death. This text, written more than a half millennium after Masakado's lifetime, is scarcely reliable, however, and the date it cites seems improbable. As noted in the main text, Shōmonki refers to him having young children at the time of his insurrection but makes no mention of adult children—unlikely for a man in his early fifties. Cf. Noguchi Minoru, *Densetsu no shōgun*, p. 36.

48. Kitayama Shigeo, *Taira Masakado*, pp. 57–60; Aoki Shigekazu, *Taira Masakado*, p. 52. *Sompi bummyaku* 4:11 records that Masakado was also known as Sōma Kojirō.

49. Fukuda Toyohiko, *Taira Masakado no ran*, pp. 27–28. Masakado's identification with the Takiguchi comes from *Sompi bummyaku* 4:11, but this service is not confirmed by any other source.

Tadahira was a son of Fujiwara Mototsune. In 909 he became head of the Fujiwara house (*uji no chōja*) upon the death of his elder brother Tokihira. In 914 he became Minister of the Right and then Minister of the Left in 924. He became regent in 930, when Emperor Sujaku ascended the throne. *Shōmonki* makes at least two references to Masakado's connection with Tadahira (pp. 93, 105), and most scholars accept these statements at face value. There is, however, some room for doubt, as no other source—including Tadahira's diary, *Teishin kōki*—corroborates the existence of any such relationship.

Chapter 3. Masakado and His Uncles

1. *Shōmonki*, p. 54. Scholars have identified at least four possible sites for Nomoto, ranging from what is now Hachisendai-machi, along the Kinu River, to Akeno-chō in the Makabe district of Ibaraki prefecture, between Mt. Tsukuba and Kachinami Bay. For details, see Hayashi Rokurō (ed.), *Shōmonki*, pp. 54n, 147n.

2. Mamoru's post as Hitachi *daijō*, his marriage ties to the Kammu Heishi, and his sphere of influence can be inferred from *Shōmonki*, pp. 55, 57. While some historians believe that Mamoru's third daughter was married to Kunika's son (Masakado's cousin) Sadamori rather than Kunika himself, the ages of the people involved and Sadamori's subsequent behavior toward Mamoru make this seem unlikely. Fukuda Toyohiko also believes that Kunika, not Sadamori, was Mamoru's son-in-law. See Fukuda Toyohiko, *Tōgoku heiran*, pp. 5–14; Kitayama Shigeo, *Taira Masakado*, pp. 55–56.

3. The tale of Minamoto Mitsuru's duel with Taira Yoshifumi appears in *Konjaku monogatari shū* 25.3. For an English translation, see William R. Wilson, "The Way of the Bow and Arrow," pp. 197–199, or Hiroaki Sato, *Legends of the Samurai*, pp. 19–21. This story is discussed in detail in Friday, *Samurai, Warfare and the State in Early Medieval Japan*, pp. 107–108, 141–142; H. Paul Varley, *Warriors of Japan as Portrayed in the War Tales*, pp. 25–26, 28; and Kobayashi Hiroko, *The Human Comedy of Heian Japan*, pp. 97–98.

4. There is considerable ambiguity as to whether Mamoru's third Taira son-in-law was Sadamori or his father, Kunika. *Shōmonki* seems to imply the former. On p. 57, for example, it portrays Sadamori musing that he, Mamoru, and Mamoru's sons are "all of the same band" and that he "cannot but be bound up with their family affairs." On p. 119 it relates an incident in which Sadamori's wife is captured while traveling or residing with Tasuku's widow. It is much easier to understand why the two women would have been keeping company with each other if they were sisters-in-law than if Tasuku's widow was merely Sadamori's mother's sister-in-law.

  Both Sadamori's words and the incident involving his wife are, however, open to other interpretations; neither conclusively identifies Sadamori as having been married to one of Mamoru's daughters. Mamoru's other sons-in-law (including Fujiwara Korechika, whom we will meet in chapter 5), moreover, belonged to Sadamori's father's generation, which suggests that this fourth daughter was more likely to have been wed to

Kunika—unless she was considerably younger than her sisters. Kunika's involvement in Masakado's counterattack on Tasuku and the others also points to the conclusion that he, rather than Sadamori, was Tasuku's brother-in-law.

5. Fukuda Toyohiko, *Tōgoku heiran*, pp. 11–12.

6. The image of ritual and formalism in early samurai warfare has been virtually reified in popular and textbook accounts. See, for example, Mikiso Hane, *Premodern Japan*, pp. 73–74; Stephen R. Turnbull, *The Book of the Samurai*, pp. 19, 22–36; Stephen R. Turnbull, *The Lone Samurai and the Martial Arts*, pp. 14–28; John Newman, *Bushido*, pp. 13–14, 16–17. But academic historians have also portrayed early samurai fighting as ritualized. Recent or important examples include Ishii Shirō, *Nihonjin no kokka seikatsu*, pp. 14–24; Eiko Ikegami, *The Taming of the Samurai*, pp. 97–103; Nishimata Fusō, "Kassen no rūru to manaa"; Okada Seiichi, "Kassen to girei"; Seki Yukihiko, "'Bu' no kōgen"; Varley, *Warriors of Japan*; Takahashi Masaaki, *Bushi no seiritsu*; Farris, *Heavenly Warriors*, *passim*; and Farris, "Japan to 1300."

7. For more, see Friday, *Samurai, Warfare and the State*, pp. 15–18, 135–137.

8. *Shin sarugakki*, p. 138.

9. Archer Jones, *The Art of War*, p. 83.

10. Hayashi Rokurō attributes the focus of Heian warfare on the enemy himself, rather than his lands, to the abundance of cultivatable fields relative to the availability of labor to work them. Thus, he argues, to destroy an adversary or his home was of more value than attempting to capture his lands intact, since the elimination of a rival freed valuable workers to be employed on the victor's own lands. Cf. *Kodai makki no hanran*, p. 173.

11. Rabinovitch, *Shōmonki*, p. 77n.

12. *Shōmonki*, p. 55.

13. Examples of raids appear in numerous Heian period literary and documentary sources, in addition to *Shōmonki*. See, for example, *Mutsuwaki*, p. 27; *Konjaku monogatari shū* 23.13, 25.5; *Heian ibun* docs. 797, ho 007, 2090, 2583; *Fusō ryakki* 902 9/26, 919 5/23; *Nihon kiryaku* 947 2/14; *Chōya gunsai*, pp. 179–180 (986 10/20 Sesshō ke ōsesho); *Chōshūki* 1094 3/8.

14. The size of early samurai military organizations is discussed in Thomas Donald Conlan, *In Little Need of Divine Intervention*, pp. 261–264; Farris, *Heavenly Warriors*, pp. 335–343; Friday, *Samurai, Warfare and the State*, pp. 39–40.

15. Fukuda Toyohiko, *Tōgoku heiran*, pp. 11–14.

16. Mass, *Lordship and Inheritance*, pp. 9–37.

17. Noguchi Minoru, *Bandō bushidan no seiritsu to hatten*, pp. 86–101. Friday, *Hired Swords*, pp. 113–116. Mass, *Warrior Government*, pp. 59–123, details a number of cases in which related houses fought on opposite sides during the Gempei War.

18. *Shōmonki* and *Konjaku monogatari shū* describe Yoshimasa as Masakado's "second eldest paternal uncle" or "the younger brother of Masakado's father," respectively. *Sompi bummyaku* (4:14), however, identifies him as the son of Masakado's youngest uncle, Yoshishige.

19. *Shōmonki*, pp. 59, 61.

20. *Shōmonki*, p. 61.

21. *Shōmonki*, pp. 61, 63.

22. *Shōmonki*, pp. 55, 59; *Konjaku monogatari shū* 25.1. The information on Masakado's "dispute over a woman" with Yoshikane is found in the opening lines of an abridged seventeenth-century version of *Shōmonki*, called *Shōmon ryakki*. The earliest surviving texts of *Shōmonki* itself lack the opening paragraph and begin in midsentence with Tasuku's attack on Masakado. The *Shōmon ryakki* opening paragraph is, however, widely believed to reflect the first lines of the original text.

    Shōmonki, Konjaku monogatari shū, and other accounts of the Masakado affair describe Yoshikane as assistant governor of Shimōsa, as does *Sompi bummyaku* 4:11. But *Shōmonki* also says that he was living in Kazusa at the time of the rebellion (pp. 59, 71, 73). Judith Rabinovitch (*Shōmonki*, p. 79n) suggests, accordingly, that Yoshikane's post was probably in Kazusa rather than Shimōsa. Her reasoning is reinforced by the fact that in 936 the Shimōsa provincial office filed a report with the central government that resulted in a warrant being issued for Yoshikane's arrest (*Shōmonki*, p. 107)—an unlikely occurrence if Yoshikane was in fact the second ranking official in Shimōsa at the time.

23. *Shōmonki*, pp. 61–63. Yoshimasa appears to have maintained a residence at Mimori.

24. *Shōmonki*, p. 59.

25. *Konjaku monogatari shū*, 25.1.

26. *Shōmonki*, p. 65.

27. *Shōmonki*, p. 65. Fukuda Toyohiko, *Tōgoku heiran*, p. 15; *Shōmonki*, Hayashi Rokurō, ed., p. 65n.

    The *Yō Shukei kyūzō-bon* version of *Shōmonki* has Masakado departing on the twenty-sixth day of the sixth month, whereas the *Shinpukuji-bon* version says he left on the twenty-sixth day of the tenth month. Neither date is plausible, however. The twenty-sixth day of the sixth month was (according to both versions of *Shōmonki*) the date that Yoshikane arrived in Mimori for his conference with Yoshimasa; and *Shōmonki* later relates (p. 67) that Masakado left for the capital to answer a summons from the court on the seventeenth day of the tenth month. Hayashi Rokurō (*Shōmonki*, p. 65n) suggests that the "twenty-sixth day of the sixth month" was probably just a misprint for the "twenty-sixth day of the *seventh* month."

28. Conlan, *In Little Need of Divine Intervention*, p. 261.

29. *Shōmonki* describes Masakado's force only as including "over one hundred horsemen" and gives no figures for the foot soldiers, whom it later credits with winning the battle for Masakado. Both documentary and literary sources for the Heian period commonly count armed forces in numbers of horsemen alone. (See, for example, *Midō kampakki* 1017 3/11; *Chōya gunsai* p. 284 [1058 3/29 *daijōkanpu*]; or *Heian ibun* doc. 797.) In sources that do enumerate both cavalry and infantry, the ratios of mounted to unmounted troops vary from more than 2:1 to just under 1:2. *Konjaku monogatari shū* 25.5, for example, describes a force of seventy mounted warriors and thirty foot soldiers; while *Heian ibun* doc. 372 and *Midō kampakki* 1017 3/11 refer to troops of fifteen or sixteen horsemen and twenty or more foot soldiers, and seven or eight horsemen and "ten or more foot soldiers," respectively.

Masakado's entourage in this particular battle is described as having defeated an army numbering in the thousands, which suggests that his infantry complement must have been relatively large.

30. Although textual sources tend to make only terse references to the presence of foot soldiers in battles or to ignore them altogether, battle scenes in pictorial sources, such as *Hōnen jōnin eden*, *Obusama Saburō ekotoba*, *Zenkūnen kassen ekotoba*, *Go sannen kassen ekotoba*, *Heiji monogatari ekotoba*, and *Mōko shūrai ekotoba*, feature them prominently. There are, moreover, exceptions to the generally low profile of foot soldiers in written texts. *Shōmonki* is a case in point.

31. Stephen Morillo, "The 'Age of Cavalry' Revisited," pp. 51–52; Bernard S. Bachrach, *Early Carolingian Warfare*, p. 174.

32. See Friday, *Samurai, Warfare and the State*, pp. 89–90.

33. *Shōmonki*, pp. 65, 67.

34. *Shōmonki*, p. 67. The text does not specify with whom Masakado filed his complaints, noting only that he reported the matter to "neighboring provinces." I have extrapolated the list in the main text from the list of provinces that later received orders to support Masakado in apprehending Yoshikane and his allies (*Shōmonki*, p. 77).

35. *Shōmonki*, pp. 67, 69, 71. The court's leniency may have stemmed, at least in part, from intercession by Masakado's patron, Fujiwara Tadahira. Curiously, however, neither *Shōmonki* nor Tadahira's diary, *Teishin kōki*, make any mention of Tadahira's involvement in the matter.

36. *Shōmonki*, p. 71.

37. *Shōmonki*, p. 73.

38. *Shōmonki*, pp. 73, 75. Fukuda Toyohiko, *Tōgoku heiran*, p. 17.

39. *Shōmonki*, pp. 75, 77. *Shōmonki* gives the day of Masakado's departure as "the nineteenth," which probably indicates the nineteenth day of the ninth month (October 25, according to the Gregorian calendar) of 937—about a week after his wife's escape from her father's compound in Kazusa.

A variant text (the *Yō Shukei kyūzō-bon*, aka the *Katakura-bon*), however, gives this date as the "ninth day of the tenth month (November fourteenth)." Rabinovitch (*Shōmonki*, p. 90n) and Stramigioli ("Preliminary Notes," p. 276) follow the variant text, the latter arguing that the season is described as "early winter" (*mōtō*), an alternative name for the tenth month of the lunar calendar. Nevertheless, the text also refers to the harvest still being in the fields, which seems to point to the earlier date.

40. *Shōmonki*, p. 77.
41. *Shōmonki*, p. 78; Fukuda Toyohiko, *Tōgoku heiran*, pp. 110–111.
42. *Shōmonki*, pp. 79, 81.
43. *Shōmonki*, p. 81; Iwai-shi shihennsan iinkai, *Taira Masakado shiryōshū*, p. 83n; Rabinovitch, *Shōmonki*, p. 94n.
44. *Shōmonki*, p. 83. Yoshikane left Ishida in late evening and had reached Hōjōji by 11 p.m., yet he did not begin his attack until 5 or 6 the next morning. The intervening six or seven hours is too much time to be accounted for by travel alone, which suggests that he must have stopped to rest. Iwaishi-shi hennsan iinkai, *Taira Masakado shiryōshū*, p. 83n.
45. Although historians long assumed that Heian warriors lived in heavily fortified compounds called *tachi* or *hōkeikan* that served dual purposes as residences and fortresses, recent scholarship has cast doubt upon this conjecture. For details, see Hashiguchi Teishi, "Hōkeikan wa ika ni seiritsu suru no ka"; Hashiguchi Teishi, "Chūsei hōkeikan o meguru shomondai"; Takahashi Masaaki, "Kihei to suigun"; or Nakazawa Katsuaki, *Chūsei no buryoku to jōkaku*. For an overview of Heian period fortifications and their usage, see Friday, *Samurai, Warfare and the State*, pp. 119–126.
46. *Hōnen jōnin eden* 1:8–9; Fujimoto Masayuki, *Yoroi o matō hitobito*, pp. 100–109. Fujimoto believes that the lack of armor on the defenders is probably in part an artistic exaggeration to distinguish the two sides for readers.
47. *Shōmonki*, pp. 83, 95.

Chapter 4. New Enemies and New Friends

1. *Shōmonki*, p. 77. Fukuda Toyohiko (*Tōgoku heiran to mononofu-tachi*, p. 18) argues that the warrant was issued in response to an incident of arson on a government stable in the eighth month of 937 rather than to Yoshikane's attacks on Masakado. Even if this is true, however, the warrant's deputization of Masakado was almost certainly the result of Masakado's grievance reports.
2. *Ryō no gige*, pp. 311–312.
3. *Ryō no gige*, p. 186. For details on *tsuibu kampu*, see Friday, *Hired Swords*, pp. 160–164; *Samurai, Warfare and the State*, pp. 23–26.
4. *Shōmonki*, pp. 57–59.
5. *Shōmonki*, pp. 77, 85.
6. *Shōmonki*, pp. 83–85.

7. Fukuda Toyohiko, *Taira Masakado no ran*, p. 132.

8. The history of the horse in Japan dates back to at least the early Jōmon period, by which time the animals had found their way into the archipelago from southern China through Kyushu and from the north through Korea. Although horses were used as pack animals by the Yayoi period, true equestrian culture arrived in Japan during the early fifth century, becoming widely diffused throughout Kyushu and most of Honshu by the sixth.

    Kobayashi Yukio, "Jōdai Nihon ni okeru jōba no fūshū," pp. 173–190. Mori Kōichi, ed., *Nihon kodai bunka no tankyū 9: uma*. Walter Edwards, "Event and Process in the Founding of Japan," pp. 265–295; Sasama Yoshihiko, *Nihon no kassen bugu jiten*, pp. 265–269. Takahashi Masaaki, "Bushi to ōken," pp. 18–20; Toyoda Aritsune and Nomura Shin'ichi, "Uma ga daikatsuyaku shita gempei no tatakai," pp. 11–36.

9. Toyoda and Nomura, "Uma ga daikatsuyaku," pp. 17–21. Kawai Yasushi, *Gempei kassen*, pp. 43–47; Hayashida Shigeyuki, "Chūsei Nihon no uma ni tsuite"; Hayashida Shigeyuki, *Nihon zairai uma ni kansuru kenkyū*; Nishimoto Toyohiro, "Kamakura-shi Yuhigahama-Minami kiseki no shutsudo uma ni tsuite," pp. 21–26; Saiki Hideo, "Hakkutsu chōsa kara miru umaya to uma," pp. 27–32; Matsuzaki Masumi, "Bagu kara miru uma," pp. 33–38.

10. Toyoda Aritsune and Nomura Shin'ichi, "Uma ga daikatsuyaku," pp. 27–28.

11. For more on this point, see Friday, *Samurai, Warfare and the State*, pp. 112–115. Scholars of Western military history have observed that a similar situation seems to have held in Europe during this same (tenth through thirteenth centuries) period. Contrary to the stereotype of knights as uncooperative solo fighters obsessed with the ideal of single combat, the normal practice seems to have been for groups of ten to forty horsemen to coordinate closely with each other. See, for example, Malcolm Vale, *War and Chivalry*, pp. 103–105.

12. Bottomly and Hopson, *Arms and Armour*, p. 12. Fujimoto Masayuki, *Yoroi o matō hitobito*, pp. 15–17. For more on early medieval Japanese armor, in English, see Friday, *Samurai, Warfare and the State*, pp. 90–96.

13. There are no extant examples of tenth-century armors, so historians can only guess at the early evolution of *ōyoroi*. The *Omodaka-odoshi* armor in the collection of the Ōmishima shrine in Ehime prefecture is believed by some to be the oldest surviving example of *ōyoroi*, but its precise origins are uncertain. Documentary evidence for dating the origins or surmising the development of early *ōyoroi* is also scarce. The term *ōyoroi* itself was not popularized until the early modern period. Early medieval texts most often denote this style of armor simply as *yoroi*, while later medieval warriors appear to have called it *shikishō no yoroi* ("proper/regular/formal armor"). A few documents and entries in chronicles and diaries from the mid-eleventh to the mid-twelfth centuries refer to *tojikawa* ("trussed cowhide")

armors worn by horsemen and contrast these with *haramaki*, a simpler form of armor worn by foot soldiers, leading some scholars to conclude that this was an earlier, alternative name for *ōyoroi*. If so, the first appearance of *ōyoroi* in the written record was in 1066. Tsuno Jin's analysis of the evolution of Japanese lamellae also points to the origins of *ōyoroi* as having been sometime during the early eleventh century.

Daijingū shozō jiki. Heian ibun doc. 1679; *Sochiki* 1081 10/18. Suzuki Keizō, "Shikishō no yoroi no keisei ni tsuite," pp. 1–9; Sasama Yoshihiko, *Nihon no katchū bugu jiten*, pp. 34–42; Seki Yukihiko, "'Bu' no kōgen," pp. 22–23; Takahashi Masaaki, *Bushi no seiritsu*, pp. 25–31, 269–274; Kondō Yoshikazu, "Ōyoroi no seiritsu"; Kondō Yoshikazu, *Chūsei-teki bugu*, pp. 44–49.

14. Takahashi Masaaki, *Bushi no seiritsu*, p. 269. Kondō Yoshikazu, *Chūsei-teki bugu*, p. 16; Sasama Yoshihiko, *Nihon no kassen bugu jiten*, pp. 97–98; Fujimoto Masayuki, "Bugu to rekishi I," p. 46; Fujimoto Masayuki, *Yoroi o matō hitobito*, pp. 38–53; Robinson, *Japanese Arms*, p. 17.

15. Examples of this design include the *hōryō-kei keikō* of the Kofun period and the *tankō* of the *ritsuryō* era. The latter should not be confused with the plate armors of the Kofun era, which archaeologists also call *tankō*. This usage is a modern (post-Meiji) convention. The *tankō* worn by the *ritsuryō* armies were of lamellar construction. Kondō Yoshikazu, *Chūsei-teki bugu*, pp. 21–27, offers a thorough discussion of *ritsuryō* period armors.

16. Fujimoto Masayuki, "Bugu to rekishi I," p. 46. Fujimoto Masayuki, *Yoroi o matō hitobito*, pp. 38–53; Sasama Yoshihiko, *Nihon no katchū bugu jiten*, pp. 43, 95–96.

17. Sasama Yoshihiko, *Katchū no subete*, pp. 75–78; and *Nihon no katchū bugu jiten*, pp. 296–310; Bottomly and Hopson, *Arms and Armour*, pp. 33–35; Fujimoto Masayuki, *Yoroi o matō hitobito*, p. 47.

18. For details, see Friday, *Samurai, Warfare and the State*, pp. 68–70.

19. For details, see Friday, *Samurai, Warfare and the State*, pp. 77–85.

20. Modern scholars estimate the maximum effective range for tenth-century mounted archers as somewhere between 10 and 20 meters, and the typical distance at which bowmen of the era fought as around 10 to 14 meters. (See Kondō Yoshikazu, *Yumiya to tōken*, pp. 119–121. Fujimoto Masayuki, 'Bugu to rekishi II," p. 70. Kawai Yasushi, *Gempei kassen*, pp. 41–43.) Fujimoto (p. 69) also notes that it was difficult for archers to achieve a full draw in the haste of battle when encumbered by the horse, the armor, and the need to shoot and dodge opponents' arrows at the same time. This made the shots even weaker than they would already have been.

21. Mounted archery tactics are discussed in depth in Friday, *Samurai, Warfare and the State*, pp. 106–111.

22. *Shōmonki*, pp. 85–87.

23. *Shōmonki*, p. 87.

24. *Shōmonki*, p. 87.
25. Hayashi Rokurō, *Shijitsu Taira Masakado*, pp. 121–122.
26. *Shōmonki*, pp. 87, 107. *Teishin kōki* 939 2/12. Anaho Sumiyuki, a watch captain (*banchō*) in the Inner Palace Guard (*kon'efu*), had also been one of the officers sent to deliver the warrant inspired by Minamoto Mamoru's complaint to Hitachi, Shimōsa and Shimozuke in 936.

    The dates of Sadamori's arrival in the capital, the court's dispatch of Sumiyuki to deliver the interrogation order to Masakado, and Sumiyuki's return to the capital are not known. But *Shōmonki* notes that there was still snow on the ground when Sadamori and his beleaguered troops crossed into Yamashiro, which suggests that his entrance to the capital could not have been too long after his battle with Masakado on the twenty-ninth day of the second month of 938. *Teishin kōki* reports a discussion between the regent (*sesshō*), Fujiwara Tadahira, and the senior councillor (*dainagon*), Fujiwara Yoshimochi, concerning "the envoy detailed to interrogate Masakado" on the twelfth day of the second month of 939. This conversation, which took place nearly a year after Sadamori's initial complaint, could, of course, have been part of the original decision to *dispatch* an interrogation officer, but if so, it indicates a strangely prolonged gap between the complaint and the court's decision to act on it. It seems more likely therefore that Tadahira and Yoshimochi were discussing Sumiyuki's report after his return to Heian-kyō. Even so, unless Sumiyuki lingered in Shimōsa for several months, he must have been back in the capital for quite some time before this conversation took place.
27. *Shōmonki*, p. 87, says that this meeting happened during the tenth month of 938. *Teishin kōki*, however, records a farewell party for Koresuke prior to his departure to Mutsu held by Fujiwara Tadahira on 939 8/17.
28. *Shōmonki*, p. 87.
29. *Shōmonki*, p. 89.
30. *Shōmonki*, p. 89.
31. Okiyo was, according to Ōmori Kingorō, a fifth-generation descendant of Emperor Kammu, which would make him a distant cousin of Masakado, who was also a fifth-generation descendant. While Okiyo does not appear in any reliable genealogies, Ōmori's surmise has generally been accepted as credible by subsequent historians. Ōmori Kingorō, *Buke jidai no kenkyū*, v. 1, pp. 75–76; Hayashi Rokurō, *Shijitsu Taira Masakado*, p. 124.
32. *Shōmonki*, p. 91. For information on the Heian tax system and the role of provincial governors therein, see Dana Robert Morris, "Peasant Economy in Early Japan"; Morris, "Land and Society." Kiley, "Provincial Administration and Land Tenure in Early Heian"; Yoneda Yūsuke, *Kodai kokka to chihō gōzoku*; Morita Tei, *Zuryō*, pp. 136–138. Morita estimates that a typical governor was able to skim off about 10 percent of the total production of his province—an enormous sum for an individual.

As noted in chapter 2, Tsunemoto did not actually receive the Minamoto surname until 961 (cf. *Sompi bummyaku* 3:221); prior to that, he was known as Prince Tsunemoto or Prince Rokuson (literally, "Prince Sixth Grandson," a sobriquet deriving from his status as the son of Emperor Seiwa's sixth son, Sadazumi). Nevertheless, *Teishin kōki, Nihon kiryaku, Honchō seiki, Fusō ryakki, Shōmonki, Kojidan, Konjaku monogatari-shū*, and other sources for the Masakado affair all refer to "Minamoto Tsunemoto," following the historiographic convention of posthumously correcting names and titles. Although this usage is, strictly speaking, anachronistic, I have retained it in this book to minimize confusion for readers familiar with other studies or with primary sources in translation.

33. *Shōmonki*, p. 89.
34. Hayashi Rokurō, *Shijitsu Taira Masakado*, pp. 125–126.
35. Kiley, "Provincial Administration," pp. 254–257, 334. Morita Tei, *Zuryō*, pp. 28–34. Batten, "State and Frontier," pp. 45–53. Yoneda Yūsuke, *Kodai kokka*, pp. 39–42, 51–52.
36. Morita Tei, *Zuryō*, pp. 65–73, 196–200.
37. Batten, "State and Frontier," pp. 79–81.
38. Yoneda Yūsuke, *Kodai kokka*, pp. 59–60, 80–81. Kiley, "Provincial Administration," p. 334. Iyanaga Teizō, "Ritsuryōseiteki tōchi shōyū." Nagahara Keiji, *Shōen*, p. 29.
39. Hayashi Rokurō, *Shijitsu Taira Masakado*, pp. 127–130. Fukuda Toyohiko, *Taira Masakado no ran*, pp. 135–137.
40. *Shōmonki*, p. 93.
41. *Shōmonki*, p. 93.
42. Hayashi Rokurō, *Shijitsu Taira Masakado*, pp. 132–133.
43. Hayashi Rokurō, *Shijitsu Taira Masakado*, pp. 132–133. Kitayama Shigeo, *Taira Masakado*, pp. 115–116.
44. *Konjaku monogatari shū* 25.1.
45. *Teishin kōki* 939 3/3, 3/9. *Nihon kiryaku* 939 3/4. *Honchō seiki* 939 6/7.
46. *Shōmonki*, pp. 91–95. *Honchō seiki* 939 6/7.
47. *Teishin kōki* 939 10/3, 10/22, 11/12, 12/4, 12/19, 940 1/9. *Nihon kiryaku* 940 1/9. *Honchō seiki* 942 3/1, 3/20.
48. *Shōmonki*, pp. 91–95. *Teishin kōki* 939 6/7, 6/9. *Honchō seiki* 939 6/7.
49. *Shōmonki*, p. 93. Kitayama Shigeo, *Taira Masakado*, pp. 116–117.
50. *Shōmonki*, p. 95. *Ruijū fusenshō* 939 5/17.
51. Kitayama Shigeo, *Taira Masakado*, pp. 119–120.
52. *Teishin kōki* 938 4/15, 4/16, 4/17, 4/18, 4/19, 4/20. *Nihon kiryaku* 938 4/15, 5/22.
53. Friday, *Hired Swords*, pp. 96–97. Farris, *Heavenly Warriors*, pp. 127–131; Toda Yoshimi, "Kokka to nōmin"; Toda Yoshimi, "Kokuga gunsei," pp. 18–20; Takahashi Masaaki, "Masakado no ran," pp. 31–42. Koyama Yasunori, "Kodai makki," pp. 245–246; Hayashi Rokurō, *Kodai makki,*

pp. 79–83. Endō Motō, "Shuba no tō," pp. 3–17; Nishiyama Ryōhei, "Ritsuryōsei shakai no henyō." Okuno Nakahiko, "Heian jidai no guntō," pp. 5–27; Hodate Michihisa, "Kodai makki," pp. 3–7.

54. *Teishin kōki* 938 5/23, 939 3/4, 4/11, 4/17, 4/18, 5/6, 8/11, 8/18; *Nihon kiryaku* 939 3/4, 4/17, 5/6, 8/11; *Honchō seiki* 938 11/3, 939 4/18, 4/19, 4/28, 4/29, 5/23, 5/25, 6/14, 6/21, 6/28, 6/29, 7/15, 7/16, 7/18.

55. *Teishin kōki* 938 5/23, 939 3/22, 3/4, 5/5, 6/15, 7/5, 8/11, 8/12, 11/12; *Nihon kiryaku* 939 6/15, 8/11; *Honchō seiki* 938 11/3, 939 6/21.

Chapter 5. Insurrection

1. *Sompi bummyaku* 2:497.
2. *Shōmonki*, p. 95.
3. *Shōmonki*, pp. 95–97.
4. *Shōmonki*, p. 97.
5. Hayashi Rokurō, *Shijitsu Taira Masakado*, pp. 137–140.
6. *Shōmonki*, p. 109.
7. *Shōmonki*, pp. 97, 99, 109.
8. *Shōmonki* (p. 83) and *Konjaku monogatari shū* 25.5, for example, relate that two tenth-century warrior leaders had only "less than ten" or "four or five" warriors at their disposal when they were taken by surprise in night attacks on their homes. Similarly, a 987 complaint filed with the Office of Imperial Police (*Heian ibun* doc. 372) describes a night attack on the residence of Minu Kanetomo by 16 mounted warriors and "20 or more foot soldiers" led by a handful of his kinsmen. A document from 1086 (*Heian ibun* doc. 4652) numbers Minamoto Yoriyoshi's "sons and immediate followers" at "20 men in all"; while a document from 1058 (*Chōya gunsai* p. 284, 1058 3/29 *daijō kanpu*) describes five notable warriors as having 32 followers between them—a figure that includes women and boys, as well as adult men.

Surviving evidence further suggests that the range of warband sizes remained relatively constant between the mid-tenth and late thirteenth centuries. A roster of warriors from Izumi in 1272 (*Kamakura ibun* doc. 11115) lists nineteen warriors; of these, one led eighteen warrior followers, six led four to nine men each, three led three retainers, four led two, and five had only one follower each. A document from 1276 (*Kamakura ibun* doc. 12275) catalogs the warband of a samurai in Higo as consisting of three followers and a horse, in addition to the man himself (for a translation of this document, see Conlan, *In Little Need of Divine Intervention*, p. 216). And a report (*Kamakura ibun* doc. 12276) "concerning the warband [*gunzei*] of Nakamura Yajirō Minamoto no Tsuzuku, a resident of Haruzuchi estate in Chikuzen province," lists "Tsuzuku, mounted and clad in *ōryoroi*; his younger brother, Saburō Nami, mounted and clad in *haramaki*;

his retainer, Gorō Tarō, mounted; and his foot soldiers, Matajirō, the lay monk [*nyūdō*] Hōren, Gentōji, Gentō Jirō, Matatarō, Sūtarō, and Inujirō."

9. Friday, *Hired Swords*, pp. 112–113. Some scholars have described warrior alliances as analogous to land-commendation agreements (see, for example, Yasuda Motohisa, "Bushidan no keisei," pp. 127–128), but the absence of legal paperwork in the former represents a crucial—and fundamental—difference between the two phenomena. Commendation instruments exist in abundance, but one searches in vain for a single document formalizing a military alliance prior to the agreements issued by Minamoto Yoritomo in the 1180s. As in the case of patron-client relationships between court nobles, a warrior entering the service of another presented his new master with his name placard (*myōbu*). There is, however, no evidence that the junior party to the arrangement ever received any written confirmation in exchange. For examples of warriors offering *myōbu* as gestures of submission, see *Heian ibun* doc. 2467 or *Konjaku monogatari shū* 25.9.

10. On this point, see Mass, *Warrior Government*, pp. 33–35, 45–54.

11. See, for example, *Heian ibun* doc. 1663, 1682, 4652; *Denryaku* 113 3/13; *Chūyūki* 1114 5/16, 5/17, 6/8, 6/30, 7/18, 7/22, 8/13, 8/16, 8/21, 9/3, 9/4; *Shōmonki*, pp. 95–97; *Fusō ryakki* 939 11/21; *Nihon kiryaku* 939 12/2.

12. *Shōmonki*, p. 99; *Fusō ryakki* 939 11/21; *Nihon kiryaku* 939 12/2. *Shōmonki* paints an even grimmer picture of the battle: "Thus," it intones, "the two sides did battle, upon which all 3000 of the provincial army were struck down, to a man."

13. *Shōmonki*, p. 99.

14. *Fusō ryakki* 939 11/21.

15. *Shōmonki*, p. 99.

16. *Shōmonki*, p. 99.

17. *Shōmonki*, p. 109.

18. Kitayama Shigeo, *Taira Masakado*, p. 128.

19. Masakado's identification of Haruaki as a *jūhyō* appears in his letter to Fujiwara Tadahira, dated 939 12/15 (quoted in *Shōmonki*, pp. 105–111).

20. Hayashi Rokurō, *Shijitsu Taira Masakado*, p. 143. Hayashi locates Haruaki's and Harumochi's familial lands in the Naka and Kuji districts of northern Hitachi. *Shōmonki* (p. 105) identifies Harumochi only as "secretary" (*jō*) of Hitachi, but he must actually have been the junior secretary. As we have seen, Taira Sadamori had been serving as senior secretary (*daijō*) since 936.

21. *Shōmonki*, p. 109.

22. Hayashi Rokurō (*Shijitsu Taira Masakado*, p. 151) and Kitayama Shigeo (*Taira Masakado*, pp. 135–136) also believe that Masakado may have gone to Hitachi simply to forcibly press his case and had no intention of fighting, much less occupying the *kokuga*.

23. *Shōmonki*, p. 99; *Fusō ryakki* 939 11/29.

24. Kitayama Shigeo, *Taira Masakado*, p. 137.
25. *Shōmonki*, p. 119.
26. *Shōmonki*, p. 103.
27. *Nihon kiryaku* 939 12/29.
28. *Shōmonki*, pp. 99–105, 115. Curiously, this list does not include Musashi, even though *Shōmonki* later notes that Masakado's tour of provincial capitals "extended to Musashi and Sagami," and the Council of State edict condemning the insurrection (940 1/11 Daijōkanpu, quoted in *Fusō ryakki* 940 1/11) refers to nine provinces under his control.
29. *Nihon kiryaku* 939 12/2, 12/27, 12/29; *Honchō seiki* 939 12/29.
30. *Shōmonki*, p. 117.
31. *Nihon kiryaku* 939 12/29, 940 1/1, 1/9; *Honchō seiki* 939 12/29; *Teishin kōki* 940 1/6, 1/7, 1/9. For more on *tsuibushi*, see Friday, *Hired Swords*, pp. 148–159.
32. 940 1/11 Daijōkanpu, quoted in *Fusō ryakki* 940 1/11; also quoted in *Honchō monzui* v. 2.
33. *Teishin kōki* 940 1/18; *Nihon kiryaku* 940 1/19.
34. *Ryō no gige*, pp. 187, 190.
35. At the time of his appointment as *seitō taishōgun*, Fujiwara Tadabumi was sixty-eight years old and held senior fourth rank, lower grade. He was serving as an imperial adviser (*sangi*) and director of the Office of Palace Repairs (*Shūri daibu*). *Sompi bummyaku* 2:526.
36. *Teishin kōki* 940 1/14; *Ruijū fusenshō* 940 1/27; *Fusō ryakki* 940 2/8. Fujiwara Kunimoto was named assistant governor of Sagami, Taira Kiyomoto was named assistant governor of Kōzuke, and Taira Kintsura was named acting junior secretary of Shimōsa.
37. Shōmonki, p. 95.
38. *Teishin kōki* 940 1/12, 1/25, 2/5; *Nihon kiryaku* 940 1/25.
39. Koyama Yasunori, "Kodai makki no Tōgoku to Saigoku," pp. 234–235, 244. For an English-language version of this article, see Koyama Yasunori, tr. by Bruce L. Batten, "East and West in the Late Classical Age"; Takahashi Tomio, "Kodai kokka to henkyō," pp. 229–260. An English-language version of this article appears as Takahashi Tomio, tr. by Karl Friday, "The Classical Polity and Its Frontier."
40. Koyama Yasunori, "Kodai makki no tōgoku to saigoku," pp. 245–246; Hayashi Rokurō, *Shijitsu Taira Masakado*, pp. 206–208; Hayashi Rokurō, *Kodai makki no hanran*, p. 79; Fukuda Toyohiko, *Taira Masakado no ran*, pp. 156–157.
41. *Nihon sandai jitsuroku* 867 11/10.
42. Hayashi Rokurō, *Kodai makki*, pp. 145–149; Fukuda Toyohiko, *Taira Masakado no ran*, p. 160; Hayashi Rokurō, *Shijitsu Taira Masakado*, pp. 204–214; Bruce Batten, *Gateway to Japan*, pp. 93–95; Farris, *Heavenly Warriors*, pp. 142–149, offers overviews of the Sumitomo affair.

43. *Fusō ryakki* 940 11/21; *Ribuōki* 936 third month; *Nihon kiryaku* 936 sixth month.

44. *Honchō seiki* 939 4/21; *Kokin wakashū mokuroku*, vol. 19; *Ribuōki* 936 third month; *Nihon kiryaku* 936 sixth month.

45. *Fusō ryakki* 940 11/21.

46. *Honchō seiki* 939 4/21; *Nihon kiryaku* 939 4/19; *Teishin kōki* 939 12/17, 4/21; *Fusō ryakki* 940 11/21. Fukuda Toyohiko, *Taira Masakado no ran*, pp. 161–162.

47. *Fusō ryakki* 940 11/21; *Nihon kiryaku* 939 12/26; *Honchō seiki* 939 12/26.

48. *Honchō seiki* 939 12/29, 941 11/5; *Nihon kiryaku* 939 12/29; *Teishin kōki* 940 1/16, 2/8.

49. *Fusō ryakki* 940 11/21. Fukuda Toyohiko, *Taira Masakado no ran*, pp. 155–156.

50. Helen C. McCullough, trans., *Okagami*, p. 178.

51. *Shōmon jun'yū tōzai gunki*, p. 1.

52. Hayashi Rokurō, *Shijitsu Taira Masakado*, pp. 204–206.

Chapter 6. Apotheosis

1. *Shōmonki*, p. 101. Masakado was, of course, a fifth-generation descendant of Emperor Kammu, not a third-generation descendant as this passage alleges. The interesting question here is whether this error represents poor arithmetic skills on the part of the *Shōmonki* author or a deliberate attempt to suggest greater hubris—and perhaps diminishing contact with reality—on Masakado's part.

2. *Shōmonki*, p. 105.

3. *Shōmonki*, p. 105.

4. *Shōmonki*, p. 115.

5. *Shōmonki*, pp. 111–113.

6. Hayashi Rokurō, *Shijitsu Taira Masakado*, pp. 173–176.

7. For more on Hachiman, see Ross L. Bender, "Hachiman Cult and the Dōkyō Incident," pp. 125–153.

8. Hayashi Rokurō, *Kodai makki*, pp. 128–130. Hayashi makes a similar argument concerning another key component of the oracle's speech: her invocation of Sugawara Michizane as the author of a document anointing Masakado emperor. *Shōmonki*, notes Hayashi, describes Michizane as "Minister of the Left and holder of the senior second rank," but he never held these credentials at the same time. His highest post while alive was Minister of the Right, and his highest rank was junior second rank. He was promoted (posthumously) to senior second rank in the fourth month of 923, but he was not raised to Minister of the Left until 993—fifty-three years after the oracle is supposed to have delivered her message to Masakado! Michizane was, like Masakado, a man who died violently and was therefore, Hayashi argues, a natural figure for the *Shōmonki* author(s)

to invoke. But the errors in the text prove that at least the details of the ora-cle's speech were created several decades after Masakado's death and make it very likely that the entire incident was simply a fabrication. Hayashi Rokurō, *Shijitsu Taira Masakado*, pp. 160–163.

9. Masakado's conversation with Okiyo is also related, in slightly varied form, in *Fusō ryakki* 939 11/29. It is, however, clear from the vocabulary and sentence structure that the *Fusō ryakki* passage was based on the *Shōmonki* one and cannot therefore be taken as independent corroboration of the incident. See Iwai-shi shihennsan iinkai, *Taira Masakado shiryōshū / tsuki Fujiwara Sumitomo shiryō*, p. 121.

10. See, for example, *Nihon kiryaku* 939 12/2, 12/27, 12/29; *Tei noō hennenki* 939 11/21.

11. The literary style of Masakado's letter to Fujiwara Tadahira differs markedly from the rest of the prose in *Shōmonki*, enhancing the document's aura of authenticity. Uwayokote Masataka was among the first historians to argue for giving more weight to this letter as a reflection of Masakado's version of events than to other parts of the text. See Uwayokote Masataka, "Taira Masakado no ran," pp. 276–279.

  To date, the best challenge to Uwayokote's position comes from Kitayama Shigeo (*Taira Masakado*, pp. 170–176), whose strongest argument centers on reservations concerning the circumstances under which the *Shōmonki* author could have gotten his hands on this document. It is, he observes, unlikely that a private letter of this sort would have been pub-lished and circulated in Kyoto or that Tadahira would have shared the letter with anyone who might have passed a copy to the *Shōmonki* author. Nor, he argues, could the author have found the letter somewhere in the provinces, for even if Masakado had retained a copy, it would almost cer-tainly have been burned in the raid on his home.

  But while Kitayama raises some piquant questions, his case remains less convincing than those of Uwayokote and others in favor of accepting the letter as authentic. There is, for example, no real basis for Kitayama's assumption that Tadahira would have kept the letter secret; one might just as easily presume he would have shared it with anyone interested— although his failure to mention it in his diary is more than a little odd in this context. Similarly, there is no compelling reason to believe that any copies of the letter that Masakado kept would have been destroyed. In point of fact, *Fusō ryakki* 940 2/14 records the capture of a cache of "treasonous documents" (*muhonsho*) along with various weapons following Masakado's final battle. The letter to Tadahira might well have been among them.

12. Masakado's letter to Fujiwara Tadahira appears in *Shōmonki*, pp. 105–111. An alternative English translation can be found in Rabinovitch, *Shōmonki*, pp. 113–116.

13. This is very close to the conclusion argued by Hayashi Rokurō. *Shijitsu Taira Masakado*, p. 163.

14. Kitayama Shigeo, *Taira Masakado*, pp. 153–154. Hayashi Rokurō, *Shijitsu Taira Masakado*, pp. 177–179. Intriguingly, Masakado appointed Taji Tsuneakira as governor, not assistant governor, of Kōzuke, which was also a *shinnō ninkoku*, raising the question of why he failed to follow the precedent in this case. Hayashi suggests that this may simply reflect ignorance on Masakado's part: Hitachi and Kazusa were within his own bailiwick, and he would therefore certainly have been familiar with the appointment traditions in those provinces, but Kōzuke was far enough away that he could have been unaware of its *shinnō ninkoku* status. If Hayashi's surmise is correct, it adds support to the conclusion that the appointments were actually made as *Shōmonki* reports them. The courtier who wrote *Shōmonki* should, after all, have been well aware of gubernatorial protocols in all three provinces and would not have introduced the error on his own—unless he had a specific reason for inventing a discrepancy between the appointments in Hitachi, Kazusa and Kōzuke. The absence of elaboration or commentary on this point, however, suggests that the author was reporting a real appointment list verbatim rather than inventing one.

15. G. Cameron Hurst, III, "The Kōbu Polity," discusses Yoritomo's creation of an independent state in the east and his subsequent reintegration of his kingdom into the central polity. Kawajiri Akio, "Shimōsa kokufu o yakiuchi shita Taira Koreyoshi," offers a detailed analysis of Koreyoshi's insurrection.

16. *Shōki mokuroku* 1003 1/16, 2/8, 5/3, 9/5, 9/8, 1018 8/19, 1022 4/13; *Hyakurenshō* 1003 2/8. *Gonki* 1003 2/28, 4/26. *Shōyūki* 1005 1/20, 1014 2/7; *Midō kampakki* 1012 intercalary 10/16, 1015 11/3, 1016 11/6, 1018 8/19, 8/29. Kawajiri Akio, "Shimōsa kokufu o yakiuchi shita Taira Koreyoshi."

17. *Shōmonki*, p. 119.

18. As I noted in chapter 3 (n. 4), Sadamori's wife was either Tasuku's sister (which would have made her a sister-in-law to Tasuku's widow) or a daughter-in-law to one of Tasuku's sisters (which would have made Tasuku's widow her mother-in-law's sister-in-law). The latter relationship seems too distant to explain why the two women would have been keeping company at this time, but it is entirely possible that they may have been related in some other fashion as well.

19. *Shōmonki*, p. 119; *Konjaku monogatari shū* 25.1. *Shōmonki* says only that the women were captured and that Sadamori's wife was stripped of her clothing "and rendered helpless" (*hagitorare katachi o arawashi ni shite, sara ni sengata nashi*). The *Konjaku* account of this incident, however, relates that the women were raped (*okasaretari*). It notes that Minamoto Mamoru's wife (or widow) was also a victim.

20. See, for example, *Mutsuwaki*, pp. 27, 31–34; *Chōya gunsai Sesshō ke ōsesho* 986 10/20, pp. 179–180; *Konjaku monogatari shū* 23.13, 25.1, 25.5; *Heian ibun*

docs. 797, *ho* 007, 2090, 2583; *Fusō ryakki* 902 9/26, 919 5/23; *Nihon kiryaku* 947 2/14; *Chōshūki* 1094 3/8.

21. This topic is explored at length in Karl Friday, *Samurai, Warfare and the State*, pp. 19–33, 155–162.

22. For a fuller description of the role of temples in the sociopolitical and economic structure of early medieval Japan, see Mikael Adolphson, "Enryakuji"; Martin Collcutt, *Five Mountains*; or Joan R. Piggott, "Hierarchy and Economics in Early Medieval Todaiji." Adolphson, *Teeth and Claws of the Buddha*, offers a comprehensive discussion of the military forces maintained by Buddhist temples.

23. *Shōmonki*, p. 121.

24. My analysis of this poetic exchange follows that of Murakami Haruaki. See Murakami Haruki, *Shōmonki shinkai*, pp. 205–206.

25. *Shōmonki*, p. 121. The poems recorded in *Shōmonki* (and nowhere else) are, of course, almost certainly apocryphal. In fact, the entire incident may very well be. I have included it in my narrative, however, because of its value in highlighting two very real components of the culture of Masakado's world.

26. *Shōmonki*, p. 121.

27. *Sompi bummyaku* 2:267-68. Hayashi Rokurō, *Kodai makki no hanran*, 130–31.

28. *Nihon kiryaku* 822 5/4; *Azuma kagami* 1209 12/15; Noguchi Minoru, *Fujiwara Hidesato*, 24–25, 35.

29. *Sompi bummyaku* 2:385–386. Noguchi Minoru, *Densetsu no shōgun: Fujiwara Hidesato*, pp. 25–27.

30. Hidesato's birth date is unknown, but as Noguchi Minoru points out, he was apparently well into late middle age at the time of the Masakado rebellion. He must therefore have been born shortly before the turn of the tenth century. Yasugi Saburō calculates his birth year to have been 885 but offers no explanation as to how he arrived at that date. Noguchi Minoru, *Densetsu no shōgun: Fujiwara Hidesato*, p. 3; Yasugi Saburō, *Fujiwara Hidesato shōgun*, pp. 43–44.

31. Hayashi Rokurō, *Kodai makki*, p. 131; Noguchi Minoru, *Densetsu no shōgun: Fujiwara Hidesato*, pp. 5–9.

32. There are no records of Hidesato's early sojourn in Kyoto and none that clearly identify who his patron might have been. *Teishin kōki* 947 7/24, however, describes Hidesato reporting an attempted insurrection by Masakado's surviving brothers through offices of Takaaki, who at the time was serving as acting middle counselor (*gon chūnagon*) and therefore outside the normal public chain of command for such reports. As Noguchi Minoru argues, this strongly suggests the existence of a patron-client relationship between Hidesato and Takaaki. Noguchi Minoru, *Densetsu no shōgun: Fujiwara Hidesato*, 45.

33. *Nihon kiryaku* 916 8/12; *Fusō ryakki* 929 5/20; Hayashi Rokurō, *Kodai*

makki, pp. 130–135. *Azuma kagami* 1209 12/15 claims that Hidesato's father and grandfather had also served as *ōryōshi*.

34. Friday, *Hired Swords*, pp. 141–148; Friday, "Teeth and Claws." The earliest extant occurrence of the term *ōryōshi* is in an edict issued by the Council of State in 795 (*Ruijū sandai kyaku* 2:548 [795 11/22 *daijōkanpu*]), but the phrase "in accordance with precedent" in the document suggests that the office did not originate with this order.

    Although most *ōryōshi* were local figures, their appointments came from the central, not the provincial, government. The normal process called for provincial governors to recommend suitable candidates to the Council of State, which would then consider the requests and issue edicts ordering the appointments. This process was hardly expeditious—it commonly took eight to ten months and occasionally as long as three years from start to finish—but it allowed the court to maintain a voice in military and police affairs in the provinces. Appointments continued to be made by the Council of State until well into the thirteenth century, when the offices faded from importance.

35. For detailed information on the *tsuibushi* post, see Friday, *Hired Swords*, pp. 148–159.

36. Kitayama Shigeo, *Taira Masakado*, p. 144.

37. Fukuda Toyohiko, *Taira Masakado no ran*, p. 173. Fukuda calculates the first day of the second month of 940 to have fallen on March 17, according to the Gregorian calendar.

38. Masakado was probably outnumbered but not as badly as *Shōmonki* seems to suggest at first glance. The text (p. 121) and *Fusō ryakki* 940 2/1 relate that just over four thousand troops (*jinpei*) followed Sadamori and Hidesato into Shimozuke (*Fusō ryakki* also notes that "one text says 19,000 troops"), while Masakado's reconstituted army is described (*Shōmonki* p. 121) as "just under 1000 warriors." The expression "*jinpei*" applied to Sadamori and Hidesato's army, however, implies that their four thousand troops included foot soldiers, peasant conscripts, and probably support personnel, as well as mounted warriors. Masakado's army is counted as "just under 1000 *tsuwamono*," a term usually reserved for elite mounted warriors. The 4:1 ratio insinuated by the *Shōmonki* narrative thus compares Hidesato's and Sadamori's full force to the core of Masakado's. The actual ratio would therefore have been much smaller; and the actual numbers probably amounted to only a few hundred men on either side. Cf. chapter 3, p. 87.

39. *Shōmonki*, pp. 121–123; *Fusō ryakki* 940 2/1. These texts hint that Hidesato had been lying in wait for Masakado and attributes his victory to the use of "age-old tactics," in particular the "*sampyō no te*" (literally, "three warriors trick" or "three weapons device"), which Rabinovitch (p. 127, n. 249), Hayashi Rokurō (*Shōmonki*, p. 122, n. 6), and others interpret to mean dividing his forces into three parts. Nevertheless, as Hayashi notes elsewhere

(Hayashi Rokurō, *Shijitsu Taira Masakado*, p. 194), *Shōmonki*'s descriptions of the battles in this final campaign (and by extension, *Fusō ryakki*'s, which are based on *Shōmonki*'s) borrow heavily from battle accounts in ancient Chinese chronicles, including Ssu-ma Ch'ien's (Sima Qian, c. 145–193 B.C.) *Shih chi* (*Shiji*; best known in English as "Records of the Grand Historian"), the fourth-century B.C. *Tso chuan* (*Zuo zhuan*; "Chronicles of Tso"), and the sixth-century B.C. *Shang shu* ("The Book of Documents" or "The Classic of History") and are not, therefore, reliable accounts of the fighting.

40. *Shōmonki*, p. 123; *Fusō ryakki* 940 2/8; Kitayama Shigeo, *Taira Masakado*, pp. 194–196.

41. *Shōmonki*, p. 123.

42. *Teishin kōki* 940 2/8, 2/9, 2/10; *Nihon kiryaku* 940 2/8; Fukuda Toyohiko, *Taira Masakado no ran*, p. 175.

43. *Shōmonki*, pp. 125–127; *Kojidan* 312; *Fusō ryakki* 940 2/13; Fukuda Toyohiko, *Taira Masakado no ran*, pp. 175–177.

44. Fukuda Toyohiko, *Taira Masakado no ran*, p. 176; *Shōmonki*, p. 127.

45. *Shōmonki*, p. 127; Kitayama Shigeo, *Taira Masakado*, pp. 197–198.

46. *Shōmonki*, p. 127.

47. *Shōmonki*, p. 129.

48. *Fusō ryakki* 940 2/13; *Kojidan* 312; *Shōmonki*, p. 129.

49. *Shōmonki*, p. 129; *Konjaku monogatari shū* 25.1; *Fusō ryakki* 940 2/8; *Kojidan* 312.

50. *Fusō ryakki* 940 2/14. The *Kokushi taikei* edition of this text describes the shields confiscated as "flat shields" (*heijun*), but two other versions indicate they were "hand shields" (*tedate*). *Wamyō ruijūshō*, p. 252, cites this passage as an example of the appearance of this term. It seems unlikely, however, that three hundred of these very unusual weapons would have been deployed in this single battle. See Friday, *Samurai, Warfare and the State*, p. 90.

51. *Teishin kōki* 940 3/18, 4/2; *Nihon kiryaku* 940 3/18; *Shōmonki*, p. 133; *Ichidai yōki* 940 2/19.

52. *Shōmonki*, p. 133.

53. *Shōmonki*, pp. 133–135.

54. *Shōmonki*, p. 137.

55. *Shōmonki*, pp. 131–133.

Epilogue

1. *Shōmonki*, p. 133; *Nihon kiryaku* 940 2/25, 3/5; *Teishin kōki* 940 3/5; *Kyūreki* 940 2/26.

2. *Teishin kōki* 940 3/18, 4/2, 4/25; *Nihon kiryaku* 940 3/18, 4/25. Hayashi Rokurō observes that numerous local legends and stories, often at variance with one another, exist concerning Tadanobu's roundup of Masakado's men and allies. Hayashi Rokurō, *Shijitsu Taira Masakado*, p. 200.

3. *Nihon kiryaku* 940 5/15; *Teishin kōki* 940 5/13, 5/15.
4. *Teishin kōki* 940 1/20, 2/5, 2/21, 2/27, 3/1, 3/7.
5. *Teishin kōki* 940 1/30, 2/3, 6/18, 6/19; *Nihon kiryaku* 940 3/4.
6. W. S. Gilbert and Arthur Sullivan, *The Pirates of Penzance or the Slave of Duty* (1879).
7. *Nihon kiryaku* 940 8/26; *Moromori ki* 1347 12/17 (940 8/26, 8/28). *Fusō ryakki* 940 11/21.
8. *Nihon kiryaku* 940 8/22; *Moromori ki,* quoted in 1347 12/17 (940 8/27, 8/28); *Fusō ryakki* 940 11/21.
9. *Nihon kiryaku* 940 10/21, 11/7, 12/19.
10. *Fusō ryakki* 940 11/21; *Nihon kiryaku* 941 2/9.
11. *Nihon kiryaku* 941 5/19; *Fusō ryakki* 940 11/21.
12. *Nihon kiryaku* 941 5/19.
13. *Fusō ryakki* 940 11/21; *Honchō seiki* 941 11/5.
14. *Fusō ryakki* 940 11/21.
15. *Fusō ryakki* 940 11/21; *Moromori ki* 941 6/20, 7/6. *Nihon kiryaku* 941 7/7; *Honchō seiki* 941 7/27, 8/7, 9/19, 11/5, 11/29. Sources disagree on how Sumitomo met his end. *Fusō ryakki* maintains that he died in prison, while *Moromori ki* and *Honchō seiki* contend that he was killed during his capture.
16. Inoue Mitsuo, *Heian jidai no gunji seido*, pp. 149–150.
17. *Teishin kōki* 940 3/9; *Nihon kiryaku* 940 3/9, 11/16; *Fusō ryakki* 940 3/9.
18. *Fusō ryakki* 940 3/9; *Shōmonki*, p. 135.
19. *Nihon kiryaku* 940 3/25; *Shōmonki*, p. 131.
20. *Sompi bummyaku* 3:57–62; *Shōmonki* p. 93; Oboroya Hisashi, *Seiwa Genji*, pp. 43–47. Some scholars have questioned this genealogy, suggesting instead that Tsunemoto was in fact descended from Emperor Yōzei, not Seiwa. See Takeuchi Rizō, *Bushi no tōjō*, pp. 40–43. For a short summary of the controversy in English, see G. Cameron Hurst, III, "Structure of the Heian Court," p. 50, n. 30.
21. *Sompi bummyaku* 3:62; *Fusō ryakki* 960 10/2; Oboroya Hisashi, *Seiwa Genji*, p. 50.
22. *Teishin kōki* 947 intercalary 7/24. There is no record of any revolt by Masakado's siblings in 947. The rewards may have been sought (belatedly) for Hidesato's actions in 940. Noguchi Minoru, *Densetsu no shōgun: Fujiwara Hidesato*, p. 46.

   Similarly, while we have multiple sources that document Hidesato's appointments to the governorships of Musashi and Shimozuke as a reward for his service against Masakado, no records of later appointments, including the *Chinjufu shōgun* title, survive. Nevertheless, the circumstantial evidence suggesting that he did hold this post late in his lifetime is compelling. For details, see Noguchi Minoru, *Densetsu no shōgun: Fujiwara Hidesato*, pp. 56–72.

23. *Honchō seiki* 967 6/14; *Sompi bummyaku* 2:386; *Nihon kiryaku* 969 3/25, 4/2, 4/3; Noguchi Minoru, *Bandō bushidan*, pp. 26–29; Noguchi Minoru, *Densetsu no shōgun: Fujiwara Hidesato*, pp. 46–51.

24. *Sompi bummyaku* 2:268, 386–411; Noguchi Minoru, *Bandō bushidan*.

25. Takahashi Tomio, *Hiraizumi no seikai*; Shōji Hiroshi, *Henkyō no sōran*; Ōya Kuninori, *Ōshū Fujiwara godai*; Mimi Hall Yiengpruksawan, *Hiraizumi*.

26. *Azuma kagami* 1187 8/15; Noguchi Minoru, "Ikusa to girei," pp. 130–153; Noguchi Minoru, *Buke no tōryō*, pp. 56–64; Futaki Ken'ichi, *Chūsei buke no sakuhō*, pp. 13–18; Takahashi Masaaki, "Nihon chūsei no sentō," pp. 197–199, 213–226; Nakazawa Katsuaki, *Chūsei no buryoku to jōkaku*; Kondō Yoshikazu, "Umayumi to yabusame"; Kondō Yoshikazu, *Chūsei-teki bugu no seiritsu to bushi*, pp. 223–225.

27. *Sompi bummyaku*, 4:11–17. *Gonki*, 998 12/14, 12/26. *Heian ibun*, doc. 4573; *Konjaku monogatari shū*, 25.4, 25.9; Noguchi Minoru, *Bandō bushidan*, pp. 64–66; Takahashi Masaaki, *Kiyomori izen*, 11; Takeuchi Rizō, *Bushi no tōjō*, pp. 16–17; Fukuda Toyohiko, *Tōgoku heiran*, pp. 56–61.

28. *Sompi bummyaku* 4:15–34. Yasuda Motohisa, *Bushi sekai no jōmaku*, pp. 69–72. According to *Sompi bummyaku* (2:17), Koretoki was actually Sadamori's son but was adopted by Koremasa.

29. *Shōyūki* 988 intercalary 5/9, 996 eleventh month, 1018 5/15, 1023 4/11, 1024) 3/16, 1025 11/26; *Midō kampakki* 1016 10/19; *Nihon kiryaku* 994 3/6. *Honchō seiki* 994 3/6; *Fusō ryakki* 1016 10/18, 10/26; *Dainihon shiryō*, 2:11, p. 31; Fukuda Toyohiko, "Ōchō gunsei," pp. 110–111; Fukuda Toyohiko, *Tōgoku heiran*, p. 61.

30. *Sakeiki* 1028 6/21; *Shōki mokuroku* 1030 7/08; *Nihon kiryaku* 1030 9/2; Fukuda Toyohiko, "Ōchō gunsei," pp. 111–112. Fukuda Toyohiko, *Tōgoku heiran*, pp. 61–63; Noguchi Minoru, *Bandō bushidan*, pp. 48–58. For detailed accounts of the Tadatsune Insurrection, see Karl Friday, "Lordship Interdicted," pp. 329–354; Wm. Wayne Farris, *Heavenly Warriors*, pp. 192–200; Takeuchi Rizō, "The Rise of Warriors." For more on *tsuitōshi*, see Friday, *Hired Swords*, pp. 159–160.

31. Yasuda Motohisa, *Bushi sekai*, pp. 69–74, 79–80. Takahashi Masaaki, *Kiyomori izen*, pp. 11–19, 47–94; Jeffrey P. Mass, *Yoritomo and the Founding of the First Bakufu*, pp. 12–36. For more on the role of retired emperors in late Heian political affairs, see G. Cameron Hurst III, *Insei*.

32. Comprehensive analyses of legends told about Masakado include: Kajiwara Masaaki and Yashiro Kazuo, *Masakado densetsu*; Murakami Haruki, *Taira Masakado densetsu*; Oda Kan'e, *Taira Masakado koseki kō*; Aoki Shigekazu, *Taira Masakado: sōgen no nobi*.

33. *Konjaku monogatari shū* 25.1.

34. *Konjaku monogatari shū* 29.25.

35. The text refers to Sadamori's son only by his post, secretary of the Left Palace Guard (*saemon no jō*), except in its first reference to him, where it is

missing two characters following this title. *Sompi bummyaku* (4:15–22) does not identify any of Sadamori's sons as having held this title. It does, however, describe his eldest son, Korenobu, as having once been secretary of the *Right* Palace Guard. The *Konjaku* authors may simply have confused these offices. Another possibility is that the son in this yarn was Koretoki, whom *Sompi bummyaku* (2:17) describes as having been Sadamori's son, adopted by his brother Koremasa, and who is identified in *Shōyūki* 996 10/11 as *saemon no jō*.

The timing of this yarn, set between 972 and 974 when Sadamori was governor of Tamba (Nishioka Toranosuke, *Shin Nihonshi nenpyō*, 396), argues in favor of Korenobu, however. Both Koretoki and Korenobu went on to posts higher than *saemon no jō* and should not therefore have been identified by this title, unless the identification was intended to refer to a title held at the time of the incident. Koretoki was serving as *saemon no jō* in 996 and would likely have been little more than a child in the early 970s.

36. *Konjaku monogatari shū* 29.5. Sadamori was appointed governor of Mutsu in the eleventh month of 974 (Nishioka Toranosuke, *Shin Nihonshi nenpyō*, p. 382) and should therefore have returned to Kyoto four years later, in late 978. This would put him arriving in the capital sometime in the first month of 979.

37. *Konjaku monogatari shū* 29.5.

38. Extensive discussions of the legends concerning Hidesato appear in Noguchi Minoru, *Fujiwara Hidesato*, pp. 140–148; Yasugi Saburō, *Fujiwara Hidesato shōgun*, pp. 84–93.

39. *Konjaku monogatari shū* 25.5; *Taiheiki* (*Tenshōbon*) 15 *kan* "Ryūgūjō kane no koto," vol. 2, p. 237.

40. This story appears in several medieval texts, including *Taiheiki* and *Tawara Tōda monogatari*. Unless otherwise noted, all quotations in the account that follows are from *Taiheiki* (*Tenshōbon*) 15 *kan* "Ryūgūjō kane no koto."

41. *Tawara Tōda monogatari*, p. 115.

42. *Tawara Tōda monogatari*, p. 116.

43. *Tawara Tōda monogatari*, pp. 126–27. *Morokado monogatari*, which appeared during the late Muromachi era, contends that Masakado had seven doubles (p. 263).

44. *Tawara Tōda monogatari*, p. 127.

45. *Tawara Tōda monogatari*, p. 135.

46. Jeffrey P. Mass, "The Kamakura Bakufu," p. 49.

BIBLIOGRAPHY

Primary Sources

Azuma kagami. Shintei zōho kokushi taikei 32–33, 2 vols. Tokyo: Yoshikawa kōbunkan, 1968.

Ban dainagon ekotoba. Nihon no emaki, vol. 2. Komatsu Shigemi, gen. ed. Tokyo: Chūō kōronsha, 1987.

Chōshūki. Zōho shiryō taisei. Kyoto: Rinsen shoten, 1965.

Chōya gunsai. Kokushi taikei. Tokyo: Yoshikawa kōbunkan, 1964.

Chūyūki. Zōho shiryō taisei. Kyoto: Rinsen shoten, 1965.

Daijingū shozō jiki. In *Jingibu 1.3.* Vol. 2 of *Gunsho ruijū*, edited by Hanawa Hōkinoichi. Tokyo: Zoku gunsho ruijū kanseikai, 1932.

Dainihon shiryō. Edited by Tōkyō daigaku shiryō hensanjo. Series 1–3. Tokyo: Tōkyō daigaku shuppankai, 1901–.

Engi shiki. Shintei zōho kokushi taikei. Tokyo: Yoshikawa kōbunkan, 1937.

Fusō ryakki. Kokushi taikei. Tokyo: Yoshikawa kōbunkan, 1965.

Gonki. Zōho shiryō taisei, vols. 4–5. Kyoto: Rinsen shoten, 1965.

Go-sannen ekotoba. Nihon no emaki, vol. 20. Komatsu Shigemi, gen. ed. Tokyo: Chūō kōronsha, 1988.

Heian ibun. Edited by Takeuchi Rizō. 15 vols. Tokyo: Tōkyōdō, 1965–1980.

Heihanki. Zōho shiryō taisei. Kyoto: Rinsen shoten, 1965.

Heiji monogatari. Shin Nihon koten bungaku taikei, vol. 43. Tochigi Yoshitada et al., gen. ed. Tokyo: Iwanami shoten, 1992.

Heiji monogatari ekotoba. Nihon no emaki, vol. 12. Komatsu Shigemi, gen. ed. Tokyo: Chūō kōronsha, 1988.

Heike monogatari (Engyōbon). 4 vols. Edited by Kitahara Yasuo and Ogawa Eiichi. Tokyo: Bensei shuppan, 1990.

Heike monogatari (Kakuichi-bon). Edited by Takagi Ichinosuke et al. Nihon koten bungaku taikei, vols. 32-33. Tokyo: Iwanami shoten, 1960.

Honchō monzui. Kokushi taikei. Tokyo: Yoshikawa kōbunkan, 1964.

Honchō seiki. Kokushi taikei. Tokyo: Yoshikawa kōbunkan, 1964.

Hōnen jōnin eden. Zoku Nihon no emaki, vols. 1–3. Komatsu Shigemi, gen. ed. Tokyo: Chūō kōronsha, 1990.

Hyakurenshō. Kokushi taikei. Tokyo: Yoshikawa kōbunkan, 1965.

Ichidai yōki. In *Dainihon shiryō.* Edited by Tōkyō daigaku shiryō hensanjo. Series 1. Tokyo: Tōkyō daigaku shuppankai.

Kojidan. Koten bunko, vols. 60–62. Tokyo: Gendai shichōsha, 1981.

Kokon chomonjū. Shintei zōho kokushi taikei. Tokyo: Yoshikawa kōbunkan, 1985.

Konjaku monogatari shū. Nihon koten bungaku zenshū, vols. 21–24. Tokyo: Shōgakkan, 1971.

Kugyō bunin. Shintei zōhō kokushi taikei. Tokyo: Yoshikawa kōbunkan, 1928.

Midō kampakki. Dainihon kokiroku. Tokyo: Iwanami shoten, 1952.

Mōko shūrai ekotoba. Nihon no emaki, vol. 13. Komatsu Shigemi, gen. ed. Tokyo: Chūō kōronsha, 1988.

Morokado monogatari. In *Muromachi monogatari shū ge*, edited by Ichiko Teiji et al., pp. 361–402. Shin Nihon koten bungaku taikei, vol. 55. Tokyo: Iwanami shoten, 1992.

Moromori ki. In *Taira Masakado shiryōshū/tsuki Fujiwara Sumitomo shiryō*, edited by Iwai-shi shihennsan iinkai. Tokyo: Shinjimbutsu ōraisha, 1996.

Mutsuwaki. In *Kassen bu*. Gunsho ruijū. Tokyo: Shoku gunsho ruijū kanseikai, 1941.

Nihon kiryaku. Shintei zōho kokushi taikei. Tokyo: Yoshikawa kōbunkan, 1985.

Nihon shoki. Shintei zōho kokushi taikei. Tokyo: Yoshikawa kōbunkan, 1985.

Obusuma Saburō ekotoba—Ise shimmeisho eutaawase. Zoku nihon no Emaki, vol. 18. Komatsu Shigemi, gen. ed. Tokyo: Chūō kōronsha, 1992.

Ōtoku gannen nōdaiki. In *Zoku zoku gunsho ruijū*, edited by Haniwa Hōkinoichi. Tokyo: Takeiki insatsusho, 1909–.

Ribuōki. In *Taira Masakado shiryōshū/tsuki Fujiwara Sumitomo shiryō*, edited by Iwaishi shihennsan iinkai. Tokyo: Shinjimbutsu ōraisha, 1996.

Ritsu. Shintei zōho kokushi taikei. Tokyo: Yoshikawa kōbunkan, 1982.

Ruijū fusenshō. Kokushi taikei. Tokyo: Yoshikawa kōbunkan, 1964.

Ruijū kokushi. Shintei zōho kokushi taikei. Tokyo: Yoshikawa kōbunkan, 1986.

Ruijū sandai kyaku. Shintei zōho kokushi taikei. Tokyo: Yoshikawa kōbunkan, 1983.

Ryō no gige. Shintei zōho kokushi taikei. Tokyo: Yoshikawa kōbunkan, 1985.

Ryō no shūge. Shintei zōho kokushi taikei. Tokyo: Yoshikawa kōbunkan, 1985.

Seiji yōryaku. Shintei zōho kokushi taikei, vol. 28. Tokyo: Yoshikawa kōbunkan, 1984.

Shin sarugakki. Nihon shisō taikei, vol. 8 Kodai seiji shakai shisō. Tokyo: Iwanami shoten, 1986.

Shobon shūsei wamyō ruijūshō. Tokyo: Rinsen shoten, 1968.

Shōki mokuroku. Dainihon kokiroku. Tokyo: Iwanami shoten, 1959–.

Shōmon jun'yū tōzai gunki. In *Taira Masakado shiryōshū/tsuki Fujiwara Sumitomo shiryō*, edited by Iwai-shi shihennsan iinkai, pp. 195-201. Tokyo: Shinjimbutsu ōraisha, 1996.

Shōmonki. Edited by Hayashi Rokurō. Tokyo: Imaizumi seibunsha, 1975.

Shōyūki. Dainihon kokiroku. Tokyo: Iwanami shoten, 1959.

Sochiki. Zōho shiryō taisei, vol. 5. Kyoto: Rinsen shoten, 1965.

Sompi bummyaku. Shintei zōho kokushi taikei. Tokyo: Yoshikawa kōbunkan, 1983.

Taiheiki emaki. Edited by Miya Tsugio and Satō Kazuhiko. Tokyo: Kawade shobō shinsha, 1992.

Taiheiki (Keichōbon). 5 vols. Edited by Yamashita Hiroaki. Shinko Nihon koten shūsei. Tokyo: Shinkosha, 1977–1988.

Taiheiki (Tenshōbon). Edited by Hasegawa Tadashi. Shimpen Nihon koten bungaku zenshū, vols. 54–57. Tokyo: Shōgakkan, 1998.

Tawara Tōda monogatari. In *Fukutomi sōshi/Tawara Tōda monogatari,* edited by Iwase Hiroshi, pp. 40–134. Osaka: Wasen shoin, 1984.

Tawara Tōda monogatari. In *Muromachi monogatarishū ge,* edited by Ichiko Teiji et al., pp. 87–139. Shin Nihon koten bungaku taikei, vol. 55. Tokyo: Iwanami shoten, 1992.

Teishin kōki. Dainihon kiroku. Tokyo: Iwanami shoten, 1956.

Ujishūi monogatari. Edited by Kobayashi Chishō. Nihon koten bungaku zenshū. Tokyo: Shōgakkan, 1973.

Utsubō monogatari. Edited by Kōno Tama. Nihon koten bungaku taikei, vol. 10. Tokyo: Iwanami shoten, 1959.

Zenkūnen kassen ekotoba—Heiji monogatari emaki—Yūki kassen ekotoba. Zoku Nihon no emaki, vol. 17. Komatsu Shigemi, gen. ed. Tokyo: Chūō kōronsha, 1992.

Secondary Sources

Abe Takeshi. *Nihon kodai kanshoku jiten.* Tokyo: Kōka shoten, 1995.

Abe Yukio. "Heiji monogatari Hachiman Tarō Yoshiie no kenkyū rombunshū." *Miyashrio gakuin jo dai* 57 (1982): 25–44.

Adolphson, Mikael. "Enryakuji: An Old Power in a New Era." In *The Origins of Japan's Medieval World: Courtiers, Clerics, Warriors, and Peasants in the Fourteenth Century,* edited by Jeffrey Mass, pp. 237–260. Stanford, CA: Stanford University Press, 1997.

———. *Teeth and Claws of the Buddha: Monastic Warriors and Sohei in Japanese History.* Honolulu: University of Hawaii Press, 2007.

Adolphson, Mikael, Edward Kamens, and Stacie Matsumoto, eds. *Heian Japan: Centers and Peripheries.* Honolulu: University of Hawaii Press, 2007.

Akagi Shizuko. "Gutei no Heishi." *Kodai bunka shiron* 3 (1982): 1–7.

Akashi Kazunori. "Kodai-chūsei kazokuron no mondaiten." *Kaihō* 23 (1985): 1–7.

Akita Shō. "Chihō kanga to sono shūhen: kokushisei no keisei o megutte." *Shōnai kokōgaku* 19 (1985): 1–11.

Akutagawa Tatsuo. *Saikoku bushidan kankei shiryōshū.* Tokyo: Bunken shuppan, 1997.

Amino Yoshihiko. "Shōen koryōsei no keisei to kōzō." In *Tōchiseidoshi,* edited by Takeuchi Rizō, pp. 173–274. Tokyo: Yamakawa shoten, 1973.

———. *Chūseishi o minaosu.* Tokyo: Yushisha, 1994.

———. "Umino ryōshu umi no bushidan." In *Bushi to wa nan darō ka,* edited by Takahashi Masaaki and Yamamoto Kōji, pp. 44–57. Tokyo: Asahi shimbunsha, 1994.

———. *Chūsei ni nani ga okita ka.* Tokyo: Nihon Editor's School, 1997.

Amino Yoshihiko, Sasamatsu Hiroshi, and Ishii Susumu. *Chūsei no tsumi to batsu.* Tokyo: Tōkyō daigaku shuppankai, 1983.

Aoki Shigekazu. *Taira Masakado: Sōgen no nobi*. Tokyo: Shinjimbutsu ōraisha, 1996.

Arnn, Barbara L. "Local Legends of the Gempei War: Reflections of Medieval Japanese History." *Asian Folk Studies* 38, no. 2 (1979): 1–10.

Asakawa Kan'ichi. *Land and Society in Medieval Japan*. Edited by Committee for the Publication of Dr. K. Asakawa's Works. Tokyo: Japan Society for the Promotion of Science, 1965.

Bachrach, Bernard S. *Early Carolingian Warfare: Prelude to Empire*. Philadelphia: University of Pennsylvania Press, 2001.

Batten, Bruce L. "Foreign Threat and Domestic Reform: The Emergence of the Ritsuryō State." *Monumenta Nipponica* 41, no. 2 (1986): 199–219.

———. "State and Frontier in Early Japan: The Imperial Court and Northern Kyushu, pp. 645–1185." Ph.D. dissertation. Stanford, CA: Stanford University, 1989.

———. "Provincial Administration in Early Japan: From *Ritsuryo Kokka* to *Ocho Kokka*." *Harvard Journal of Asiatic Studies* 53, no. 1 (June 1993): 103–134.

———. *To the Ends of Japan: Premodern Frontiers, Boundaries and Interactions*. Honolulu: University of Hawaii Press, 2003.

———. *Gateway to Japan: Hakata in War and Peace, 500–1300*. Honolulu: University of Hawaii Press, 2006.

Bay, Alexander R. "Bugei and Heihō: Military Skills and Strategy in Japan from the Eighth to Eleventh Centuries." Master's thesis. Eugene: University of Oregon, 1998.

Bender, Ross L. "Hachiman Cult and the Dōkyō Incident." *Monumenta Nipponica* 34, no. 2 (1979): 125–153.

Bock, Felicia, tr. *Engi-Shiki: Procedures of the Engi Era Books I–IV*. Tokyo: Monumenta Nipponica Monograph, 1970.

Borgen, Robert. "Origins of the Sugawara: A History of the Haji Family." *Monumenta Nipponica* 30, no. 4 (1975): 406–422.

———. *Sugawara no Michizane and the Early Heian Court*. Cambridge, MA: Harvard University Press, 1985.

Bottomly, I., and A. P. Hopson. *Arms and Armour of the Samurai: The History of Weaponry in Ancient Japan*. New York: Crescent Books, 1988.

Brazell, Karen. "Three Tales of Michinaga." *Journal of Japanese Studies* 10, no. 1 (1984): 185–196.

Brown, Delmer, and Ishida Ichirō, trans. and ed. *The Future and the Past: A Translation and Study of the Gukansho, An Interpretive History of Japan Written in 1219*. Berkeley: University of California Press, 1979.

Butler, Kenneth D. "The Heike Monogatari and the Japanese Warrior Ethic." *Harvard Journal of Asian Studies* 29 (1969): 93–108.

Chūsei toshi kenkyūkai. *Kodai kara chūsei e*. Tokyo: Shinjimbutsu ōraisha, 1995.

Cogan, Thomas J., trans. *The Tale of the Soga Brothers*. Tokyo: University of Tokyo Press, 1987.

Conlan, Thomas Donald. *In Little Need of Divine Intervention: Scrolls of the Mongol Invasions of Japan*. Ithaca, NY: East Asia Program, Cornell University, 2001.

———. *State of War: The Violent Order of Fourteenth Century Japan*. Michigan

Monograph Series in Japanese Studies. Ann Arbor: University of Michigan Center for Japanese Studies, 2003.

Deguchi Hisanori. "Monogatari to shite no byōbue: Ichinotani kassen-zu byōbu o megutte." *Gunki to katarimono* 36, (no. 3 2000): 63–73.

"Denki densetsu kenkyūjō." *Taira Masakado no ran to kanren denshō.* www31.ocn.ne.jp/~denkidensetu/ddk/m1.htm. Accessed 10/6/2005.

Edwards, Walter. "Event and Process in the Founding of Japan." *Journal of Japanese Studies* 9, no. 2 (1983): 265–295.

Egami Yasushi. "The River Style Garden and the Problem of 'Nosuji' in Early Medieval Japan." *France-Asie* 19, no. 180 (1963): 905–920.

Endō Motō. "Masakado no ran zengo no kantō chiiki no shingyō girei." *Nihon kodaishi ronsō* 1983, pp. 389–410.

Farris, Wm. Wayne. *Population, Disease, and Land in Early Japan, 645–900.* Cambridge, MA: Harvard University Press, 1985.

———. *Heavenly Warriors: The Evolution of Japan's Military, 500–1300.* Cambridge, MA: Harvard University Press, 1992.

———. "Japan to 1300." In *War and Society in the Ancient and Medieval Worlds: Asia, the Mediterranean, Europe, and Mesoamerica*, edited by Kurt Raaflaub and Nathan Rosenstein, pp. 47–70. Cambridge, MA: Center for Hellenic Studies, Harvard University, 1999.

Florenz, Karl. "Ancient Japanese Rituals." *Transactions of the Asiatic Society of Japan* 1, no. 27 (1900): 1–112.

Friday, Karl. *Hired Swords: The Rise of Private Warrior Power in Early Japan.* Stanford, CA: Stanford University Press, 1992.

———. "Teeth and Claws: Provincial Warriors and the Heian Court." *Monumenta Nipponica* 43, no. 2 (1988): 153–185.

———. "Valorous Butchers: The Art of War During the Golden Age of the Samurai." *Japan Forum* 5, no. 1 (April 1993): 1–19.

———. "Pushing Beyond the Pale: The Yamato Conquest of the *Emishi* and Northern Japan." *Journal of Japanese Studies* 23, no. 1 (1997): 1–24.

———. "Kisha no ayumi no ikkōsatsu: Chūsei Nihon ni okeru kokka to bunka to gijutsu." *Tōkyō daigaku shiryō hensanjō kenkyū kiyō* 11 (March 2000): 21–35.

———. *Samurai, Warfare and the State in Early Medieval Japan.* London: Routledge, 2004.

———. "Lordship Interdicted: Taira Tadatsune & the Limited Horizons of Warrior Ambition." In *Centers and Peripheries in Heian Japan*, edited by Mikael Adolphson, Edward Kamens, and Stacie Matsumoto, pp. 329–354. Honolulu: University of Hawaii Press, 2007.

Fujimoto Masayuki. "Bugu to rekishi I: tate." *Rekishi to chiri* 418 (1990): 40–52.

———. "Bugu to rekishi II: yumiya." *Rekishi to chiri* 421 (1990): 58–72.

———. "Bugu to rekishi III: katchū." *Rekishi to chiri* 424 (1990): 41–59.

———. *Yoroi o matō hitobito.* Tokyo: Yoshikawa kōbunkan, 2000.

Fujioka Kenjiro. "Historical Development of Japanese Cities: Ancient and Feudal Ages." In *Japanese Cities: A Geographical Approach*, pp. 13–16. Tokyo: Association of Japanese Geographers, 1970.

Fukuda Keikichi. "Zenkyūnen kassen to Sadatō densetsu." *Kawauchi Kodaishi Ronshū* 5 (1989): 47–67.

Fukuda Toyohiko. "Tetsu to uma to Taira Masakado." *Gekkan hyakka* 196 (1974): 6–11.

———. "Ōchō gunsei kikō to nairan." In *Iwanami kōza Nihon rekishi 4 (Kodai)*, pp. 81–120. Tokyo: Iwanami shoten, 1976.

———. *Taira Masakado no ran.* Tokyo: Iwanami shoten, 1981.

———. "Taira Masakado o meguru eio densetsu no keisei." *Gakkan hyakka* 238 (1982): 38–43.

———. "Fujiwara Sumitomo to sono ran." *Nihon rekishi* 471 (1987): 1–21.

———. "Fujiwara Sumitomo no ran." In *Heian ōchō no bushi*, edited by Yasuda Motohisa, pp. 76–83. Senran Nihonshi. Tokyo: Daiichi hōgen, 1988.

———. "Taira Masakado no ran." In *Heian ōchō no bushi*, edited by Yasuda Motohisa, pp. 65–74. Senran Nihonshi. Tokyo: Daiichi hōgen, 1988.

———. "Kodai makki no yōhei to yōhei taichō." In *Chūsei Nihon no shosō*, edited by Yasuda Motohisa sensei tainin kinen ronshū kangyō iinkai, vol. 5, pp. 459–489. Tokyo: Yoshikawa kōbunkan, 1989.

———. ed. *Ikusa.* Chūsei o kangaeru. Tokyo: Yoshikawa kōbunkan, 1993.

———. "Senshi to sono shūdan." In *Ikusa*, edited by Fukuda Toyohiko, pp. 76–129. Tokyo: Yoshikawa kōbunkan, 1993.

———. "Tōgoku no uma to tetsu." *Rekishi chiri kyōiku* 518 (1994): 14–19.

———. *Tōgoku heiran to mononofu-tachi.* Tokyo: Yoshikawa kōbunkan, 1995.

———. "Bushi = zaichiryōshu-ron to bushi = geinōjin-ron no kankei." *Nihon rekishi* 601, (1998): 98–104.

———, ed. *Chūsei no shakai to buryoku.* Tokyo: Yoshikawa kōbunkan, 1994.

Fukuei Suiken. *Nihontō yomoyama hanashi.* Tokyo: Yūsankaku shuppan, 1989.

Fukui Toshihiko. "Seii to zōto ryakunempyō." In *Kodai tōhoku rekishi to minzoku*, edited by Kimoto Yoshinobu, pp. 171–183. Tokyo: Kōryō shoten, 1989.

———. "Seii, zōto to kanjin." *Minkan* 120 (1989): 45–81.

Futaki Ken'ichi. *Chūsei buke no sakuhō.* Tokyo: Yoshikawa kōbunkan, 1999.

Giei Akio. "Ōchō kokka moto no kokuga keibatsu saiteitai." In *Bunka-shi no shokiri*, edited by Okuma Kazuo, pp. 204–238. Tokyo: Yoshikawa kōbunkan, 2003.

Gilbert, W. S., and Arthur Sullivan. "Pirates of Penzance or the Slave of Duty," 1879.

Goble, Andrew E. "War and Injury: The Emergence of Wound Medicine in Medieval Japan." *Monumenta Nipponica* 60, no. 31 (2005): 297–338.

Gomi Fumihiko. *Fukugen no Nihon shi: kassen emaki.* Tokyo: Mainichi shimbunsha, 1990.

———. "Kubi no fechishizumu." In *Fukugen no Nihon shi: kassen emaki*, edited by Gomi Fumihiko, pp. 74–75. Tokyo: Mainichi shimbunsha, 1990.

———. "Shi-Kassen no seikai." In *Fukugen no Nihon shi: kassen emaki*, edited by Gomi Fumihiko, pp. 58–59. Tokyo: Mainichi shimbunsha, 1990.

———. "Tachi no shakai to sono hensen." In *Shiro to tachi o horu yomu*, edited by Satō Makoto and Gomi Fumihiko, pp. 225–242. Tokyo: Yamakawa shuppan kai, 1994.

————. *Sassei to shinkō: bushi o saguru.* Tokyo: Kadokawa sensho, 1997.

Grapard, Allan. *The Protocol of the Gods: A Study of the Kasuga Cult in Japanese History.* Berkeley, CA: University of California Press, 1992.

Haga Noboru. "Emishi to henkyō." *Hikaku bunka* 2 (1986): 1–38.

Hall, John W. *Government and Local Power in Japan 500–1700: A Study Based on Bizen Province.* Princeton, NJ: Princeton University Press, 1966.

————. "Kyoto as Historical Background." In *Medieval Japan: Essays in Institutional History,* edited by John W. Hall and Jeffrey P. Mass, pp. 3–38. New Haven, CT: Yale University Press, 1974.

Haruda Takayoshi. "Masakado no ran ni okeru buryoku soshiki: toku ni banrui ni tsuite." *Shigen* 2, no. 3 (1967): 44–51.

————. "Taira Masakado no ran no buryoku." In *Kantō no kodai shakai kodaishi ronshū,* edited by Endō Motō, pp. 127–162. Tokyo: Meicho shuppan, 1989.

Hashiguchi Teishi. "Chūsei hōkeikan o meguru shomondai." *Rekishi hyōron* 454 (1988).

————. "Hōkeikan wa ika ni seiritsu suru no ka." In *Sōten Nihon no rekishi 4: chūsei hen.* Tokyo: Shin jimbutsu ōraisha, 1991.

Hashimoto Hisakazu. "Bushi no daitō to shizen." In *Kōkogaku ni yoru Nihon rekishi 16 shizen kankyō to bunka,* edited by Ōtsuka Shoji et al., pp. 83–96. Tokyo: Yūsankaku shuppan, 1996.

Hattō Sanae. "Kodai ni okeru kazoku to kyōdōtai." *Rekishi hyōron* 424 (1985): 14–23.

————. "Sekkanki ni okeru zuryō no ie to kazoku keitai." *Nihon rekishi* 442 (1985): 1–18.

Hayashi Rokurō. *Shijitsu Taira Masakado.* Tokyo: Shinjimbutsu ōraisha, 1975.

————. *Kodai makki no hanran.* Tokyo: Kyōikusha, 1977.

Hayashi Rokurō, ed. *Ronshū Taira Masakado kenkyū.* Tokyo: Gendai shisosha, 1975.

Herail, Francine. *Yodo no Tsukai: Ou le Système Des Quatre Envoyés.* Paris: Presses Universitaires de France, 1966.

————. *Fonctions et Fonctionnaires Japonais Au Début Du XIème Siècle.* Paris: Bibliothèque Japonaise, 1971.

Hirada Kōji, ed. "Nihon kodaishi sōgō bunken mokuroku." *Kenkyū to shiryō* 7 (1990): 1–147.

Hirano Hiroyuki. "Heian shoki ni okeru kokushi gunji no kankei ni tsuite." *Shien* 72 (1955).

Hodate Michihisa. "Kodai makki no tōgoku to ryūjū kizoku." In *Chūsei Tōgokushi no kenkyū,* edited by Chūsei tōgokushi kenkyūkai, pp. 3–22. Tokyo: Tōkyō daigaku shuppankai, 1988.

————. *Heian jidai.* Nihon no rekishi, vol. 3. Tokyo: Iwanami juniya shinsho, 1999.

Horiguchi Teishi. "Chūsei hōkeikan o meguru shomondai." *Rekishi hyōron* 454 (1988).

————. "Hōkeikan wa ika ni seiritsu suru no ka." In *Sōten Nihon no rekishi 4: Chūsei hen.* Tokyo: Shin jimbutsu ōraisha, 1991.

Horiuchi Kazuaki. "Heian chūki no kebiishi no buryoku ni tsuite." In *Ronkyū*

Nihon kodai shi, edited by Yamaō Yukihisa, pp. 341–362. Tokyo: Gakuseisha, 1979.

The Hour of the Ox: A Trip into the Japanese World of the Supernatural. www.tokyo teleport.com/teleport/soul/essays/ausa2004b.htm. Accessed 9/6/2005.

Hurst, G. Cameron, III. "Structure of the Heian Court: Some Thoughts on 'Familial Authority' in Medieval Japan." In *Medieval Japan: Essays in Institutional History*, edited by John W. Hall and Jeffrey P. Mass, pp. 39–59. New Haven, CT: Yale University Press, 1974.

———. *Insei: Abdicated Sovereigns in the Politics of Late Heian Japan 1086–1185.* New York: Columbia University Press, 1976.

———. "Michinaga's Maladies: A Medical Report on Fujiwara Michinaga." *Monumenta Nipponica* 34, no. 1 (1979): 101–112.

———. "The Kōbu Polity: Court-Bakufu Relations in Kamakura Japan." In *Court and Bakufu in Japan*, edited by Jeffrey P. Mass, pp. 3–28. New Haven, CT: Yale University Press, 1982.

———. "*Kugyō* and *Zuryō*: Center and Periphery in the Era of Fujiwara no Michinaga." In *Centers and Peripheries in Heian Japan*, edited by Mikael Adolphson, Edward Kamens, and Stacie Matsumoto, pp. 66–101. Honolulu: University of Hawaii Press, 2007.

Ike Tōru. "Nihon chūsei no sensō to heiwa." *Ikkō ronsō* 101, no. 4 (1989): 50–69.

Ikegami, Eiko. *The Taming of the Samurai: Honorific Individualism and the Making of Modern Japan.* Cambridge, MA: Harvard University Press, 1995.

Ikenari Yuko. "Kodai no dōro gyōsei ni tsuite: yōro o chūshin ni." *Tachibana shigaku* 15, no. 10 (2000): 13–28.

Imai Seinosuke. "Kassen no kikō." In *Gunki monogatari no seisei to hyōgen*, edited by Yamashita Hiroaki, pp. 31–46. Tokyo: Wasen shoin, 1995.

Imaizumi Takao. "Kodai Tōhoku jōsaku no jōshisei." In *Kita Nihon chūseishi no kenkyū*, edited by Hanamoto Yasuhisa, pp. 3–23. Tokyo: Yoshikawa kōbunkan, 1990.

Inoue Katsuhiro. "Nihon kodai ni okeru 'kō' to 'shi' ni tsuite no kisōteki kōan." In *Rekishi to hōhō 1 Nihonshi ni okeru kō to shi*, edited by Rekishi to hōhō henshū iinkai, pp. 119–146. Tokyo: Aoki shoten, 1996.

Inoue Mitsuo. "Masakado no ran to chūō kizoku." *Shirin* 50, no. 6 (1967): 1–26.

———. *Heian jidai no gunji seido no kenkyū.* Tokyo: Yoshikawa kōbunkan, 1980.

Inoue Mitsusada. "The Ritsuryō System in Early Japan." *Acta Asiatica* 31 (1977): 83–112.

Inoue Mitsusada with Delmer Brown. "The Century of Reform." In *Ancient Japan.* Vol. 1 of *The Cambridge History of Japan*, edited by Delmer M. Brown, pp. 163–220. New York and London: Cambridge University Press, 1993.

Irumada Nobuo. *Musha no yō ni.* Nihon no rekishi. Tokyo: Shūeisha, 1991.

Ishibashi Shōzō. "Emishi no seikai to hachinohe." *Hachinohe chiiki shi* 13 (1988): 2–50.

Ishii Masakuni. *Kodai katana to tetsu no kagaku.* Tokyo: Yūsankaku shuppan, 1995.

Ishii Ryōsuke. "Gunji, keisatsu oyobi kotsu seido." In *Nihon hōseishi gaisetsu*, pp. 128–134. Tokyo: Kōbundō, 1948.

Ishii Shirō. *Nihonjin no kokka seikatsu.* Nihon kokuseishi kenkyū, vol. 2. Tokyo: Tōkyō daigaku shuppankai, 1986.

Ishii Susumu. "Chūsei seiritsuki gunsei kenkyū no isshiten: kokuga o chūshin to suru gunjiryoku soshiki ni tsuite." *Shigaku zasshi* 78, no. 12 (1969): 1–32.

———. "Bushidan no hatten." In *Kanagawa kenshi, tsushihen,* vol. 1, pp. 347–442. Yokohama: Kanagawa-ken, 1981.

———. "The Formation of Bushi Bands (Bushidan)." *Acta Asiatica* 49 (1985): 1–14.

———. *Kamakura bushi no jitsuzo.* Tokyo: Heibonsha, 1987.

Ishimoda Shō. *Kodai makki seijishi jōsetsu.* Tokyo: Miraisha, 1956.

———. "Taira Tadatsune no ran ni tsuite." In *Kodai makki seijishi josetsu,* pp. 182–196. Tokyo: Miraisha, 1956.

———. "Kodai makki no hanran." In *Ronshū Taira Masakado kenkyū,* edited by Hayashi Rokurō, pp. 151–159. Tokyo: Gendai shisosha, 1975.

———. "Masakado no ran ni tsuite." In *Ronshū Taira Masakado kenkyū,* edited by Hayashi Rokurō, pp. 192–199. Tokyo: Gendai shisosha, 1975.

Isomura Yukio. "Hokubu kyūshū no kodai bōei shisetsu." In *Shiro to tachi o horu yomu,* edited by Satō Makoto and Gomi Fumihiko, pp. 119–156. Tokyo: Yamakawa shuppan kai, 1994.

Itō Kaoru. "Nishinotani iseki shutsudo ibutsu no kinzokugakuteki kaiseki." In *Tsuwamono no jidai: kodai makki no Tōgoku shakai,* edited by Maizō bunkazai sentaa, pp. 134–143. Tokyo: Yokohama-shi rekishi hakubutsukan, 1998.

Itō Katsuya. *Zenkunen no eki, Gosannen no eki.* Akita: Mumeisha shuppan, 1993.

Iyanaga Teizō. "Ritsuryōseiteki tōchi shōyū." In *Iwanami kōza Nihon rekishi kodai 3,* pp. 33–78. Tokyo: Iwanami shoten, 1962.

Izumiya Yasuo. "Heian jidai ni okeru kokuga kikō no henka: mokudai o chūshin to shite." *Kodai bunka* 29, no. 1 (1977): 1–18.

Jones, Archer. *The Art of War in the Western World.* Chicago: University of Illinois Press, 1987.

Kajiwara Masaaki. "Setsuwashū no naka no buyūshi." In *Heian ōchō no bushi,* edited by Yasuda Motohisa, pp. 98–101. Senran Nihonshi. Tokyo: Daiichi hōgen, 1988.

Kajiwara Masaaki and Kajiwara Masaaki. "Sensei koki kinen ronshū kangyōkai." eds. *Gunki bungaku no keifu to tenkai.* Tokyo: Kyūko shoin, 1998.

Kajiwara Masaaki and Yashiro Kazuo. *Masakado densetsu: Minshū no kokoro ni ikiru eiyū.* Tokyo: Shindoku shosha, 1966.

Kamii Keikichi. "Zen kūnen no eki minaoshi no tame ni." In *Tōhoku kodaishi no kenkyū,* edited by Takahashi Tomio, pp. 407–440. Tokyo: Yoshikawa kōbunkan, 1986.

Kamon Nammi. *Taira Masakado mahōjin.* Tokyo: Kawade shobō shinsha, 1996.

Kanda Keikichi. "Zenkyūnen kassen to sadatō densetsu." *Kawauchi kodaishi ronshū* 5 (1989): 47–67.

Kanegae Hiroyuki. "Heian jidai no 'kuni' to 'tachi.'" In *Shiro to tachi o horu yomu,* edited by Satō Makoto and Gomi Fumihiko, pp. 91–118. Tokyo: Yamakawa shuppan kai, 1994.

Kaneko Arichika. *Nihon no dentō bajutsu: bajō bugei hen.* Tokyo: Nichibō shuppansha, 1995.

Kanezashi Shōzō. "Suigun to senjutsu." In *NHK rekishi e no shōtai 5: muteki*

Yoshitsune gundan, edited by Toyoda Aritsune and Nomura Shin'ichi, pp. 99–105. Tokyo: Nihon hōsō shuppan kyōkai, 1990.

Kasamatsu Hiroshi. "Omae no kasan . . ." In *Chūsei no tsumi to batsu*, edited by Amino Yoshihiko et al., pp. 1–14. Tokyo: Tōkyō daigaku shuppankai, 1983.

———. "Youchi." In *Chūsei no tsumi to batsu*, edited by Amino Yoshihiko et al., pp. 89–102. Tokyo: Tōkyō daigaku shuppankai, 1983.

Kashiyama Iwao. *Ōshū sennen senki*. Tokyo: Sōeishuppan, 1995.

Kawai Yasushi. *Gempei kassen no kyozō o hagu*. Tokyo: Kōdansha, 1996.

———. "Kawachi Ishikawa Genji No 'Hōki' to Heike monogatari." *Jimbun gakuhō* 306 (March 2000): 45–78.

Kawajiri Akio. "Masakado no ran to Hitachi no kuni." *Nihon rekishi* 527 (1992): 1–18.

———. "Shimōsa kokufu o yakiuchi shita Taira Koreyoshi." *Chiba shigaku* 20 (1992): 26–35.

———. "Taira Yoshifumi to Masakado no ran." *Chiba kenshi kenkyū* 1 (1993): 36–52.

Kawane Yoshiyasu. "Heian makki no zaichi ryōshusei ni tsuite." In *Chūsei hōkensei shiron*. Tokyo: Tokyo daigaku shuppankai, 1971.

Kawashima Shigehiro. "Suruga no kuni ni okeru Taira Masakado no ran." *Chihōshi Shizuoka* 20, (no. 4 1992): 44–70.

Kazusa Takeshi. "Mutsuwaki to Fujiwara Akihira." *Kodaigaku kenkyū* 129 (1993): 22–31.

Kelsey, W. Michael. *Konjaku Monogatarishū*. Twayne, 1982.

Kiley, Cornelius J. "Estate and Property in the Late Heian Period." In *Medieval Japan: Essays in Institutional History*, edited by John W. Hall and Jeffrey P. Mass, pp. 109–126. New Haven, CT: Yale University Press, 1974.

———. "Provincial Administration and Land Tenure in Early Heian." In *Cambridge History of Japan, Vol. 2, Heian Japan*, edited by Donald H. Shively and William McCullough, pp. 236–340. New York and Cambridge, UK: Cambridge University Press, 1999.

Kimura Hideaki. "Bushidan Akashi-shi ni tsuite." *Rekishi to Kōbe* 193 (1995): 23–32.

Kimura Shigemitsu. *'Kokufū no bunka' no jidai*. Tokyo: Aoki shoten, 1997.

Kitagawa Hiroshi, and Bruce T. Tsuchida, trans. *The Tale of the Heike*. Tokyo: University of Tokyo Press, 1975.

Kitakawa Tadahiko. *Gunjimono ronkō*. Tokyo: Miyai shoten, 1989.

Kitamura Yūki. "Heiankyō no shihai kōzō." *Shigaku zasshi* 94, no. 1 (1985): 1–37.

Kitatsune Shinsao. "Kamakura bakufu seiritsuki ni okeru Ōshū Fujiwara-shi to Minamoto Yoshitsune." In *Nihon chūsei seiji shakai no kenkyū*, edited by Ogawa Shin sensei no koki kinen ronshū o kangyō suru kai, pp. 67–100. Tokyo: Zoku gunsho ruijū kanseikai, 1991.

Kitayama Shigeo. "Sekkan seiji." In *Iwanami kōza Nihon rekishi kodai 4*, pp. 1–40. Tokyo: Iwanami shoten, 1962.

———. *Taira Masakado*. Tokyo: Asahi shimbunsha, 1993.

Kobashi Seiji. "Ōshū kassen to nijūkutsu." In *Kyōdo no kenkyū*. Fukushima: Fukushima-ken Kunimi-chō, 1979.

Kobayashi Hiroko. *The Human Comedy of Heian Japan: A Study of the Secular Stories in the 12th Century*. Tokyo: Centre for East Asian Cultural Studies, 1979.

Kobayashi Shōji. "Fujiwara Sumitomo no ran sairon." *Nihon rekishi* 499 (1989): 1–19.

———. "Fune ikusa." In *Ikusa*, edited by Fukuda Toyohiko, pp. 210–239. Tokyo: Yoshikawa kōbunkan, 1993.

Kobayashi Yukio. "Jōdai Nihon ni okeru jōba no fūshū." *Shirin* 34, no. 3 (1951): 173–190.

Kodai gakkyōkai, ed. *Kodai Tōgoku no bujintachi*. Saitama: Saitama kenritsu saki-tama shiryōkan, 1989.

Kodaigaku Kyōkai and Kodaigaku kenkyūjo, eds. *Heian jidaishi jiten*. Tokyo: Kadokawa shoten, 1994.

Kondō Yoshikazu. "Chūsei bushiron no ichi zentei: ritsuryōsei-ka ni okeru yumiya no ichi." In *Chūsei no kūkan o yomu*, edited by Gomi Fumihiko, pp. 212–246. Tokyo: Yoshikawa kōbunkan, 1995.

———. "Chūsei bushiron no ichi zentei: ritsuryōseika ni okeru yumiya no ichi." In *Chūsei no kūkan o yomu*, edited by Gomi Fumihiko, pp. 212–246. Tokyo: Yoshikawa kōbunkan, 1995.

———. *Yumiya to tōken: chūsei kassen no jitsuzō*. Tokyo: Yoshikawa kōbunkan, 1997.

———. "Ōyoroi no sciritsu: yūshoku kojitsu no kenchi kara." In *Tsuwamono no jidai: kodai makki no Tōgoku shakai*, edited by Maizō bunkazai sentaa, pp. 144–154. Tokyo: Yokohama-shi rekishi hakubutsukan, 1998.

———. "Buki kara mita chūsei bushiron." *Nihonshi kenkyū* 416 (1997): 26–47.

———. "Chūsei sentō shiryō to shite no gunki monogatari no ichi: *Zenkūnen kassen emaki* to *Heike monogatari* no kankei o chūshin ni." In *Gunki bungaku to sono shūen*, edited by Kajiwara Masaaki, pp. 135–157. Tokyo: Kyūko shoin, 2000.

———. *Chūsei-teki bugu no seiritsu to bushi*. Tokyo: Yoshikawa kōbunkan, 2000.

———. "Gunki monogatari kara mita chūsei no buki no shiyō to sentō." *Gunki to katarimono* 36 (2000): 3–14.

Koromogawa Jin. "Chūsei zenki no kemmon jiin to buryoku." *Nempō chūsei shi kenkyū* 25 (May 2000): 1–28.

Kotofuji Sanae. *Heianchō no otoko to onna*. Tokyo: Chūō kōronsha, 1995.

Koyama Yasunori. "Nihon chūsei seiritsuki no mibun to kaikyū." *Rekishigaku kenkyū* 328 (1967): 26–41.

———. "Kodai makki no Tōgoku to Saigoku." In *Iwanami kōza Nihonshi kodai 4*, pp. 231–269. Tokyo: Iwanami shoten, 1976.

Koyama Yasunori, tr. by Bruce L. Batten. "East and West in the Late Classical Age." In *Capital & Countryside in Japan, 300–1180: Japanese Historians Inter-preted in English*, edited by Joan R. Piggot, pp. 366–401. Ithaca, NY: Cornell University East Asia Series, 2006.

Kudō Keiichi. "Tōi no raikō." In *Heian ōchō no bushi*, edited by Yasuda Moto-hisa, pp. 88–89. Senran Nihonshi. Tokyo: Daiichi hōgen, 1988.

Kudō Masaki. "Tōhoku kodaishi to jōsaku." *Nihonshi kenkyū* 136 (1973): 17–33.

———. "Kodai emishi no shakai: kōeki to shakai soshiki." *Rekishi hyōron* 434 (1986): 13–35.

———. *Jōsaku to emishi*. Kōkogaku raiburari. Tokyo: Nyū saiensusha, 1989.

———. "Kodai emishi to sono bunka." *Miyashiro rekishi kagaku kenkyū* 30 (1989): 1–6.

Kumagai Kimio. "Emishi no seiyaku." *Nara kodaishi ronshū* 1 (1985): 15–26.

Kuroda Hideo. *Sugata to shigusa no chūsei shi: ezu to emaki no fukei kara.* Tokyo: Heibonsha, 1986.

———. "Kubi o kakeru." *Gekkan hyakka* 306 (1988): 13–21.

———. *Gempei no kōbō.* Tokyo: Gakushū kenkyūsha, 1989.

———. *Nazo kaki Nihon shi: ega shiryō o yomu.* NHK Ningen Daigaku, nos. 1–3 gekki. Tokyo: Nihon hōsō shuppan kyōkai, 1999.

Kuroda Toshio. *Nihon chūsei no kokka to shūkyō.* Tokyo: Iwanami shoten, 1975.

Kuwabara Shigerō. "Tōhoku no jōkaku." In *Shiro*, edited by Ueda Masaaki, pp. 103–128. Tokyo: Shakai shisōsha, 1977.

Kuwada Tadachika. *Shimpen Nihon bushō retsuden.* Tokyo: Akita shoten, 1989.

———. *Shimpen Nihon kassen zenshū.* Tokyo: Akita shoten, 1989.

Maizō bunkazai sentaa, ed. *Tsuwamono no jidai: kodai makki no Tōgoku shakai.* Tokyo: Yokohama-shi rekishi hakubutsukan, 1998.

Mass, Jeffrey P. *Warrior Government in Medieval Japan: A Study of the Kamakura Bakufu, Shugo and Jitō.* New Haven, CT: Yale University Press, 1974.

———. *Lordship and Inheritance in Early Medieval Japan: A Study of the Kamakura Sōryō System.* Stanford, CA: Stanford University Press, 1989.

———. "The Kamakura Bakufu." In *Medieval Japan*, edited by Kozo Yamamura, pp. 46–88. The Cambridge History of Japan, vol. 3. New York: Cambridge University Press, 1990.

———. *Yoritomo and the Founding of the First Bakufu.* Stanford, CT: Stanford University Press, 1999.

Masuda Toshinobu. "Shōmonki Ron." In *Kodai chūsei no seiji to chiiki shakai*, edited by Inoue Tatsuo, pp. 164–197. Tokyo: Oyama kyaku, 1986.

———. "Masakado no ran no seijishiteki bunseki." In *Kodaishi kenkyū no kadai to hōhō*, edited by Inoue Tatsuo, pp. 173–192. Tokyo: Kokusho kangyōkai, 1989.

Matsuhara Hironobu. *Kodai no chihō gōzoku.* Tokyo: Yoshikawa kōbunkan, 1988.

Matsumoto Shimpachirō. "Shōmonki no inshō." *Bungaku* 19, no. 10 (1951): 6–21.

———. "Shōmonki no inshō." In *Ronshū Taira Masakado kenkyū*, edited by Hayashi Rokurō, pp. 160–177. Tokyo: Gendai shisosha, 1975.

Matsumoto Yūsuke. "8 seiki kara 9 seiki shōtō ni kakete no Mutsu-Dewa azetchi." *Shishu* 24 (1989): 44–48.

Matsuzaki Masumi. "Bagu kara miru uma." In *Kamakura no bushi to uma*, edited by Uma no hakubutsukan, pp. 33–38. Tokyo: Meicho shuppan, 1999.

McCullough, Helen C. "A Tale of Mutsu." *Harvard Journal of Asiatic Studies* 25 (1964–1965): 178–211.

———. "Social and Psychological Aspects of Heian Ritual and Ceremony." In *Studies on Japanese Culture*, vol. 2, edited by the Japan P.E.N. Club, pp. 275–279. Tokyo: The Japan P.E.N. Club, 1973.

———, trans. *Okagami, The Great Mirror: Fujiwara Michinaga and His Times.* Princeton, NJ: Princeton University Press, 1980.

————, trans. *Tale of the Heike*. Stanford, CA: Stanford University Press, 1988.

McCullough, William H. "Japanese Marriage Institutions in the Heian Period." *Harvard Journal of Asian Studies* 27 (1967): 103–167.

————. "The Heian Court, 794–1070." In *Cambridge History of Japan, Vol. 2, Heian Japan*, edited by Donald H. Shively and William H. McCullough, pp. 20–96. New York and Cambridge, UK: Cambridge University Press, 1999.

Minamoto Yasushi. *Gekiroku Nihon no kassen: Masakado to Sumitomo no hanran*. Tokyo: Tokyo supotsu shimbunsha, 1979.

Miya Tsugio. *Kassen emaki*. Tokyo: Kadokawa shoten, 1977.

Miyake Chōhyōe. "Masakado no ran no kenkyū zentei: toku ni shūba no tō o chūshin to shite." In *Ronshū Taira Masakado kenkyū*, edited by Hayashi Rokurō, pp. 178–191. Tokyo: Gendai shisosha, 1975.

Miyanaga Tetsuo and Morita Yasushi. "Heian zenki Tōgoku no gunji mondai ni tsuite." *Kanezawa daigaku kyōiku gakubu kiyō* 24 (1975): 49–61.

Miyawaki Shunzō. *Heian Kamakura shi kikō*. Tokyo: Kōdansha, 1997.

Mizuno Yū. *Nihon kodai ōchō shiron josetsu*. Tokyo: Komiyama shoten, 1954.

Mori Kōichi, ed. *Nihon kodai bunka no tankyu 9: uma*. Tokyo: Shakai shisōsha, 1974.

Mori Toshio. "Yumiya no hattatsu." In *Fukugen no Nihon shi: Kassen emaki*, edited by Gomi Fumihisa, pp. 42–43. Tokyo: Mainichi shimbunsha, 1990.

————. "Yumiya no iryoku (1)." In *Fukugen no Nihon shi: Kassen emaki*, edited by Gomi Fumihisa, pp. 38–39. Tokyo: Mainichi shimbunsha, 1990.

————. "Yumiya no iryoku (2)." In *Fukugen no Nihon shi: Kassen emaki*, edited by Gomi Fumihisa, pp. 40–41. Tokyo: Mainichi shimbunsha, 1990.

Morillo, Stephen. "The 'Age of Cavalry' Revisited." In *The Circle of War in the Middle Ages: Essays on Medieval Military and Naval History*, edited by Donald J. Kagay and L. J. Andrew Villalon, pp. 45–58. Woodbridge, New York: Boydell Press, 1999.

Morita Tei. "Kodai sentō ni tsuite." In *Heian shōki kokka no kenkyū*, pp. 170–190. Tokyo: Gendai sōzōsha, 1970.

————. "Heian zenki o chūshin shita kizoku no shiteki buryoku ni." *Shigen* 15 (1972): 70–84.

————. *Zuryō*. Tokyo: Kyōikusha, 1978.

————. *Kenkyūshi ōchō kokka*. Tokyo: Yoshikawa kōbunkan, 1980.

————. "Heian zenki Tōgoku no gunji mondai ni tsuite." In *Kaitaiki ritsuryō seiji shakaishi no kenkyū*. Tokyo: Kokusho kangyōkai, 1983.

————. "Heianki nōmin shihai no jitsuzo." *Kyōka kyōiku kenkyū* 21 (1985): 141–152.

————. "Sumitomo no ran ni tsuite." *Jimbun kagaku shakai kagaku kiyō* 40 (1991): 15–23.

Morris, Dana Robert. "Peasant Economy in Early Japan, 650–950." Ph.D. dissertation. Berkeley: University of California, 1980.

————. "Land and Society." In *Cambridge History of Japan, Vol. 2, Heian Japan*, edited by Donald H. Shively and William McCullough, pp. 183–235. New York and Cambridge, UK: Cambridge University Press, 1999.

Morris, Ivan. *The World of the Shining Prince: Court Life in Ancient Japan*. New York: Knopf, 1964.

———. "Marriage in the World of Genji." *Asia* 11 (1968): 54–77.

Motogi Yasuo. *Bushi no seiritsu.* Tokyo: Yoshikawa kōbunkan, 1994.

Murai Yasuhisa, ed. *Heian ōchō no bushi: senran Nihonshi, Vol. 2.* Tokyo: Daiichi hōgen shuppan kabushiki kaishi, 1988.

———. "Meibō o tatematsuru." In *Heian ōchō no bushi*, edited by Yasuda Motohisa, pp. 104–105. Senran Nihonshi. Tokyo: Daiichi hōgen, 1988.

———. "Shūba no tō to shūsen no tomogara." In *Heian ōchō no bushi*, edited by Yasuda Motohisa, pp. 84–87. Senran Nihonshi. Tokyo: Daiichi hōgen, 1988.

Murakami Haruki. *Taira Masakado densetsu.* Tokyo: Kumifuru shoin, 2001.

Murano Takao, ed. *Nihon no katana: tetsu no waza to bu no kokoro.* Tokyo: Tōkyō kokuritsu hakubutsukan, 1997.

Nagahara Keiji. "Land Ownership under the Shoen-Kokugaryo System." *Journal of Japanese Studies* 1, no. 2 (1975): 269–296.

———. *Shōen.* Tokyo: Hyōronsha, 1978.

Nagai Hajime. "Gundansei teihaigo no Heishi." *Kokugakuin zasshi* 89, no. 9 (1988): 46–59.

Nagaoka Hideo. "'Gunki mono' no zentei hōga." *Kokugakuin kō kiyō* 20 (1987): 25–66.

Nakahara Toshiaya. "Shishi shinchū no mushi: sōhei." In *Heian ōchō no bushi*, edited by Yasuda Motohisa, pp. 94–97. Senran Nihonshi. Tokyo: Daiichi hōgen, 1988.

———. "Zuishin." In *Heian ōchō no bushi*, edited by Yasuda Motohisa, pp. 102–103. Senran Nihonshi. Tokyo: Daiichi hōgen, 1988.

Nakamura Ken. "Chūsei no daiku tōkō imonoshi to gijutsu." In *Kodai chūsei no gijutsu to shakai*, edited by Miura Keiichi. Gijutsu no shakaishi, vol. 1. Tokyo: Yūhikaku, 1982.

Nakazawa Katsuaki. "Kūkan to shite no 'jōkaku' to sono tenkai." In *Shiro to tachi o horu yomu*, edited by Satō Makoto and Gomi Fumihiko, pp. 191–224. Tokyo: Yamakawa shuppan kai, 1994.

———. *Chūsei no buryoku to jōkaku.* Tokyo: Yoshikawa kōbunkan, 1999.

Newman, John. *Bushido: The Way of the Warrior.* Wigston, Leicester: Magna Books, 1989.

Nickerson, Peter. "The Meaning of Matrilocality: Kinship, Property, and Politics in Mid-Heian." *Monumenta Nipponica* 48, no. 4 (1993): 429–468.

Niino Naokichi. "Kodai ni okeru jōsaku to miyako mura." In *Rekishi no naka no toshi to sonranku shakai*, edited by Tanaka Yoshio, pp. 383–402. Tokyo: Shibunkaku shuppan, 1994.

Nishimata Fusō. "Kassen no rūru to manaa." In *Gempei no sōran*, edited by Yasuda Motohisa, pp. 146–147. Tokyo: Daiichi hōgen, 1988.

Nishioka Toranosuke. "Bushi kaikyū kessei no ichiyoin to shite no 'maku' no hatten." In *Shōenshi no kenkyū*, pp. 301–407. Tokyo: Iwanami shoten, 1953.

———. *Shin Nihonshi nempyō.* Tokyo: Chūō kōronsha, 1955.

Nishiyama Ryōhei. "Kodai no tatakai, bōryoku, arasoi." *Nihonshi kenkyū* 452 (April 2000): 46–53.

Noguchi Minoru. *Bandō bushidan no seiritsu to hatten.* Tokyo: Kōseisho rinseishūsha, 1982.

————. "11–12 Seiki, okuwa no seiji kenryoku o meguru shomondai." In *Kōki sekkan jidaishi no kenkyū*, edited by Kodai gakkyōkai, pp. 397–415. Tokyo: Yoshikawa kōbunkan, 1990.

————. "Ikusa to girei." In *Ikusa*, edited by Fukuda Toyohiko, pp. 130–153. Tokyo: Yoshikawa kōbunkan, 1993.

————. *Buke no tōryō no jōken: chūsei bushi o minaosu.* Tokyo: Chūō kōronsha, 1994.

————. "Kokka to buryoku: chūsei ni okeru bushi buryoku." *Rekishi hyōron* 564, (1997): 60–73.

————. "Bandō bushi to uma." In *Kamakura bushi to uma*, edited by Baji bunka zaidan/uma no hakubutsukan, pp. 51–70. Tokyo: Meicho shuppan, 1999.

————. *Densetsu no shōgun: Fujiwara Hidesato.* Tokyo: Yoshikawa kōbunkan, 2001.

Nomura Shin'ichi. "Nihon no zairai uma to un'yū uma." In *NHK rekishi e no shōtai 5: muteki Yoshitsune gundan*, edited by Toyoda Aritsune and Nomura Shin'ichi, pp. 11–36. Tokyo: Nihon hōsō shuppan kyōkai, 1990.

Nozaki Jun. "Tōgoku bushi no gijutsu bunka." *Tōhoku gakuin daigaku tōhoku bunkaken kiyō* 24, (no. 8 1992): 39–46.

Nuta Raiyū. *Nihon monshōgaku.* Tokyo: Shin jimbutsu ōraisha, 1968.

Ōbinata Katsumi. *Kodai kokka to nenjū gyōji.* Tokyo: Yoshikawa kōbunkan, 1993.

Oborotani Hisashi. "Bushi no jōdō shinkō." In *Heian ōchō no bushi*, edited by Yasuda Motohisa, pp. 142–143. Senran Nihonshi. Tokyo: Daiichi hōgen, 1988.

————. "Miyako no samurai hina no musha: sekkanke to musha." In *Heian ōchō no bushi*, edited by Yasuda Motohisa, pp. 137–141. Senran Nihonshi. Tokyo: Daiichi hōgen, 1988.

Oboroya Hisashi. *Seiwa Genji.* Tokyo: Kyoikusha, 1984.

Oda Kan'e. *Taira Masakado koseki kō.* Tokyo: Binkan kyōkai (Ronshobō), 1908 report, 1973.

Ogasawara Nobuo. "Tōken gaisetsu." In *Nihon no katana: tetsu no waza to bu no kokoro*, edited by Murano Takao, pp. 8–34. Tokyo: Tōkyō kokuritsu hakubutsukan, 1997.

Ogata Takashi. *Genji to Ōshū Fujiwara-shi yondai no kyōbō.* Tokyo: Kōfūsha shuppan, 1993.

Ōhira Satoshi. "Hori no keifu." In *Shiro to tachi o horu yomu*, edited by Satō Makoto and Gomi Fumihiko, pp. 57–90. Tokyo: Yamakawa shuppan kai, 1994.

Okada Seiichi. "Kassen to girei." In *Ikusa*, edited by Fukuda Toyohiko, pp. 154–181. Tokyo: Yoshikawa kōbunkan, 1993.

————. "Ōshū Fujiwara-shi no ōu shihai." *Seiji keizai shigaku* 348, (1995): 1–14.

Okuda Masahiro. *Chūsei bushidan to shingyō.* Tokyo: Kashiwa shoten, 1980.

Okuno Nakahiko. "Heian ji dai no guntō ni tsuite." In *Minashū undō to sabetsu-jōsei*, edited by Minshūshi kenkyūkai, pp. 5–27. Tokyo: Ōyama kaku, 1985.

————. "Kodai Tōhoku to Tōgoku." *Minshūshi kenkyū* 37 (1989): 33–48.

————. "Bushidan keiseishijō yori mita Taira Tadatsune no ran: shisen ron hihan." *Komeizawa shigaku* 6 (1990): 1–10.

———. "Ōshū gosannen no eki no shinshiryō." *Komezawa shigaku* 7 (1991): 18–49.

———. "Tōhoku gunseishijō kara mita Ōshū Fujiwara-shi tōjō no igi." *Minshūshi kenkyū* 43, no. 5 (1992): 1–16.

Ōmiwa Tatsuhiko. "Bushi no daitō." In *Kōkogaku ni yoru Nihon rekishi 5 seiji*, edited by Ōtsuka Shoji et al., pp. 75–88. Tokyo: Yūsankaku shuppan, 1996.

Ōmori Kingorō. *Buke jidai no kenkyū*. Tokyo: Fukuyamabō, 1924.

———. "Taira Masakado jiseki kō." In *Ronshū Taira Masakado kenkyū*, edited by Hayashi Rokurō, pp. 139–150. Tokyo: Gendai shisosha, 1975.

Ōya Kuninori. *Ōshū Fujiwara godai: Michinoku ga hitotsu ni natta jidai*. Tokyo: Kawade shobō shinsha, 2001.

"Ōyoroi no tanjō." In *Tsuwamono no jidai: Kodai makki no Tōgoku shakai*, edited by Maizō bunkazai sentaa, pp. 33–84. Tokyo: Yokohama-shi rekishi hakubutsukan, 1998.

Piggott, Joan R. *Capital & Countryside in Japan, 300–1180: Japanese Historians Interpreted in English*. Ithaca, NY: Cornell University East Asia Series, 2006.

Ponsonby-Fane, Richard. *Sovereign and Subject*. Kyoto, Japan: Ponsonby-Fane Memorial Society, 1962.

———. *Imperial Cities: The Capitals of Japan from the Oldest Times Until 1229*. Lanham, MD: University Press of America, 1979.

"Prosperity and Vice: Facts about the Kokushi 1000 Years Ago." *East* 17, nos. 5–6 (1981): 53–61.

Raaflaub, Kurt, and Nathan Rosenstein, eds. *War and Society in the Ancient and Medieval Worlds: Asia, the Mediterranean, Europe, and Mesoamerica*. Cambridge, MA: Center for Hellenic Studies, Harvard University, 1999.

Rabinovitch, Judith N. *Shōmonki: The Story of Masakado's Rebellion*. Tokyo: Monumenta Nipponica Monograph, 1986.

Robinson, H. Russell. *Japanese Arms and Armor*. New York: Crown Publications, 1969.

Saeki Arikiyo et al. *Masakado no ran*. Tokyo: Yoshikawa kōbunkan, 1976.

Saiki Hideo. "Hakkutsu chōsa kara miru umaya to uma." In *Kamakura bushi to uma*, edited by Baji bunka zai dan and Uma hakubutsukan, pp. 27–32. Tokyo: Meicho shuppan, 1999.

Saitō Toshio. "Gunji kizoku buke to henkyō shakai." *Nihonshi kenkyū* 427 (1998): 27–58.

Sakai Hideya. "Chō to tachi, shūraku to yashiki: Tōgoku kodai iseki ni miru tachi no keisei." In *Shiro to tachi o horu yomu*, edited by Satō Makoto and Gomi Fumihiko, pp. 21–56. Tokyo: Yamakawa shuppan kai, 1994.

Sakamoto Akira. "Tōgoku bushi no sōbi kōjō o horu: Yokohama-shi Nishinotani iseki no chōsa seika." In *Tsuwamono no jidai: kodai makki no Tōgoku shakai*, edited by Maizō bunkazai Sentaa, pp. 117–133. Tokyo: Yokohama-shi rekishi hakubutsukan, 1998.

Sakamoto Tarō Hakase Kanreki Kinenkai, ed. *Nihon kodaishi ronshū*. Tokyo: Yoshikawa kōbunkan, 1962.

Sasagi Muneo. "Heian chūki no tōchi shōyū nintei ni tsuite." *Nihonshi kenkyū* 239 (1982): 32–62.

Sasai Jun'ichi. "Heian shoki kokushi kansatsu seido no tenkai o megutte." *Hisutoria* 70 (1976): 1–19.

Sasaki Hiroyasu. "Ōshū 12 nen kassen no koshō." *Iwate shigaku kenkyū* 80 (1997): 172–185.

Sasaki Jun'ichi. "Heian shoki kokushi kansatsu seido no tenkai o megutte." *Hisutoria* 70 (1976): 1–19.

Sasaki Ken'ichi. "Masakado no ran to Tōgoku gōzoku: toku ni Musashi Takeshiba o chūshin to shite." In *Kodai tennōsei to shakai kōzō*, edited by Takeuchi Rizō, pp. 235–256. Tokyo: Kōsō shobō, 1980.

Sasaki Minoru. "Tetsu to Nihon-tō." In *Ikusa*, edited by Fukuda Toyohiko, pp. 39–75. Tokyo: Yoshikawa kōbunkan, 1993.

———. "Nihon-tō to ōyoroi no seiritsu katei: Kinzoku kōkogakuteki tachiba kara no kōsatsu." *Rekishi gaku kenkyū* 730, no. 11 (1999): 35–44.

Sasaki Muneo. "Heian chūki no tōchi shōyū nintei ni tsuite." *Nihonshi kenkyū* 239 (1982): 32–62.

———. "10–11 seiki no zuryō to chūō seifu." *Shigaku zasshi* 96, no. 9 (1987): 1–36.

Sasaki Susumu. "Hiraizumi Fujiwara-shi to bunji 5 nen ōshū kassen." *Minshūshi kenkyū* 46, (1993): 13–26.

Sasama Yoshihiko, ed. *Katchū no subete*. Tokyo: PHP kenkyūsho, 1997.

———. *Nihon no kassen bugu jiten*. Tokyo: Kashiwa shobō, 1999.

Sasayama Haruo. *Nihon kodaishi nempyō*. Tokyo: Tōkyōdō shuppan, 1993.

Sato Hiroaki. *Legends of the Samurai*. Woodstock, NY: Overlook Press, 1995.

Satō Makoto. "Kodai · Chūsei no shiro to tachi." In *Shiro to tachi o horu yomu*, edited by Satō Makoto and Gomi Fumihiko, pp. 3–21. Tokyo: Yamakawa shuppan kai, 1994.

Satō Makoto and Gomi Fumihiko. *Shiro to kan wo horu yomu: kodai kara chūsei e.* Tokyo: Yamakawa shuppansha, 1994.

Seki Yukihiko. *Bushidan kenkyū no ayumi: gakusetsu shiteki tenkai*. Tokyo: Shin jimbutsu ōraisha, 1988.

———. "Kokuga gunsei to bushi no hassei ha dono yō ni kanren suru ka." In *Sōten no Nihon-shi 4*, edited by Minegishi Sumio, pp. 14–26. Tokyo: Shinjimbutsu ōraisha, 1991.

———. "'Bu' no kōgen: Kōchū to yumiya." In *Ikusa*, edited by Fukuda Toyohiko, pp. 1–38. Tokyo: Yoshikawa kōbunkan, 1993.

Sekiguchi Akira. "Kodai emishi no dokuya shiyō ni kansuru ikkōsatsu." In *Rekishi to kokoro*, edited by Enomoto Moriyoshi hakase taikan o iwau kai, pp. 35–41. Tokyo: Enomoto Moriyoshi hakase taikan o iwau kai, 1988.

Sekiguchi Hiroko. "Kodai kazoku to kon'in keitai." In *Koza Nihonshi 2*, edited by Rekishigaku kenkyūkai and Nihonshi kenkyūkai, pp. 287–326. Tokyo: Tokyo daigaku shuppankai, 1984.

Shima Setsuko. "Masakado no ran no zaichi kōzō." *Nara shien* 13 (1965): 1–11.

Shimomukai Tatsuhiko. "Ōchō kokka kokuga gunsei no seiritsu." *Shigaku kenkyū* 144 (1979): 1–27.

———. "Ōchō kokka kokuga gunsei no kōzō to tenkai." *Shigaku zasshi* 51 (1981): 44–67.

———. "Ōryōshi, tsuibushi no shoruikei." *Hisutoria* 94 (1982): 17–33.

———. "Nihon ritsuryō gunsei no kihon kōzō." *Shigaku kenkyū* 175 (1987): 17–43.

———. "Ōchō kokka gunsei kenkyū no kihon shikaku: 'tsuibu kampu' o chūshin ni." In *Ōchō kokka seishi*, edited by Sakamoto Shōzō, pp. 285–345. Tokyo: Yoshikawa kōbunkan, 1987.

———. "'Fujiwara Sumitomo no ran' saikentō no tame no ichi shiryō." *Nihon rekishi* 495 (1989): 15–32.

———. "Tenkei Fujiwara Sumitomo no ran ni tsuite no seijishiteki kōan." *Nihonshi kenkyū* 348 (1991): 1–32.

———. "Sumitomo tsuitōki ni tsuite." *Seto Naikai chiikishi kenkyū* 4 (1992): 163–194.

———. "Ritsuryō gunsei to kokuga gunsei." In *Jinrui ni totte tatakai to wa 2, tatakai no shisutemu to taigai senryaku*, edited by Matsugi Takehiko and Udagawa Takehisa, pp. 81–121. Tokyo: Tōyō shorin, 1999.

Shimomura Itaru. *Bushi*. Tokyo: Tōkyōdō shuppan, 1993.

Shiro to Kassen. Asahi Hyakka Nihon no rekishi bessatsu: rekishi o yominaosu, vol. 15. Tokyo: Asahi shimbunsha, 1993.

Shively, Donald H. and William H. McCullough, eds. *Heian Japan*. The Cambridge History of Japan, vol. 20. New York: Cambridge University Press, 1999.

Shōji Hiroshi. *Henkyō no sōran*. Tokyo: Kyōikusha, 1977.

Snellen, J. B. "Shoku Nihongi." *Transactions of the Asiatic Society of Japan* 11, 14 (1934, 1937): 151–239, 209–278.

Stramigioli, Giuliana. "Preliminary Notes on the Masakadoki and Taira No Masakado Story." *Monumenta Nipponica* 28, no. 3 (1973): 261–293.

———. "Masakadoki." *Rivista Studi Orientali* 53, nos. 1–2 (December 1979): 1–69.

Sugihashi Takao. "Chūsei bushi no seiritsu wo meguru kingyō ni yosete." *Ritsumeikan bungaku* 542 (1995): 74–86.

Sugimoto Keizaburō. "Konjaku monogatari no bushi setsuwa: Heike monogatari to no kanren ni oite." *Hōsei daigaku bungakubu kiyō* 9 (1963): 26–53.

Sugimoto Masayoshi and David L. Swain. *Science and Culture in Traditional Japan, AD 600–1854*. Cambridge, MA: MIT Press, 1978.

Suzuki Hironari. "Kodai Mutsu kuni no gunsei." *Rekishi* 77 (1991): 19–36.

———. "Kodai Dewa no kuni no gensei." *Kokushi danwakai zasshi* 33 (1992): 1–16.

Suzuki Keizō. "Ya no kōsei: yūshoku kojitsu no kenkyū." *Kokugakuin kōtō gakkō kiyō* 1 (1959): 3–44.

———. "Shikishō no yoroi no keisei ni tsuite." *Kokugakuin zasshi* 63, no. 4 (1962): 1–9.

Suzuki Masaya. *Teppō to Nihonjin: "teppō shinwa" ga kakushite kita koto*. Tokyo: Yōsuisha, 1997.

———. *Katana to kubi-tori: sengoku kassen isetsu*. Tokyo: Heibonsha shinsho, 2000.

Suzuki Takeo. "Heian jidai ni okeru nōmin no uma." *Nihon rekishi* 239 (1968): 42–55.

Suzuki Tetsuyū. "Masakado no ran kara Kamakura bushi e." In *Chūsei no fūkyō*

o yomu 2 toshi Kamakura to Bandō no umi ni kurasu, edited by Amino Yoshihiko and Ishii Susumu, pp. 123–154. Tokyo: Shinjimbutsu ōraisha, 1994.

Suzuki Tōru. *Nihon kassen-shi hyakuwa.* Tokyo: Chūō kōronsha, 1997.

Tabata Yasuko. "Kodai, chūsei no 'ie' to kazoku: yōshi o chūshin to shite."
Tachibana jōshi daigaku kenkyū kiyō 12 (1985): 41–67.

Tahara, Mildred M. *Tales of Yamato: A 10th Century Poem-Tale.* Honolulu:
Hawaii University Press, 1980.

Taira Masakado ni matsuwaru densetsu. www.xiangs.com/Masakado/legend/
index1.shtml. Accessed 9/6/2005.

Takahashi Masaaki. "Masakado no ran no hyōka o megutte." *Bunka shigaku* 26
(1971): 25–44.

———. "Kihei to suigun." In *Nihonshi 2 chūsei 1,* edited by Toda Yoshimi, pp.
68–98. Tokyo: Yūhikaku, 1978.

———. *Kiyomori izen.* Tokyo: Heibonsha, 1984.

———. "Bushi o minaosu." In *Bushi to wa nan darō ka,* edited by Takahashi
Masaaki and Yamamoto Kōji, pp. 2–7. Tokyo: Asahi shimbunsha, 1994.

———. "Bushi to ōken." In *Bushi to wa nan darō ka,* edited by Takahashi Masaaki
and Yamamoto Kōji, pp. 8–23. Tokyo: Asahi shimbunsha, 1994.

———. "Kodai no bun to bu." In *Senren to soya,* edited by Shimizu Akitoshi.
Tokyo: Tokyo daigaku shuppan kai, 1995.

———. "Tsurugaoka Hachimangū yabusame gyōji no seiritsu." *Atarashii rekishigaku no tame ni* 224 (1996): pp. 1–12.

———. "Chūsei seiritsuki ni okeru kokka shakai to buryoku." *Nihonshi kenkyū*
427 (1998): pp. 3–26.

———. *Bushi no seiritsu: bushizō no sōshutsu.* Tokyo: Tōkyō daigaku shuppankai,
1999.

———. "Nihon chūsei no sentō: yasen no kijōsha o chūshin ni." In *Tatakai no
shisutemu to taigai senryaku (jinrui ni totte tatakai to ha #2),* edited by Matsugi
Takehiko and Udakawa Takehisa, pp. 193–224. Tokyo: Tōyō shorin, 1999.

Takahashi Masaaki and Yamamoto Kōji. *Bushi to wa nan darō ka.* Asahi Hyakka
Nihon no rekishi bessatsu: rekishi o yominaosu, vol. 8. Tokyo: Asahi shimbunsha, 1994.

Takahashi Osama. "Chūsei bushidan no keisei to chiiki shakai." *Hisutoria* 149
(1995): 22–41.

Takahashi Takashi. "Fushū no ran." In *Heian ōchō no bushi,* edited by Yasuda
Motohisa, pp. 28–36. Senran Nihonshi. Tokyo: Daiichi hōgen, 1988.

———. "Bushidan no shihai ronri to sono hyōzō: meiei hassho iseki no
seititsu." *Rekishi hyōron* 611 (March 2001): 17–33.

Takahashi Tomio. *Emishi.* Tokyo: Yoshikawa kōbunkan, 1963.

———. *Hiraizumi no seikai: Fujiwara Kiyohira.* Tokyo: Kiyomizu shinsho, 1983.

———. *Kodai emishi o kangaeru.* Tokyo: Yoshikawa kōbunkan, 1991.

———. *Bushi no kokoro, nihon no kokoro.* Tokyo: Kondō shuppansha, 1991.

———. *Ōshū Fujiwara-shi.* Tokyo: Yoshikawa kōbunkan, 1993.

———. "The Classical Polity and Its Frontier," tr. by Karl Friday. In *Capital &
Countryside in Japan, 300–1180: Japanese Historians Interpreted in English,* edited

by Joan R. Piggot, pp. 130–145. Ithaca, NY: Cornell University East Asia Series, 2006.

Takahashi Tomio et al., eds. *Zusetsu Ōshū Fujiwara-shi to Hiraizumi*. Tokyo: Kawaide shobō shinsha, 1993.

Takashima Hideyuki. "Masakado no ōken." *Gumma shiryō kenkyū* 15 (Oct. 2000): 1–19.

Takeuchi Rizō. *Bushi no tōjō*. Nihon no rekishi. Tokyo: Chūō kōronsha, 1965.

———. "The Rise of Warriors." In *Heian Japan*, edited by Donald H. Shively and William H. McCullough, pp. 644–711. The Cambridge History of Japan, vol. 2. New York: Cambridge University Press, 1999.

Takinami Sadako. "Heian-kyō no kōzō." In *Kodai o kangaeru: Heian no miyako*, edited by Sasayama Haruo. Tokyo: Yoshikawa kōbunkan, 1991.

Tanaka Katsuya. *Emishi kenkyū*. Tokyo: Shinsensha, 1992.

"Tetsu o kagaku suru." In *Tsuwamono no jidai: kodai makki no Tōgoku shakai*, edited by Maizō bunkazai Sentaa, pp. 107–115. Tokyo: Yokohama-shi rekishi hakubutsukan, 1998.

Toby, Ronald P. "Why Leave Nara? Kammu and the Transfer of the Capital." *Monumenta Nipponica* 40, no. 3 (1985): 331–348.

Toda Yoshimi. "Heian shōki no kokuga to fugōsō: kokugaryō keisei katei no ichi sokumen." *Shirin* 42, no. 2 (1959): 86–93.

———. "Kokuga gunsei no keisei katei." In *Chūsei no kenryoku to minshū*, edited by Nihonshi kenkyūkai shiryō kembukai, pp. 5–44. Tokyo: Sōgensha, 1970.

Tode Hiroshi and Tanaku Migaku, eds. *Kenryoku to kokka to sensō*. Tokyo: Shōgakkan, 1998.

Togawa Tomoru. "9–10 seki no zaichi seisei to Masakado no ran kioi." *Shigaku* 3 (1983): 27–58.

"Tōgoku bushidan no genzō." In *Tsuwamono no jidai: Kodai makki no Tōgoku shakai*, edited by Maizō bunkazai Sentaa, pp. 93–106. Tokyo: Yokohama-shi rekishi hakubutsukan, 1998.

Toyoda Aritsune and Nomura Shin'ichi, eds. "Uma ga daikatsuyaku shita gempei no tatakai." In *NHK rekishi e no shōtai 5: Muteki Yoshitsune gundan*, edited by Toyoda Aritsune and Nomura Shin'ichi, pp. 11–36. Tokyo: Nihon hōsō shuppan kyōkai, 1990.

Toyoda Takeshi. "Eiyū to densetsu." In *Chūsei no seiji to shakai*. Tokyo: Yoshikawa kōbunkan, 1983.

Tsumie Hisayoshi. *Nihon no kassen: Kō sureba kateta*. Tokyo: Chūō kōronsha, 1997.

Tsuno Jin. "Kodai kozane yoroi no tokuchō." In *Tsuwamono no jidai: kodai makki no Tōgoku shakai*, edited by Maizō bunkazai sentaa, pp. 155–164. Tokyo: Yokohama-shi rekishi hakubutsukan, 1998.

———. "Kodai tekkō kara mita buki shozoku to buki seisaku." *Utsuki shigaku* 16 (2002): 40–69.

Tsutao Kazuhiro. "Konjaku monogatari-shū no tsuwamono setsuwa o megutte." *Kokugo to kokubungaku* 76, no. 10 (1999): 15–26.

Turnbull, Stephen R. *The Samurai: A Military History*. New York: Macmillan, 1976.

———. *The Book of the Samurai: The Warrior Class of Japan.* New York: Gallery Books, 1982.

———. *Samurai Warriors.* Poole, UK: Blandford Press, 1987.

———. *The Lone Samurai and the Martial Arts.* London: Arms and Armour Press, 1990.

Ury, Marian, trans. *Tales of Times Now Past: 62 Stories from a Medieval Japanese Collection.* Berkeley, CA: University of California Press, 1979.

Uwasugi Kazuhiko. "'Tsuwamono' kara bushi e." *Rekishi chiri kyōiku* 518 (1994): 8–13.

Uwayokote Masataka. "Heian chūki no keisatsu jōtai." In *Ritsuryō kokka to kizoku shakai*, edited by Takeuchi Rizō hakase kanreki kinenkai, pp. 511–540. Tokyo: Yoshikawa kōbunkan, 1969.

———. *Nihon chūsei seiji-shi kenkyū.* Tokyo: Haniwa shobō, 1970.

———. "Heian jidai no nairan to bushidan." In *Shimpojium Nihon rekishi 5 chūsei shakai no keisei*, edited by Toda Yoshimi, pp. 141–291. Tokyo: Gakuseisha, 1972.

———. "Taira Masakado no ran." In *Ronshū Taira Masakado kenkyū*, edited by Hayashi Rokurō, pp. 267–287. Tokyo: Gendai shisosha, 1975.

Vale, Malcolm. *War and Chivalry: Warfare and Aristocratic Culture in England, France and Burgundy at the End of the Middle Ages.* Athens: University of Georgia Press, 1981.

Varley, H. Paul, trans. *A Chronicle of Gods and Sovereigns: Jinnō Shōtōki of Kitabatake Chikafusa.* New York: Columbia University Press, 1980.

———. *Warriors of Japan as Portrayed in the War Tales.* Honolulu: University of Hawaii Press, 1994.

Wakita Haruko. "Marriage and Property in Premodern Japan from the Perspective of Women's History." *Journal of Japanese Studies* 1, no. 2 (1984): 321–345.

Wheatley, Paul, and Thomas See. *From Court to Capital: A Tentative Interpretation of the Japanese Urban Tradition.* Chicago: University of Chicago Press, 1978.

Whipple, Charles. *Masakado's Revenge.* www.charlest.whipple.net/masakado .html. Accessed 9/6/2005.

Wilson, William R. "The Way of the Bow and Arrow: The Japanese Warrior in the Kojaku Monogatari." *Monumenta Nipponica* 28, nos. 1–4 (1973): 177–233.

Yamagishi Ryōji. *Sōran no Nihon kodaishi.* Tokyo: Kōsaidō shuppan, 1995.

Yamaguchi Hideo. "Heian jidai no kokuga to zaichi seiryoku." *Kokushigaku* 156 (1995): 91–102.

Yamamoto Kōji. "Chijoku to waruguchi." In *Kotoba no bunkashi chūsei 2*, edited by Yamamoto Kōji, pp. 33–118. Tokyo: Heibonsha, 1989.

———. "Kassen ni okeru bunka tairitsu." In *Bushi to wa nan darō ka*, edited by Takahashi Masaaki and Yamamoto Kōji, pp. 26–43. Tokyo: Asahi shimbunsha, 1994.

Yamashita Tomoyuki. "Awa no kuni ni okeru bushidan no seiritsu to tenkai." *Ritsumeikan bungaku* 521 (1991): 145–172.

Yashiro Kazuo. "Shōmonki no sekai: Sadamori, Masakado o chūshin ni." In *Shōmonki: Kenkyū to shiryō*, pp. 8–44. Tokyo: Shindoku shosha, 1963.

Yasuda Motohisa. *Bushi sekai no jōmaku.* Tokyo: Yoshikawa kōbunkan, 1973.

————, ed. *Gempei no sōran*. Senran Nihonshi. Tokyo: Daiichi hōgen, 1988.

————, ed. *Heian ōchō no bushi*. Senran Nihonshi. Tokyo: Daiichi hōgen, 1988.

————, ed. *Kassen no Nihonshi*. Tokyo: Shufu to seikatsu sha, 1990.

Yasuda Takayoshi. "Taira Masakado no ran no buryoku." In *Kantō no kodai shakai*, edited by Endō Motō, pp. 237–262. Tokyo: Meicho shuppan, 1989.

Yasugi Saburō. *Fujiwara Hidesato shōgun*. Tokyo: Seiunsha, 2006.

Yiengpruksawan, Mimi Hall. *Hiraizumi: Buddhist Art and Regional Politics in Twelfth-Century Japan*. Cambridge, MA: Harvard University Press, 1998.

Yoneda Yūsuke. *Kodai kokka to chihō gōzoku*. Tokyo: Kyōikusha, 1979.

Yoneya Toyonosuke. "Masakado no ran ni kansuru 2–3 no mondai." *Nihonshi kenkyū* 50 (1960): 6–26. Report in *Ronshū Taira Masakado kenkyū*, edited by Hayashi Rokurō, pp. 200–221. Tokyo: Gendai shisosha, 1975.

————. "In Hokumen bushi tsuikō: Toku ni sōshiki ni tsuite." *Ōsaka sangyō daigaku jimbun kagaku ronshū* 70 (1990): 29–61.

Yoshida Akira. "Heian chūki no buryoku ni tsuite." *Hisutoria* 47 (1967): 1–16.

Yoshie Akio. "Shōki chūsei sonraku no keisei." In *Kōza Nihonshi*, vol. 2, edited by Rekishigaku kenkyūkai to Nihonshi kenkyūkai, pp. 105–130. Tokyo: Tokyo daigaku shuppankai, 1970.

Yoshii Hiroshi. "Ikusa to minshū." In *Ikusa*, edited by Fukuda Toyohiko, pp. 182–209. Tokyo: Yoshikawa kōbunkan, 1993.

Yoshimura Shigeki. "Takiguchi no kenkyū." *Rekishi chiri* 53, no. 4 (1929): 1–30.

————. "In hokumen kō." *Hōseishi kenkyū* 2 (1953): 45–71.

Yoshizawa Mikio. "Kodai gunsei to kiba heiryoku ni tsuite." In *Ritsuryō kokka to kōzō*, edited by Seki Akira sensei koki kinenkai, pp. 147–177. Tokyo: Yoshikawa kōbunkan, 1989.

CREDITS

Maps on pages vii, 22, 46, 66, 105, 111, 135 by Karl Friday and Wendy Giminski; photos on page 6 by Karl Friday and Atsuko Tanaka; genealogical chart on page 36 by Karl Friday.

Illustration credits: page 46 by Karl Friday after *Taiheiki emaki* in Miya Tsuigio and Satō Kazuhiko, eds., *Taiheiki emaki* (Tokyo: Kawade shobō shinsha, 1992; page 70 by Karl Friday after *Mōko shūrai ekotoba*, reproduced in Komatsu Shigemi, ed., *Mōko shūrai ekotoba*, vol. 13 of *Nihon no emaki* (Tokyo: Chūō kōron sha, 1988); pages 86–90 and 92–94 by Nicholas Adams: "The arrival of Masakado's head in the capital" after *Tawara Tōda emaki* (aka *Tawara Tōda zōshi*), as reproduced in Noguchi Minoru, *Densetus no shōgun: Fujiwara Hidesato* (Tokyo: Yoshikawa kōbunkan, 2001); "A provincial government compound" after photographs of various models; "A provincial governor en route to his province of appointment" after *Inaba dō engi emaki*, reproduced in *Shūkan Asahi hyakka Nihon no rekishi 61* (1987); "An ambush" after *Obusama Saburō ekotoba*, reproduced in Komatsu Shigemi, ed., *Obusama Saburō ekotoba / Ise shinmeisho e-utaawase*, vol. 18 of *Zoku Nihon emaki* (Tokyo: Chūō kōron sha, 1992); "Hidesato and Sadamori raid Masakado's home" after *Hidesato zōshi*, as reproduced in Yasuda Motohisa, ed., *Heian Ōchō no bushi*, vol. 2 of *Senran no Nihonshi: kassen to jinbutsu* (Tokyo: Daiichi hōgen, 1988); "Sumitomo's final battle" after *Rakuonji engi*, as reproduced in *Shūkan Asahi hyakka Nihon no rekishi 59* (1987); "Hidesato battles the centipede" after *Tawara Tōda monogatari*, reproduced in http://www.lib.hiroshima-u.ac.jp/dc/kyodo/naraehon/research/05/; page 91 by Chie Friday after *Hōnen jōnin eden*, reproduced in Komatsu Shigemi, ed., *Hōnen jōnin eden chū*, vol. 1 of *Zoku Nihon emaki* (Tokyo: Chūō kōron sha, 1992).

INDEX

NOTE: Page numbers in *italics* refer to illustrations or maps.

Printed in the USA
CPSIA information can be obtained
at www.ICGtesting.com
JSHW012015140824
68134JS00025B/2431